Endangered Wildlife and Plants of the World

Volume 8
PAL–RAB

Marshall Cavendish
New York • London • Toronto • Sydney

Marshall Cavendish Corporation
99 White Plains Road
Tarrytown, NY 10591-9001

Created by Brown Partworks Ltd.
Project Editor: Anne Hildyard
Associate Editors: Paul Thompson, Amy Prior
Managing Editor: Tim Cooke
Design: Whitelight
Picture Research: Helen Simm
Index Editor: Kay Ollerenshaw
Production Editor: Matt Weyland
Illustrations: Barbara Emmons, Jackie Harland, Tracy Williamson

Library of Congress Cataloging-in-Publication Data

Endangered wildlife and plants of the world
p.cm.
Includes bibliographical references (p.).
ISBN 0-7614-7194-4 (set)
ISBN 0-7614-7202-9 (vol. 8)
1. Endangered species--Encyclopedias. I. Marshall Cavendish Corporation.

QH75.E68 2001
333.95'22'03--dc21
99-086194

Printed in Malaysia
Bound in the United States of America
07 06 05 04 03 02 01 00 7 6 5 4 3 2 1

39365465

Photo Credits
Cover: Natural History Photographic Agency, Kevin Schafer
Title Page: Natural History Photographic Agency, Martin Harvey
Contents page: Robert Meinke

American Fisheries Society: James E. Johnson/U.S.F.W.S. 1130, 1134, John N. Rinne/U.S.F.W.S., William N. Roston 1135; Erwin & Peggy Bauer: 1110, 1114; Biological Photo Services: Ken Lucas 1129; Birdlife International: M. Lammertinck 1142; Bruce Coleman Inc.: Edward Degginger 1033, Norman Tomalin, 1072, 1073; Bruce Coleman Ltd.: Dr. P. Evans 1061; Jose A. Colon: 1031; Corbis: Tom Bean 1122, Susan Middleton & David Liitschwager 1117; D.R.K. Photo: Tom & Susan Bean Inc. 1028, John Cancalosi 1054, Stephen J. Krasemann 1051; Martin Gibbons: 1014; Chuck Hubbuch: 1015; I.C.C.E.: Dr M. A. Haque 1017; Life File:

Louise Oldroyd 1044; Allan Maltz: 1148; Robert Meinke: 1041; R. Miller: 1057, 1098; Robert & Linda Mitchell: 1052; Natural History Photographic Agency: Martin Harvey 1079; Hugh & Carol Nourse: 1091; H. Douglas Pratt: 1107; Phil Sheridan: 1090, 1092; Warren D. Thomas: 1038, 1046, 1137; VIREO: B. Chudleigh 1102S Dremeaux 1075, J. Dunning 1035, A. Morris 1100, T.J. Ulrich 1053, C. Volpe 1143; Wildlife Conservation Society (H.Q. at the Bronx Zoo): 1094; Rod Williams: 1067; Zoological Society of San Diego: 1019, 1069, 1070, 1111, 1119, 1120, J. Dolan 1081, Ron Garrison 1060, 1068, 1113, 1124, 1147

Cover: Klipspringer. Natural History Photographic Agency: Kevin Schafer
Title page: Blue-crowned pigeon. Natural History Photographic Agency: Martin Harvey
Contents page: Bradshaw's desert parsley. Robert Meinke

TABLE OF CONTENTS/VOLUME 8

ESA and IUCN

In this set of endangered animals and plants, each species, where appropriate, is given an ESA status and an IUCN status. The sources consulted to determine the status of each species are the Endangered Species List maintained by the U.S. Fish and Wildlife Service and the Red Lists compiled by IUCN–The World Conservation Union, which is a worldwide organization based in Switzerland.

ENDANGERED SPECIES ACT

The Endangered Species Act (ESA) was initially passed by the U.S. Congress in 1973, and reauthorized in 1988. The aim of the ESA is to rescue species that are in danger of extinction due to human action and to conserve the species and their ecosystems. Endangered plants and animals are listed by the U.S. Fish and Wildlife Service (USFWS), which is part of the Department of Interior. Once a species is listed, the USFWS is required to develop recovery plans, and ensure that the threatened species is not further harmed by any actions of the U.S. government or U.S. citizens. The act specifically forbids the buying, selling, transporting, importing, or exporting of any listed species. It also bans the taking of any listed species in the U.S. and its territories, on both private and public lands. Violators can face heavy fines or imprisonment. However, the ESA requires that the protection of the species is balanced with economic factors.

The ESA recognizes two categories of risk for species:

Endangered: A species that is in danger of extinction throughout all or a significant part of its range.

Threatened: A species that is likely to become endangered in the foreseeable future.

RECOVERY

Recovery takes place when the decline of the endangered or threatened species is halted or reversed, and the circumstances that caused the threat have been removed. The ultimate aim is the recovery of the species to the point where it no longer requires protection under the act.

Recovery can take a long time. Because the decline of the species may have occurred over centuries, the loss cannot be reversed overnight. There are many factors involved: the number of individuals of the species that remain in the wild, how long it takes the species to mature and reproduce, how much habitat is remaining, and whether the reasons for the decline are clear cut and understood. Recovery plans employ a wide range of strategies that involve the following: reintroduction of species into formerly occupied habitat, land aquisition and management, captive breeding, habitat protection, research, population counts, public education projects, and assistance for private landowners.

SUCCESS STORIES

Despite the difficulties, recovery programs do work, and the joint efforts of the USFWS, other federal and state agencies, tribal governments, and private landowners have not been in vain. Only seven species, less than 1 percent of all the species listed between 1968 and 1993, are now known to be extinct. The other 99 percent of listed species have not been lost to extinction, and this confirms the success of the act.

There are some good examples of successful recovery plans. In 1999, the peregrine falcon, the bald eagle, and the Aleutian goose were removed from the endangered species list. The falcon's numbers have risen dramatically. In 1970, there were only 39 pairs of falcons in the United States. By 1999, the number had risen to 1,650 pairs. The credit for the recovery goes to the late Rachel

Carson, who highlighted the dangers of DDT, and also to the Endangered Species Act, which enabled the federal government to breed falcons in captivity, and took steps to protect their habitat.

Young bald eagles were also successfully translocated into habitat that they formerly occupied, and the Aleutian Canada goose has improved due to restoration of its habitat and reintroduction into former habitat.

IUCN–THE WORLD CONSERVATION UNION

The IUCN (International Union for Conservation of Nature) was established in 1947. It is an alliance of governments, governmental agencies, and nongovernmental agencies. The aim of the IUCN is to help and encourage nations to conserve wildlife and natural resources. Organizations such as the Species Survival Commission is one of several IUCN commissions that assesses the conservation status of species and subspecies globally. Taxa that are threatened with extinction are noted and steps are taken for their conservation by programs designed to save, restore, and manage species and their habitats. The Survival Commission is committed to providing objective information on the status of globally threatened species, and produces two publications: the *IUCN Red List of Threatened Animals*, and the *IUCN Red List of Threatened Plants*. They are compiled from scientific data and provide the status of threatened species, depending on their existence in the wild and threats that undermine that existence. The lists for plants and animals differ slightly.

The categories from the *IUCN Red List of Threatened Animals* used in *Endangered Wildlife and Plants of the World* are as follows:

Extinct: A species is extinct when there is no reasonable doubt that the last individual has died.

Extinct in the wild: A species that is known only to survive in captivity, well outside its natural range.

Critically endangered: A species that is facing an extremely high risk of extinction in the wild in the immediate future.

Endangered: A species that is facing a very high risk of extinction in the wild in the near future.

Vulnerable: A species that is facing a high risk of extinction in the wild in the medium-term future.

Lower risk: A species that does not satisfy the criteria for designation as critically endangered, endangered, or vulnerable. Species included in the lower risk category can be separated into three subcategories:

Conservation dependent: A species that is part of a conservation program. Without the program, the species would qualify for one of the threatened categories within five years.

Near threatened: A species that does not qualify for conservation dependent, but is close to qualifying as vulnerable.

Least concern: A species that does not qualify for conservation dependent or near threatened.

Data deficient: A species on which there is inadequate information to make an asssessment of risk of extinction. Because there is a possibility that future research will show that the species is threatened, more information is required.

The categories from the *IUCN Red List of Threatened Plants*, used in *Endangered Wildlife and Plants of the World*, are as follows:

Extinct: A species that has not definitely been located in the wild during the last 50 years.

Endangered: A species whose survival is unlikely if the factors that threaten it continue. Included are species whose numbers have been reduced to a critical level, or whose habitats have been so drastically reduced that they are deemed to be in immediate danger of extinction. Also included in this category are species that may be extinct but have definitely been seen in the wild in the past 50 years.

Vulnerable: A species that is thought likely to move into the endangered category in the near future if the factors that threaten it remain.

Rare: A species with small world populations that are not at present endangered or vulnerable, but are at risk. These species are usually in restricted areas or are thinly spread over a larger range.

PALMS

Phylum: Anthophyta (flowering plants)

Family: Arecaceae (Palmae)

When you imagine a tropical landscape, palms probably spring to mind. The palm family, Arecaceae (or Palmae), contains between 2,500 and 3,500 species and is distributed throughout the warmer parts of the world wherever there is a sufficient amount of moisture. Palms have the most diverse range of species in the tropics, and can dominate the vegetation. More than 65 percent of the species grow in the world's rainforests. Palms are long-lived, woody monocotyledons that have solitary or clumping stems topped by a distinctive crown of feathery or fan-shaped leaves. Most species flower regularly throughout the course of their adult life.

The greatest threat to palms today is habitat destruction. Forestry, mining, land clearance for farming, and urbanization all pose major threats. Several species have been seriously endangered by the collection of the fleshy, edible growing-point leaves (heart of palm) for thatching or animal fodder, and by the bulk collection of seeds for the horticultural market. At least 100 species are currently endangered and about nine are thought to have become extinct.

Argun Palm

(Medemia argun)

IUCN: Endangered

Height: Up to 33 ft. (10 m)
Leaves: Stiff, glaucous green, fan-shaped
Fruits: Blue-black, the size and shape of plums
Habitat: Dry watercourses, arid valleys, desert
Range: Nubian Desert of northeast Sudan

ARGUN PALM
Africa

CONSIDERED BY MANY to be extinct or, at best, on the verge of extinction, the Argun palm was rediscovered in 1995 after a special expedition was mounted to look for it. The last prior record of its existence was a report of two isolated trees, now dead, at an oasis in southern Egypt. Though not a native, it was once probably cultivated widely in that country, as it is frequently portrayed in paintings on the interior walls of the tombs of the ancient Egyptian Pharaohs.

Today the Argun palm survives in some numbers in wadis (seasonally dry watercourses) in the trackless desert wastes of northern Sudan. Numerous rock paintings in the area show animals and birds, such as giraffes and ostriches, that are now entirely absent. These paintings indicate a time when the area was not as dry as it is today and suggest the Nubian Desert had a more favorable climate in the not too distant past that permitted a richer flora and fauna.

Recent studies have shown that the entire Sahara had a more humid climate only a few thousand years ago. It appears that these venerable palms and the few scarce *Acacia*, relict savanna plants, are the last survivors of those less extreme times.

Curiously for a desert plant, the Argun palm relies on flood waters for seed dispersal. Despite the arid climate, every few years there is a brief but heavy period of rainfall. The water rushes down from the surrounding mountains and fills the entire valley. These floods must be very violent, judging from the amount of debris stacked up against the palm trunks to a depth of 3 to 4

The unpredictable climate, and increasingly dry conditions in the desert, have contributed to the endangerment of the Argun palm.

feet (0.9 to 1.2 meters). The underground reservoirs are replenished, and large seeds that may have been lying on the surface for months or years are carried off by the rushing waters.

Humans have played a small part in the rarity of the Argun palm in comparison with the role played by climate change. The nearest settlement to their habitat, the gold mining town of Murrat Wells, was abandoned when the gold ran out, thereby easing any human pressure on the palm populations. Nomads on camels still wander these wastelands and occasionally cut the leaves for use in the manufacture of ropes and mats. Unless the leaves are out of reach, the nomads generally inflict no more damage than an occasional harvesting, the palm's trunk apparently being of little use even as firewood. There is no significant pollution here to harm the trees.

These palms grow in a landscape of stark, unforgiving, natural beauty. The valley floor is made of compacted sand and the palms are virtually the only living things to be seen. By day the temperatures can reach 104 degrees Fahrenheit (40 degrees Centigrade) and only plants and animals that are totally adapted to the harshness of the climate can survive. There is no surface water for hundreds of miles in every direction but, strangely, there are isolated wells, dug by the nomads, which reach well-supplied underground reservoirs just 6½ to 10 feet (2 to 3 meters) down. This water supply explains and ensures the palm's survival.

When the seed germinates it sends down a single, fragile root that extends for two or more meters. The root grows quickly until it reaches water, at which point the young plant can relax a little. Subsequent growth is then rather slow.

The scattered populations of Argun palm contain perhaps a thousand individuals. They are reproducing and could be said to be stable. However, due to the localized habitat, the unpredictable nature of the climate, and potential use of the palm by local people, these trees must be described as endangered. Recently, for the first time, seeds have been distributed to botanical gardens and enthusiasts around the world, though it is hoped that the Argun palm, a born survivor, will not have to rely on cultivation for its continued existence.

Martin Gibbons and Tobias Spanner

Carossier Palm
(Attalea crassispatha)

IUCN: Endangered

Class: Angiospermopsida
Order: Arecales
Family: Arecaceae
Subfamily: Arecoideae
Tribe: Cocoeae
Height: 66 ft. (20 m)
Leaf length: About 16 ft. (5 m)
Habitat: Lowland, moderately wet forest
Range: Southern Haiti

THE CAROSSIER PALM is similar to the coconut palm. Because it has relatively small seeds with three

The Carossier palm may reach a height of up to 65 feet (20 meters). Leaves are around 16 feet (5 meters) long.

eyes, a hard shell, and edible white meat or endosperm, the Carossier palm is known locally in Haiti as *petit coco* (French) or *koko* (Creole). Both names translate into English as "little coconut." This palm differs from the coconut palm in its straighter trunk and slightly shorter, stiffer leaves. It is, in fact, closely related to the coconut palm.

The Carossier palm is native to southern Haiti. It is a tall, sturdy palm that may reach 65 feet (20 meters) in height. The featherlike divided leaves are about 16 feet (5 meters) long with stiff, regularly spaced leaflets. Old leaves of this palm fall cleanly from the trunk, unlike those of most *Attalea* species. A woody bract surrounds short, densely branched clusters of flowers. Pollen-bearing and seed-bearing flowers are produced separately on the same flower cluster (monoecious). Mature fruits are about 1 inch (2.5 centimeters) long, orange, and fibrous. The seeds have a hard shell and a hollow cavity.

This is the only Caribbean representative of the genus *Attalea*, but there are twenty to

thirty other species ranging from Mexico to Paraguay. Some confusion regarding names exists. *Attalea crassispatha* has been known as *Maximilliana crassispatha* and *Orbignya crassispatha*. Currently, several authors place these closely related palms with *Scheelea* within the genus *Attalea*. Despite a trend toward consolidating these genera, at least one author argues for their separation and place the Carossier palm in the genus *Orbignya*. For convenience, *Attalea* is used here in the broader sense.

The Carossier palm is endangered, and it is thought to be the most endangered palm in the Americas. For several years only 25 palm plants existed in the wild. Joel Timyan, an independent researcher, discovered number 26 in the wild in August of 1999. Timyan is optimistic that a few more will be discovered with continued exploration. Known wild plants survive in fence rows, in pastures, and at garden edges. Based on the healthy seed production of isolated wild plants and cultivated plants in the United States, the insect pollinators are generalists and the plant is self-fertile. The natural seed distributor, however, is not known. It may no longer exist in the palm's natural location. In Haiti, many seeds are cracked and eaten by children.

Those that escape and germinate are plowed under by gardeners or browsed by livestock. While this species continues to exist in its normal habitat, its surroundings have been dramatically altered by humans. Because of the great extent of environmental changes to the area, it could be argued that this palm no longer exists in the wild.

This palm shows the potential for wide adaptability in warm, moist climates. In south Florida it has grown well in a variety of situations. Seedlings tolerate full sun at an early age. In bright shade, the palm will grow until it eventually emerges above the canopy. While plants can be successfully cultivated in a continually moist site in heavy soil, the best specimens are grown in sandy, well-drained soils with extra irrigation and fertilization.

In 1940 seeds of a Haitian palm, *Attalea crassispatha*, were first delivered to the Fairchild Tropical Garden in Florida. Nearly 50 years later, in 1999, one of four plants flowered and produced a few fruits for the first time. Wild plants were mapped in the late 1980s and early 1990s. During this project, extra seeds were shipped to Fairchild. While distributing seeds to botanical gardens around the world, the Fairchild staff learned that the seeds have an unusually short viability for a species of *Attalea*. Seeds are relatively quick and easy to germinate. Because of this, the storage and long-distance shipping of seeds are more difficult. At Fairchild and Florida International University in 1999, research began into the natural genetic variation that can be found within existing plants.

Conservation of this palm faces many problems. With Haiti's current political and social problems, the future of a single palm species is not a high priority. The few remaining plants survive on private lands. Natural catastrophes, human need, and natural attrition combined with the current lack of natural regeneration could decimate the remaining population. Nothing of substance stands between the last individuals and the loss of species in the wild.

The future of the Carossier palm may lie in cultivation. To conserve this species in Haiti, Timyan has proposed planting it on public, school, and hospital grounds. This is limited by the scarcity of opportunities within the palm's natural range. To initiate this project, Timyan is working with nurseries and plant enthusiasts in Haiti to collect and germinate seeds, supported by a Flora and Fauna International grant. It is likely that botanical gardens and private gardeners could contribute to the long-term survival of the palm, although this is subject to numerous dangers. Private collections come and go, and valuable specimens can fall into the hands of disinterested people. Botanical gardens may change priorities. Unintentional genetic drift is a risk in cultivation, including hybridization with related species in palm collections. The future of this palm is uncertain. While the plant seems secure in cultivation, there is a risk of extinction in its natural habitat. The efforts of individuals, botanical gardens, and agencies are all that stand in the way of this palm's extinction.

Chuck Hubbuch

Nicobar Palm

(Bentinckia nicobarica)

IUCN: Vulnerable

Order: Arecales
Family: Arecaceae (Palmae)
Subfamily: Arecaceae
Size: Up to 65 ft. (20 m) tall, with single, slender trunk, swollen at the base
Leaves: Feathery, arching, 5–13 ft. (1.5–4 m) long, with leaflets 11½–22½ in. (30–60 cm) long
Habitat: Tropical evergreen forests at low altitudes
Range: Nicobar Islands, India

THE NICOBAR ISLANDS lie in the eastern Bay of Bengal and are the peaks of a submerged mountain range that connects western Myanmar (formerly Burma) with the large Indonesian island of Sumatra. Pleasant sea breezes blow off the ocean and there is no great variation in the climate over the year. The temperature averages 86 degrees Fahrenheit (30 degrees Centigrade). The natural forest vegetation is still very rich in some places on many of the islands. When German botanist Wilhelm Kurz (1834–1878) formally described the Nicobar palm in 1875, it was said to dominate the landscape on some of the islands. Nowadays, however, it is threatened because of rapid habitat destruction.

Natural catastrophes such as storms and volcanoes pose additional threats. The palm is endemic to the Nicobar Islands and is a component of the moist forests there. The Nicobar palm

The Nicobar palm is found at low altitudes, in rich, evergreen forest on the Nicobar Islands, India.

shares these forests with other palms, such as betelnut (*Areca catechu*) and rattans (*Calamus* sp. and *Korthalsia* sp.). Wild palms are among the most important trees of the rich tropical forests that are found in the Nicobar Islands. Twelve of the 26 types of palm that grow there are endemic to the islands.

The Nicobar palm is a graceful, slender palm with a solitary trunk, swollen at the base, prominently ringed with circular leaf scars, and topped by a long, prominent crownshaft (leaf bases sheathing the stem) with about 10 gracefully arching, shortly stalked, feathery leaves.

In the Nicobar Islands, the leaves of wild Nicobar palms are used as a thatching material for roofing. In addition, the trunks are used as pillars for constructing huts. The islands are not economically rich; their main source of income is timber and plywood, supplemented by minor forest products such as bamboo, cane, and tree gum. The unique forest habitats are now being lost or broken up into isolated patches due to damage caused by humans. Habitat fragmentation is a particular problem because it adversely affects the special niches that the palm needs to survive and, ideally, thrive. The

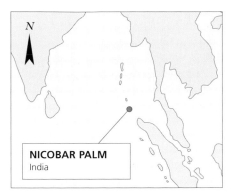

NICOBAR PALM
India

seeds rarely germinate in such disturbed forests. India has now established a National Man and the Biosphere Reserve Committee, and several Biosphere Reserves have been declared, including the Nicobar Islands and, in particular, the natural habitat of the Nicobar palm.

The Nicobar palm is also grown in several botanical gardens. The palms are often cultivated as ornamental trees.

More data is needed about seed germination to enable the palm to be more widely cultivated in tropical areas. Seeds and field-grown plants are now commercially available. Cultivated palms such as the Nicobar palm need plenty of water, mulching, and regular doses of fertilizer. Cultivation, propagation, and even seed banking could enable the reintroduction of the palm to parts of its former range.

Nick Turland

Giant Panda
(Ailuropoda melanoleuca)

ESA: Endangered

IUCN: Endangered

Class: Mammalia
Order: Carnivora
Family: Ailurpoda
Weight: 165–353 lb. (75–160 kg)
Head-body length: 47–59 in. (120–150 cm)
Tail length: 5 in. (13 cm)
Diet: Mainly bamboo shoots and stalks, roots, flowers, grasses, and occasionally fish, pikas, and small rodents
Gestation period: 150 days
Longevity: Up to 25 years
Habitat: Montane forests at a height of 7,500–12,500 ft. (2,287–3,812 m); areas with dense stands of bamboo
Range: Central China

IN 1957 A MAN in Nairobi, Kenya, was commissioned by an American ZOO to negotiate a trade with China in which the Chinese would receive a selection of East African mammals in exchange for a giant panda. In May 1958, the agent finally took charge of a panda named Chi-Chi, a six-month-old female. Unfortunately, the negotiations had taken too long. The United States had since broken off its relations with the People's Republic of China, making Chi-Chi a banned import. Chi-Chi never mated, and died in 1972.

Since then, however, political relations between China and the United States have improved enough to allow a pair of pandas to be presented as gifts to the National Zoo in Washington, D.C. They have been on public display ever since. Their attempts to mate and produce young have been the subject of regular news reports. However, breeding these endangered animals in captivity has been difficult.

For all the giant panda's visibility since the western world became aware of it in 1869, fewer than 100 individuals have been exported from China. Moreover, the animal has been seen in the wild by fewer than 50 westerners. Yet the giant panda is almost certainly one of the best-loved bears in the world. It seems appropriate that the World Wildlife Fund has chosen the giant panda for its symbol of conservation.

The giant panda ought not to be confused with the red panda. The red panda shares some space and dietary preferences with the giant panda, but the red panda does not look like a bear and is, in fact, related to the raccoon.

However much it looks like a bear, the giant panda does not always seem to act like a bear. It does not hibernate, eats little meat, and neither growls nor roars. In fact, it bleats. Such a list of unbearlike behavior is not easily explained away. Not surprisingly, until recently many scientists were persuaded that the giant panda was not a true bear.

Proof positive

This argument ended in 1985 when molecular biologists proved that the giant panda is a true bear. Apart from its coloration and seemingly gentle behavior, the giant panda resembles other bears. It has white fur with black eye patches and black legs, feet,
ears, chest, and shoulders. Sometimes the tip of its 5-inch (13-centimeter) tail is also black. This black-and-white patching is thought to provide the giant panda with ideal camouflage in the sometimes snowy places where it lives and feeds; the animal vanishes in direct sunlight or snow. The fur is thick and coarse and thins along the belly. As with other carnivores, there are scent glands under the tail.

The head is massive when compared to the rest of the body. The pad on the sole of each forepaw has an accessory lobe, a sort of sixth digit that evolved to help the bear grasp bamboo shoots. In fact, the lobe is an enlarged wrist bone and incapable of independent movement.

Bamboo eater

The average adult panda spends about 10 to 12 hours a day eating bamboo—its main source of food. It feeds on over 15 different species of this plant, eating as much as 50 pounds (23 kilograms) of the fibrous vegetation a day. To do the work of chewing, the panda uses large molar teeth.

Some scientists believe that bamboo was once a seasonal or supplemental food, and that until recently, meat played a larger role in the animal's nutrition. In fact, the modern giant panda is too slow to catch much meat, although it does manage to collect an occasional fish or rodent.

When the panda comes across a rat hole, experts think that it stomps and tramps over the

The giant panda prefers a vegetarian diet, eating mainly bamboo shoots and stalks, roots, flowers, and grasses. It will, however, occasionally eat fish, pikas, and small rodents.

nearby ground until the rat sticks its head up to observe whatever is making the commotion. At that point, the giant panda probably catches the rat by snatching it in its mouth.

The panda neither hibernates nor occupies a permanent den. Instead it takes shelter in hollow trees, rock crevices, and caves. Although it can climb trees, it prefers to remain on the ground. It can move quickly when necessary, but prefers a sedentary and solitary life. As long as a supply of edible bamboo is available, the panda is likely to remain where it is. Some pandas apparently spend their entire lives in three or four mountain valleys. Only the search for a mate seems to goad this animal into traveling any distance. With its short legs and pigeon-toed walk, the panda looks a little clumsy, but, in fact, this is not the case.

When one giant panda meets another, the reception is cool. Sometimes this bear will fight an approaching bear without any apparent provocation.

Breeding occurs during the spring between March and May, during the female's estrous period. This was thought to be seven-to-ten-days, but recent reports indicate a one-day estrous period. Although fetal development occurs in a matter of a few weeks, scientists believe that the fertilized egg does not immediately attach itself to the walls of the uterus. This is known as delayed implantation. This process enables bear cubs to be born at a time that is best for cub survival (usually in September).

The mother gives birth to one, two, or sometimes three cubs weighing a scant 3 to 5 ounces (90 to 140 grams) each.

Strangely, the mother seems to abandon all but one of her cubs. All cubs are born white and nearly hairless, but begin to darken after about one month. Independent feeding begins at three to four months of age. A cub may not go out on its own until it is around three years old. After one year a cub will weigh about 75 pounds (34 kilograms). Sexual maturity is reached at about five or six years, and females breed only once every two or three years.

Movement

Although pandas can stand on their hind legs, they never attempt to do so. When necessary, they flee at a trot and climb trees to find safety. Cubs and older individuals fall victim to leopards and wild dogs, but more often they suffer from a lack of food or water. Giant pandas are also vulnerable to diseases and internal parasites.

Highly intelligent, pandas have been taught a variety of stunts including tumbling, bicycling, eating with a knife and fork, and dunking a basketball.

About 100 giant pandas live in captivity, and probably fewer than 1,000 continue to live in the wild. More than half of the giant pandas remaining in the mountains live in genetic isolation in chains of refuges that have been created for them by the Chinese government.

Renardo Barden

N

■ **GIANT PANDA**
Asia

Ornate Paradisefish

(Malpulutta kretseri)

IUCN: Lower risk

Class: Actinopterygii
Order: Perciformes
Family: Belontiidae
Length: 1½ in. (4 cm)
Reproduction: Egg layer
Habitat: Ponds and shaded, clear streams
Range: Southwest Sri Lanka

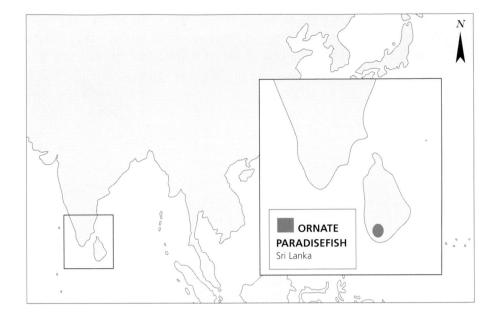

ORNATE
PARADISEFISH
Sri Lanka

THE ORNATE paradisefish is omnivorous, feeding mostly on insects and zooplankton. The fins are yellow edged with blue, while the caudal, dorsal, and anal fins have black spots. Because of its appearance, this species is in demand as an aquarium fish, which may explain why it was once threatened in the wild.

The ornate paradisefish builds a nest made of air bubbles on the undersides of floating vegetation. Deforestation across most of the island nation of Sri Lanka, resulting in subsequent soil erosion and river siltation, has been responsible for a widespread and generalized degradation of fish habitat.

William E. Manci

PARAKEETS

Class: Aves
Order: Psittaciformes
Family: Psittacidae

Parakeets are as different from parrots as toadstools are from mushrooms, or pigeons are from doves. The longer experts look for a biological difference, the more it becomes apparent that the distinction is just a quirk of the English language. Certain genera of parrots are traditionally called conures or parakeets. In recent years many ornithologists have stopped using the name conure in favor of parakeet. Many parakeets are well-known in captivity, but virtually nothing is known about their natural histories.

Cuban Parakeet

(Aratinga euops)

IUCN: Vulnerable

Length: 10–11 in. (25.4–28 cm)
Clutch size: 2–5 eggs
Diet: Primarily fruits and seeds but also flowers and leaf buds
Habitat: Forests
Range: Cuba

THE CUBAN PARAKEET was formerly one of the most common endemic birds of Cuba. It is now rare in a few remote regions and extinct on the Isle of Pines, where it was once abundant.

Cuba's 44,218 square miles (114,967 square kilometers) make it the largest island in the Greater Antilles of the Caribbean. Cuba is a little larger than Ohio, and a little smaller than Pennsylvania. After the voyages of Christopher Columbus, Spain claimed the island and maintained control until the Spanish-American War of 1898. The Cuban landscape was steadily converted to cattle grazing and tobacco production. Sugarcane, however, emerged as the island's most important crop. The use of slave labor to work on the plantations caused huge resentment and social turmoil. More agricultural output meant more exports, and those exports were desperately needed for cash in this impoverished country. Forests were cut and burned to make room for more cattle, tobacco, and sugarcane.

No matter how much land was converted, it was never

enough. Economic prosperity and social reform have always remained just out of reach for the Cuban people. Today, forest cover has been greatly reduced and a number of birds, including the Cuban parakeet, are vulnerable to extinction.

The Cuban parakeet is green overall, with scattered flecks of red about the head, neck, and yellowish green underparts. A patch of bright red and yellow shows at the end of the fleshy part of the underwing. A conspicuous bare ring around the eye is dull white, and the beak is an ivory or dull horn color. The long, slender tail shows green above and golden brown below.

The Cuban parakeet is mostly arboreal, feeding in the forest canopy or woodland treetops on fruits, buds, and flowers. It nests in either abandoned woodpecker holes in trees or in the nests of arboreal termites. Thus, as forests in Cuba disappear, the Cuban parakeet loses both its feeding and its nesting habitats. It has also suffered because of the cage bird industry.

Excessive trapping eliminated the Cuban parakeet from the Isle

GOLDEN PARAKEET
South America

of Pines off Cuba's southwestern coast early in the 1900s. Trapping continued on Cuba, where the added problem of habitat destruction has left the species very localized. However, trapping does not constitute much of a threat at present, with only ten birds recorded in trade between 1991 and 1995. It is now completely absent from some of its former haunts and is common only in the Zapata Swamp. *Common* is a relative term, of course. The Cuban parakeet exists in greater numbers in the Zapata Swamp than anywhere else in Cuba, but even there it is not as numerous as in past decades or

centuries. The species occurs in a number of protected areas, but no specific action has been taken to prevent the Cuban parakeet from becoming endangered.

Golden Parakeet
(Aratinga guaruba)

ESA: Endangered	
IUCN: Endangered	

Length: 13–14 in. (33–35.6 cm)
Clutch size: 2–4, but up to 6 eggs
Diet: Fruits and cultivated plants
Habitat: Rainforests
Range: North-central Brazil south of the Amazon River

THE GOLDEN parakeet shares a common problem with many tropical forest birds—it was becoming rare before any information was discovered about its natural history.

An overall golden yellow plumage distinguishes the golden parakeet. Dark green flight feathers look black against the otherwise yellow wing. A bare ring around the eye is dull white, and the large beak is horn colored. A fruit eater, the golden parakeet often displays the stains of fruit juices on its face and underparts. It finds all its food in the forest canopy.

The golden parakeet inhabits various forest types in Pará and adjacent northern Maranhão in northeastern Brazil, south of the Amazon River. Many of the forests in these two states are being cut. Some timber harvest is

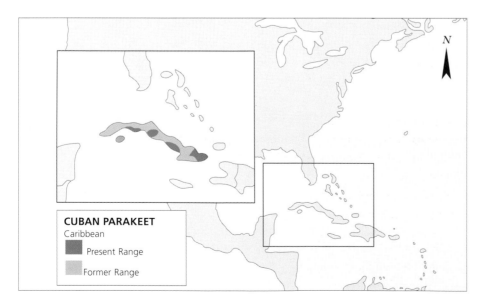

CUBAN PARAKEET
Caribbean
■ Present Range
■ Former Range

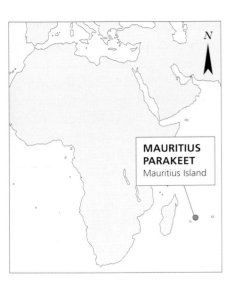

MAURITIUS PARAKEET
Mauritius Island

involved, but in many areas the forests are simply cut and burned to clear the land for agriculture. The habitat destruction obviously affects the golden parakeet, but trapping also takes a toll.

Only the international aspects of the cage bird trade make the news. The illegal sale of protected species makes good headlines when a smuggling operation is exposed. Many birds, however, never leave the general area where they are trapped. Local people prize captive birds every bit as much as foreigners do. The number of golden parakeets disappearing into the local pet trade is unknown. As well as being highly valued in both international and local bird trade markets, it is also hunted for food and sport, and persecuted to curtail crop damage.

There are very few nature reserves in this bird's natural territory, and even in such reserves the parakeet's nomadic tendencies make it difficult to protect. The violation of reserves for timber exploitation and trapping must be stopped, and effective protected areas must be developed in order to arrest the current decline of this species.

Mauritius Parakeet

(Psittacula echo)

ESA: Endangered

IUCN: Critically endangered

Length: 15¾–16½ in. (40–42 cm)
Weight: 5¾–6 oz. (163–167 g)
Clutch size: Probably 2–3 eggs
Incubation: Probably
28–32 days
Diet: Buds, leaves, flowers,
fruits and seeds, twigs,
and bark
Habitat: Primary forests
Range: Mauritius Island, east of
Madagascar in the Indian
Ocean

FEW BIRDS CAN BE ANY rarer than the Mauritius parakeet. In 1987 only eight birds were known to survive. Few birds have been rare for as long as the Mauritius parakeet. Its decline began as long ago as the 1500s, and that story may end any day.

The parakeet lived on Mauritius for possibly as long as a million years. The Alexandrine parakeet (*Psittacula eupatris*), a common bird in India and Pakistan, was probably the source of the individuals that pioneered the Mascarene Islands off Madagascar. Isolated by space and time, the Mauritius parakeet developed different behaviors that ultimately distinguished it from its relatives. Free from reptilian and mammalian predators, the Mauritius parakeet was limited only by island size and food resources available. This changed when people found the island.

Mountains, canyons, and valleys make up the 720 square miles (1,872 square kilometers) of volcanic Mauritian landscape. The island was almost completely forested when Portuguese sailors discovered it in 1507. The Dutch claimed the island in 1598, but waited until the 1640s to establish a colony there. By 1680 the dodo (*Raphanus cucullatus*), the most famous Mauritian of all, had been ushered into extinction by the actions of people. Extinctions continued through the next 350 years. Mauritius has lost about 27 unique species of birds since people found the island. All the losses are attributable to humans, either directly or indirectly.

When the Dutch arrived on Mauritius, they probably introduced the crab-eating macaque (*Macaca fasciculatus*) from its homeland in Java. An arboreal mammal, the macaque was able to climb trees and prey on the eggs and nestlings of birds that had never been afflicted by such predators before. Sailors also brought goats (*Capra hircus*) and rats (*Rattus* sp.) to Mauritius. Settlers imported sheep (*Ovis aries*), cattle (*Bos taurus*), pigs (*Sus scrofa*), and other livestock and pets. Forests were cleared to open up the land for farming and grazing. Sugar cane became important. Ebony wood (*Diospyros* sp.) became valuable. Pines (*Pinus* sp.), eucalyptus (*Eucalyptus* sp.), tea, and coffee also assumed a vital role in the island economy. In sum, the primary forests were cut both for valuable tropical woods and for agriculture development.

Grazing, farm crops, and plantations all took land area.

What primary forests were left uncut were damaged by the grazing of feral livestock and the Timor deer (*Cervus timorensis*), which was imported for recreational hunting. The damage the animals caused was compounded by exotic plants.

Less than one percent of Mauritius' primary forest survives today. Considering this thorough conversion of habitat, 27 lost species seems a small figure compared to the losses that might have been. Unfortunately, several additional species unique to Mauritius are poised for extinction, and the parakeet is one of these species.

The Mauritius parakeet sports a green plumage. The male has a rich blue tinge on the hindcrown and nape. A deep rose pink line also highlights the lower rear line of the cheek and stops short of meeting on either side at the nape. The beak has a bright red upper half and an all black lower half. The female lacks the blue wash, and her cheek lines are dark green and yellow green. Her beak is completely black.

Inhabiting only tiny patches of primary forest, the Mauritius parakeet lives an entirely arboreal life. It feeds almost exclusively on the flowers, fruits, and seeds of native plants, supplementing them with twigs, bark, leaves, and buds. Its dependence on primary forest and scrub undoubtedly has caused trouble for its population.

Estimates of population vary, but the most optimistic figure cited about 100 birds in 1970. Most ornithologists agree that no more than 50 birds were still alive in the early 1970s. Two powerful cyclones, in 1975 and 1979, were followed by reductions in parakeet numbers. Nearly complete breeding failure through the late 1970s brought the population to only 10 or 12 birds by 1980. The failure continued into the 1980s, until only eight Mauritius parakeets were known to be alive by 1987. Breeding success has since improved, and some captive-bred birds have been released into the wild. In 1998 the wild population increased to 59–73 birds, largely due to intensive management.

Contrasting the demise of the native parakeet, the ring-necked parakeet (*Psittacula krameri*) thrives on Mauritius. Introduced to the island in 1886, the ring-necked parakeet has adapted to secondary forest, tracts of exotic trees, and plantations. Before the forest cutting progressed so far, and before all the exotic trees and other plants became well established, the ring-necked parakeet competed with Mauritius parakeets for food and nesting. The future of parakeets on Mauritius seems to belong to the exotic species. The native parakeet has been rare for a long time and its survival is uncertain.

Kevin Cook

See also Parrots.

Maui Parrotbill

(Pseudonestor xanthophrys)

ESA: Endangered

IUCN: Vulnerable

Class: Aves
Order: Passeriformes
Family: Drepanididae
Length: 5½ in. (14 cm)
Weight: Males, 1 oz. (25 g); Females, ¾ oz. (20 g)
Incubation: 13–16 days
Diet: Insects, particularly larvae
Habitat: Ohia (*Metrosideros Collina*) woodlands
Range: Maui, Hawaiian Islands

THE MAUI PARROTBILL is a stocky little bird with a short tail and a large head on a squat neck. The parrotbill looks masked because of the dark olive line through the lore and eye that separates the yellow above the eye and on the cheek. Uniformly olive green above and dull yellow below, the parrotbill looks rather like a leaf, except for its beak. The thick and stout upper half curves dramatically downward, well past the tip of the lower half, to form a prominent hook.

Volcanic habitat

Fossils indicate that the parrotbill once inhabited Molokai as well as Maui. The Molokai population probably disappeared after Polynesians settled on the island, but they left well before the Europeans arrived. The parrotbill once used koa (*Acacia koa*) and dry ohia (*Metrosideros* sp.) woodlands at lower elevations than where it is found today. By 1990 the parrotbill lived only in a moderately wet belt of ohia woodlands between 4,300 and 6,800 feet (1,300 to 2,070 meters). Its last stronghold is the northeastern slope of Mount Haleakala, a volcano in eastern Maui. The decline of the Maui parrotbill is due to the influence of many factors, including the presence of exotic species and habitat destruction, but its retreat up the volcano is usually blamed on mosquitoes.

Mosquitoes became established in the Hawaiian Islands in the 1820s. They can carry the parasites that cause avian malaria, and can thus rapidly spread the disease within a bird population. Malaria is fatal to honeycreepers such as the Maui parrotbill. The mosquito does not live well at higher elevations, so fewer birds develop avian malaria higher up the mountains. This explains why the parrotbill remains above a specific altitude even though otherwise acceptable habitat is still available elsewhere. The parrotbill is sandwiched between the lower limit and the tree line above, where the trees thin out too much for its needs.

Exotic threat

Even in the narrow zone where it lives, conditions are not ideal for the parrotbill. Exotic mammals and plants have degraded the parrotbill's habitat. The Polynesians brought pigs (*Sus scrofa*) to the Hawaiian Islands. Some of

the pigs have escaped captivity and now live as feral animals on many islands. They destroy the seedlings of native plants and spread the seeds of exotic plants in their feces. Exotic plants often outcompete native plants, and they do not carry the same insects as do native plants. The parrotbill needs insects in order to survive. Creeping over tree trunks and branches, it picks at loose bark and wood to find grubs, the larval stage of beetles.

As with many bird species on the Hawaiian islands, exotic species such as rats and mongooses have contributed to the decline of the Maui parrotbill.

Fewer native plants mean there are fewer places for a parrotbill to find food.

Protective measures

Some work has been accomplished on behalf of Maui's native birds. Haleakala National Park and the Waikamoi Kamakou preserves run by The Nature Conservancy all preserve some primary woodland and forest habitat suitable for the remaining honeycreepers, including the parrotbill. Some of the important habitat areas have been fenced against feral livestock and to keep out axis deer (*Axis axis*). Several government agencies cooperate to conduct population surveys, and plans for the captive breeding of rare honeycreepers have been explored.

The Maui parrotbill population was approximately 500 birds during the 1980s and 1990s. Small populations are vulnerable to catastrophes and new threats. For example, another mosquito has been found on the islands, and this one lives at higher elevations. Also, the earlier mosquito seems to be adjusting to higher elevations, and there is always potential for new exotic predators such as the brown tree snake (*Boiga irregularis*) to become established on the Hawaiian Islands. Hopefully, habitat preservation efforts, monitoring against accidental introductions of exotic species, and public education will help preserve birds such as the Maui parrotbill.

Kevin Cook

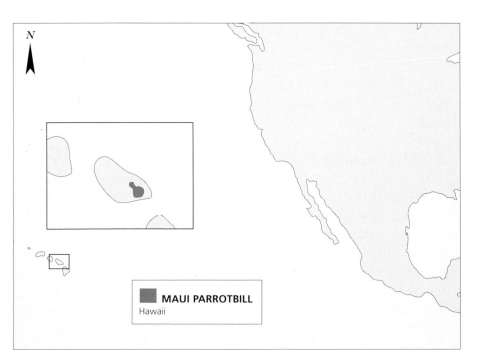

N

MAUI PARROTBILL
Hawaii

PARROTS

Class: Aves

Order: Psittaciformes

Family: Psittacidae

Subfamily: Psittacinae

Parrots make up the largest family of birds outside the songbird order. They edge out the hummingbirds and the pigeons for the honor. Counting the songbirds, parrots still rank as about the fifth largest family of birds. Moreover, they make a natural family, because all parrots look similar. Some bird families are so diverse that ornithologists still are not sure exactly how to classify them.

Parrots have always fascinated people. Their brilliant colors, large size, expressive faces, apparent intelligence, and long lives all satisfy the human desire for animal companionship. The parrots' greatest appeal, however, is undoubtedly their ability to mimic human speech. People may love the trill of the canary, but only a parrot can speak. This novel ability has worked against the parrots as a group, making them a valuable commodity in the pet trade.

Many parrot species now face immediate threats to their survival. The collection of live wild birds for the cage bird trade constitutes a major hazard to many species. Other species occupy only small geographic areas and are, therefore, vulnerable to human activities that alter habitat conditions. This problem is especially acute on islands. Many countries have signed the Convention on the Trade of Endangered Species, commonly known as the CITES Treaty. This international agreement lists species that cannot be legally imported or exported. Parrots are disproportionately represented on the CITES list, partly because they are so popular and partly because so many species are now jeopardized.

Primarily birds of the Southern Hemisphere, parrots are most numerous and diverse in South America, with the next greatest number in Australia and Indonesia. As residents of tropical forests, many parrot species have become victims of forest destruction. People have cut tropical forests both for lumber and to make space available for agriculture. Whatever the purpose of forest cutting, its effect on birds is the same. Excessive cutting causes excessive losses. Some parrots have already become extinct, and many more may follow unless human attitudes change. The loss of parrots means more than just the loss of birds.

Most parrots are specifically adapted for eating fruits, seeds, nectar, or pollen, although some may supplement their diets with insects. A long history of birds and plants evolving together usually indicates an important companionship. Certain plants may depend just as much on parrots for pollination or dispersing their seeds as the parrots do on the plants for producing edible fruits and seeds. If the parrots are removed from this relationship, known as commensalism, the plants suffer too. Studying endangered parrots for their roles in natural environments should be an ornithological priority.

Ground Parrot

(Pezoporus wallicus)

ESA: Endangered

Length: 12 in. (30 cm)

Clutch size: 3–4 eggs

Diet: Seeds, young plant sprouts

Habitat: Shrub lands, wetlands, prairies

Range: Coastal Australia

THE GROUND parrot closely resembles the night parrot (*Geopsittacus occidentalis*) and the kakapo (*Strigops habroptilus*). The kakapo occurs only in mountain areas of New Zealand, while the night parrot lives in central and western Australia, and the ground parrot inhabits coastal Australia. All of them are adorned with green feathers well mottled with yellows, browns, and black, so that they look much like low-growing plant life on the ground. The ground parrot also sports a bright orange-red colored bar on its forehead.

Whereas the kakapo is owlish in appearance, the ground parrot is much like a pheasant. It has a long, slender tail, and it runs well on its feet, with legs much longer than those of most parrots. When startled, it bursts into explosive flight, alternating rapid wing beats with long glides, just like the familiar ring-necked pheasant (*Phasianus colchicus*).

The nocturnal ground parrot inhabits coastal lowlands overgrown with small or dwarf shrubs. These shrub lands are sometimes called heath because of a low-growing heather (*Erica* sp.) that often grows abundantly in such places. The shrub lands may be wet or dry or both, and they offer dense ground cover in which the ground parrot can both hide and find ample food plants. However, the shrub lands also attract livestock grazing.

Despite its camouflaged coloration, swift running, and strong flying, the ground parrot has been unable to hide from, outrun, or outfly habitat destruction.

To improve the plant community for cattle, people burn the heath to kill off the shrubs and encourage more grass. They also drain off the water to improve grass cover. Both actions diminish the land's value to ground parrots. Furthermore, cattle trample parrot nests, causing additional problems.

There are no complete estimates of the ground parrot's population, but surveys in the early 1980s yielded grim results. The ground parrot has disappeared from some historically occupied areas and survives in drastically fragmented populations elsewhere.

Recommendations have been made for preserving habitat. Other measures should include eliminating cattle and other livestock grazing, stopping burning, and discontinuing the draining of wetlands associated with the heathland habitat.

Imperial Parrot
(Amazona imperialis)

ESA: Endangered
IUCN: Vulnerable

Length: 17–18 in. (43.2–45.7 cm)
Clutch size: Probably 2 eggs
Diet: Fruits, seeds, buds
Habitat: Montane forests
Range: Dominica in the Lesser Antilles of the Caribbean

IN A GENUS KNOWN for its brightly colored and beautiful parrots, one stands out among them all. The imperial parrot is the largest of the Amazon parrots (*Amazona*), and many believe it is the most striking. Describing the imperial parrot is difficult because its glowing colors blend so subtly.

The back and rump are green with a dark edge to each feather, causing a lightly scaled look. The folded wing appears mostly shiny green, except for a red patch along the leading edge just below the bend. The outer flight feathers are violet-blue, green, and brown. The inner flight feathers show a broad maroon patch in flight. The head and neck are dark purplish maroon, with a pale blue and green sheen. The face appears a little more maroon with a bare eye ring of dull brown encircling an orange-red eye. The throat, breast, and belly are shiny purple and are sharply offset by the blue-tinged bright green of the legs and undertail.

A bird of high mountain forests on a small island, the imperial parrot was secure for many years after Europeans colonized Dominica. According to the 1991 census, approximately 71,000 people live on the island's 290 square miles (754 square kilometers). They depend heavily on bananas as an export crop, so much of the lowland forests have been cleared and converted to plantations. Dominica is mountainous, however, and the interior mountain forests remained undisturbed well into the 1970s. Even with this habitat available, the imperial parrot still declined.

People have long hunted parrots as food, and birds such as the imperial parrot are good sport for recreational hunters. Most damaging of all, bird lovers so value the imperial parrot that they have driven the price of a bird very high. Illegal trapping and smuggling are widespread and serious enough to jeopardize the population. Whenever a wild animal population becomes severely depleted, that species becomes more vulnerable to natural events. Hurricanes that pounded Dominica in 1979 and again in 1980 left only one viable

Besides its size and beauty, the imperial parrot adds to its mystique by being shy. It is perfectly content to remain in the treetops.

population. That population is now quite small, because forest cutting has finally caught up with the native forests that are located on Dominica.

However, from a gloomy estimate of only 60 imperial parrots remaining in 1987, the population is now 250–300. This is due to governmental and non-governmental efforts to guarantee legal protection, protect habitat, and alert citizens to the bird's plight. Conservation has reduced pressure from local trade. The species' future now rests in preserving remaining montane forest and stopping trapping for the cage bird market.

Maroon-fronted Parrot

(Rhynchopsitta terrisi)

IUCN: Vulnerable

Length: 15½–17 in. (39.4–43.2 cm)
Incubation: Probably about 28 days
Diet: Seeds of cone-bearing trees, especially pines and junipers (*Juniperus*); also acorns and buds
Range: Mexico

THE MAROON-FRONTED parrot is related to the thick-billed parrot. Some experts regard the maroon-fronted as a subspecies of the thick-billed parrot, while others consider it to be a discrete species. Whatever the case, the maroon-fronted parrot differs from the thick-billed parrot in appearance by having a maroon rather than red forehead, forecrown, and eye line. The thick-billed parrot shows bright red at the wing bend and on the leg, while the maroon-fronted parrot is a duller red color. Where the thick-billed is yellow under the wing, the maroon-fronted is gray. Even the green body plumage is a darker green on the maroon-fronted parrot.

Living range

The maroon-fronted parrot occupies a smaller range than the thick-billed parrot. It is limited to a small area in northeastern Mexico and does not wander northward into the United States. Within its range it feeds extensively on pine seeds, but pines are becoming harder to find. Uncontrolled fires and overgrazing by domestic animals, compounded by clearance for agriculture and some logging, are eliminating suitable habitat for this parrot. The bird's population is considered to be relatively stable, numbering about 2,000 individuals, but the remaining habitat has dwindled in size to an area of about 4,350 square miles (7,000 square kilometers).

Decline reversal

Some action has been taken to arrest and even reverse this decline. The main breeding colony at El Taray cliffs (where up to 1,400 birds have been observed) is specially protected, and some key areas have been reforested with pine trees to provide food for these parrots.

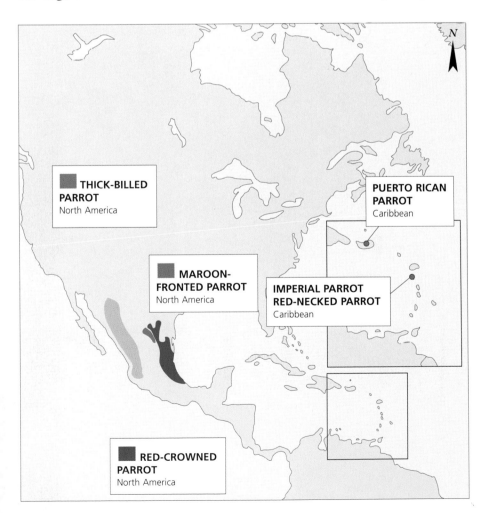

THICK-BILLED PARROT
North America

MAROON-FRONTED PARROT
North America

RED-CROWNED PARROT
North America

PUERTO RICAN PARROT
Caribbean

IMPERIAL PARROT
RED-NECKED PARROT
Caribbean

Paradise Parrot
(Psephotus pulcherrimus)

IUCN: Extinct in the wild

Length: 10–11 in. (25.4–27.9 cm)
Clutch size: 4–5 eggs
Incubation: 20–24 days
Diet: Seeds and leaves
Habitat: Savannas, prairie-shrub land mix
Range: Queensland and New South Wales, Australia

A GAUDY LITTLE parrot once inhabited the grassy countryside of eastern Australia. Known as the paradise parrot, it displayed brightly colored plumage.

Color distribution
The rump, side of the neck, lower breast, and upper belly were a curious mottling of turquoise and green. A red forehead and yellow eye ring accented an otherwise green face. A bright red wing patch matched the belly, undertail, and leg. The paradise parrot was a small bird with a very long tail that made up possibly half its total length.

Grass grazing
Being little more than sparrow-sized, the paradise parrot would frequently perch on a grass stem, bending it over to bring the seed head into reach.

The grasslands it inhabited stretched from the coast between Mackay and Brisbane inland and somewhat southwesterly to the area between Cunnamulla and Bourke. Grasslands have always been valuable to people for grazing their cattle.

The final blow
Ranchers often burned the dry grass to force a flush of new growth for their cattle. The fire served to destroy the principal food of the paradise parrot. After several consecutive years of heavy drought and grazing, the paradise parrot population diminished dramatically. No population estimates have been proposed for the species because the last verified sighting was in 1927. People occasionally make reports about having seen paradise parrots, but most sightings originate from the northern Queensland area, outside the species' historic range.

Nevertheless, the reports sustain some ornithologists' hopes that a small population of the gaudy but handsome paradise parrot might be rediscovered sometime in the future.

In contrast to the bright body, a sooty brown extended from the crown of the paradise parrot down the nape onto the back. The wing and tail were similar, with a tinge of green and blue.

Puerto Rican Parrot

(Amazona vittata)

ESA: Endangered

IUCN: Critically endangered

Length: 11–12 in. (27.9–30.5 cm)
Clutch size: 2–4 eggs
Incubation: 26 days
Diet: Many kinds of fruits
Habitat: Mature forests
Range: Puerto Rico in the Greater Antilles of the Caribbean

Given a little time, the Puerto Rican parrot may be able to recover from its desperate situation now that its island homeland is recovering.

A MILLION birds of a single species disappeared in just a few decades. This irreversible disappearance took a once abundant species to the threshold of extinction. What happens now to the Puerto Rican parrot depends largely on how people help it.

Color distribution

A small bird, the Puerto Rican parrot wears a dark green plumage. The head, neck, upper back, and upper breast have a faintly scaled look because each individual feather has a dark edge. A bright red forehead and a dark eye in a bright white eye ring distinguish the face. A deep, shiny, royal blue shows in the wings, even when they are folded. This general color scheme helps the Puerto Rican parrot blend in with the forests of its home islands. It once ranged throughout Puerto Rico and on the much smaller neighboring islands of Mona, Culebra, and probably Vieques and St Thomas. By the early 20th century, the Puerto Rican parrot had vanished from all the smaller islands and was in serious trouble on Puerto Rico. The parrot's decline corresponds with European colonization and the modern development of the West Indies.

Christopher Columbus reached Puerto Rico in 1493. The Spaniards' first interest was gold mining, but agriculture became the economic backbone of Puerto Rico for the next 450 years. The Spanish introduced sugarcane in 1515, and with it came slave labor. Pineapples, bananas, tobacco, coffee, and cattle were the vital crops. Ever more space was needed for greater productivity. By the end of the first decade of the 1900s, less than 20 percent of Puerto Rico's forests remained uncut. Originally, nearly all of Puerto Rico's 3,435 square miles (8,931 square kilometers) were forested. By the 1920s, only 1 percent of Puerto Rico had any forest cover.

While the habitat destruction progressed, the human fascination for cage birds increased. Parrots became increasingly popular. Trapping wild birds and raiding nests for nestlings grew excessive at a time when the Puerto Rican parrot population was already declining rapidly. Some people shot the parrots for sport or food, and a few people shot them to protect their fruit crops. After all the damage people did, the Puerto Rican parrot still had to contend with natural processes. Hurricanes and predatory animals have presented a constant threat to an already weakened species.

Insect threat

Given the perilous state of the species, even threats that affect very small numbers of birds are highly significant. Bot-flies (*Philornis pici*) parasitize the species, sometimes at relatively high levels. Introduced honeybees (*Apis mellifera*) and native pearly-eyed thrashers (*Margarops fuscatus*) compete with the parrot for nest sites. Predation by red-tailed hawks (*Buteo jamaicensis*) and possibly peregrine falcons (*Falco peregrinus*) is particularly damaging. Introduced rats (*Rattus* spp.) may also prey on Puerto Rican parrots.

Besides habitat loss, exotic predators, and natural competitors, the parrot must cope with the weather. In 1989 Hurricane Hugo swept across Puerto Rico, brutalizing the entire landscape. In the aftermath of the hurricane, parrot surveys were conducted. Ornithologists found only 23 birds, about half the number that were known to exist before the storm. The population fell to just 13 wild birds in the mid-1970s, but had recovered to 47 birds before Hugo. Since then, the wild population had increased to 44 birds by 1996.

Wild parrots survive only in the Luquillo Mountains of the Caribbean National Forest. A captive population of 87 birds has been successfully bred. The current conservation strategy is aimed at bolstering both wild and captive populations, rather than attempting costly and possibly premature reintroductions.

Meanwhile, Puerto Rico has been gradually moving toward a manufacturing economy and away from agriculture. Some agricultural land has been allowed to revert back to wild vegetation. Trees are growing again, but many years will be needed before they form a forest.

If captive breeding, suppression of exotic species, and public education programs against the illegal cage bird trade continues, there is some hope that the Puerto Rican parrot may recover well enough to be a part of its island's future.

Red-crowned Parrot
(*Amazona viridigenalis*)

IUCN: Endangered

Length: 13 in. (33 cm)
Incubation: 25–30 days in feral birds
Diet: Fruits, seeds, buds, and flowers
Habitat: Dry woodlands and forests
Range: Mexico

THE RED-CROWNED parrot is in an odd ecological position: its historic wild population is declining, while it thrives as an exotic species elsewhere.

The red-crowned parrot of Mexico has suffered heavy trapping and nest raiding for many years. So many birds have been sold in the cage bird trade that it has become abundant in captivity. Naive bird owners soon learn the work and inconvenience of keeping pet birds. Some owners end up by giving their parrots away, some owners sell them, and some just turn them loose. Parrots also escape regularly. Feral populations have become established in Puerto Rico and the cities of Miami, Los Angeles, San Diego, Brownsville, and Monterrey. Ironically, they can survive in urban woodlands but cannot survive in modified native habitat.

Bright plumage
The red-crowned parrot sports a bright red lore, forehead, and crown. A violet stripe originates behind the eye and sweeps around the hindcrown and down onto the nape, where it fades into a green color. A bright white eye ring sets off the golden eye from bright leaf-green cheeks. A straw gold beak completes the colorful head and face. The outer flight feathers are a blue color, but the inner flight feathers show red, which is visible when the wings are folded.

Pretty as it is, the red-crowned parrot can be a nuisance when it discovers ripening corn in a farmer's field. It also takes seeds from pine cones and eats a wide variety of fruits.

Forest food
Red-crowned parrots find their food in the dry woodlands and forests that once covered the lowlands around the Gulf of Mexico. They also range inland from the Gulf Coast to a dry ridge system well grown with pines (*Pinus* sp.) and oaks (*Quercus* sp.). These forests and woodlands have been cut for lumber and have been converted to pasture and croplands. As the native character of the land has been lost, the red-crowned parrot has correspondingly declined.

Although feral populations of red-crowned parrots have taken up living as exotic species in American cities, this does not mean they are adequately safeguarded against habitat destruction in their native range, and their absence from their native range can create a problem for other species. For example, red-crowned parrots feed quite wastefully. They take a few bites, then drop large, uneaten portions of fruit to the ground. But what appears wasteful by human standards may, in fact, be a vital part of maintaining plant communities by seed distribution.

Wild red-crowned parrots numbered between 3,000 and 6,500 birds in 1994. The rate of forest destruction and continued illegal trapping threaten to reduce red-crowned parrots even further.

Red-necked Parrot
(Amazona arausiaca)

ESA: Endangered

IUCN: Vulnerable

Length: 15¾ in. (40 cm)
Clutch size: 1–2 eggs
Diet: Fruit, buds, and cultivated oranges
Habitat: Low-elevation montane forests
Range: Dominica in the Lesser Antilles of the Caribbean

ROADS WOULD seem harmless enough to a parrot, and indeed roads by themselves pose no problem for the red-necked parrot. Roads are intended for people. When they penetrate remote areas, however, people gain access to places they would otherwise ignore. The consequences to wildlife living in those remote areas can be devastating. The red-necked parrot is an unfortunate example.

Multi-colored plumage
One of the larger Amazon parrots, the red-necked parrot is green overall, with straw yellow corners on its short, broad tail. A bit of yellow, some blue, and a little bright red on the inner flight feathers show even when the wing is folded. Individual

feathers on the back, nape, and side of the neck have dull brownish edges that give the plumage a scaled look. The golden orange eye sits in a bare white eye ring. Violet-blue or indigo colors the forecrown, forehead, lore, and front half of the cheek. A crescent of bright red on the throat gives the bird its name. This subtle blend of colors makes the red-necked parrot an attractive bird, and its appearance and abundance made it a popular cage bird. Until recently

Red-crowned parrots are doing poorly in their historic range, but are thriving in new locales.

the red-necked parrot was common on the Caribbean island of Dominica.

Inhabiting forests on the lower mountain slopes of Dominica, the red-necked parrot lives mostly inland, while Dominica's 71,000 people inhabit the coast. People have converted coastal lowlands and foothills from native vegetation to banana plan-

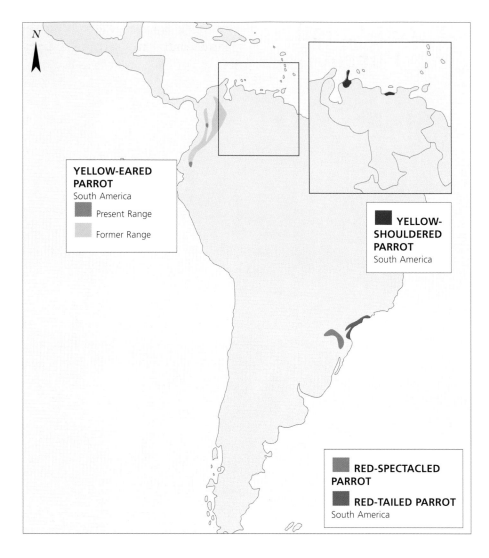

YELLOW-EARED
PARROT
South America

■ Present Range

░ Former Range

■ YELLOW-
SHOULDERED
PARROT
South America

■ RED-SPECTACLED
PARROT
■ RED-TAILED PARROT
South America

Red-spectacled Parrot
(Amazona pretrei)

ESA: Endangered

IUCN: Endangered

Length: 12½ in. (32 cm)
Clutch size: 2–4 eggs
Diet: Seeds of *Araucaria* sp. are favored, but also a wide range of other fruits, seeds, and flowers
Habitat: Savanna woodland and riverine forest
Range: Southwestern Brazil, northeastern Argentina, and extreme eastern Paraguay

NEVER ABUNDANT, the red-spectacled parrot has seriously declined as its essential habitat has been destroyed. In the non-breeding season it associates closely with, and probably depends on, forests dominated by species of *Araucaria*, a common conifer found in the Southern Hemisphere. Both the forests and the parrots that use them are unique.

The red-spectacled parrot does indeed have red around its eyes, but not in the manner its name suggests. Bare, white skin surrounds the bird's brown eye. Red encircles the white eye ring and also colors the lore, forehead, and crown. Red flecks often decorate its plain, green cheek. The overall green plumage appears heavily scaled because the feathers have dark tips. The entire leading edge of the wing is bright red, and both the inner and outer flight feathers show some blue. The undertail and tip

tations without disturbing the red-necked parrot's habitat. The parrot's fortunes began to change in the 1970s when economic development spurred road building into the island's interior.

The roads were intended to improve transportation around the island, both for tourism and for expanding agriculture. Unfortunately, the roads improved access to the interior forests for everyone, including hunters and trappers. People in the Caribbean have hunted parrots as food for centuries. In some situations, recreational hunting has replaced subsistence hunting. Despite worldwide efforts to discourage the cage bird trade, a market for parrots

still exists. These problems for the species are compounded by hurricanes (such as those in 1979 and 1980), and the array of predators and competitors that also threaten the Imperial parrot.

The combination of further forest clearing to provide land for banana plantations plus more hunting and trapping has caused the red-necked parrot population to decline to possibly as few as 150 birds in 1980. This parrot survives in only one population, which was estimated at 500 to 1,000 birds in 1997. Being large and attractive was not enough for the parrot to gain protection when it was common. Now it is rare, and habitat conservation helps ensure its survival.

of the tail are both yellow green. A few red feathers color the leg, but the foot and toe are straw colored.

The landscape where they occur is largely rolling prairie hills. The larger ravines and valleys between the hills are densely grown with *Araucaria*. Because the habitat of the red-spectacled parrot is so broadly scattered, the bird has developed a somewhat nomadic lifestyle. Since 93 percent of forest has been lost within its core range in Brazil owing to logging, over-exploitation of other forest products, and intense livestock grazing, remaining habitat is very scattered and birds concentrate at a few roost sites each evening. There is also an organized internal trade in the species, but losses of birds to this pressure appear insignificant. Some birds appear to genuinely migrate, but roost sites shift regularly depending on available food resources. In 1971 the red-spectacled parrot was observed in flocks of 30,000 birds but had apparently declined to 7,500–8,500 individuals in the early 1990s. However, counts in 1997 indicate that the species is more numerous, and that there is a total population of about 16,300 individuals.

The future of this species will depend on the protection of breeding and roost sites and on the success of current public awareness campaigns aimed at limiting both deforestation and internal trade practices.

Virtually nothing is known about the red-spectacled parrot's breeding habits, predators, natural population cycles, if any, or its inclination to wander. No population estimates were available in the early 1990s.

Red-tailed Parrot
(Amazona brasiliensis)

ESA:	Endangered

IUCN:	Endangered

Length: 14–15 in. (35.6–38 m)
Clutch size: 3–4 eggs
Habitat: Lowland and coastal forests
Range: Southeastern Brazil

THE RED-TAILED parrot has dwindled because of human ambitions. The human species needs habitat and space the same as every other animal, but humans demand more from the land than any other species. Quite often, human needs exceed the capacity of the land to produce, so that people gradually change the land. Birds such as the red-tailed parrot suffer when those changes eventually eliminate their habitat.

Coastal development
The coastal lowlands of southeastern Brazil once supported unique birds and other types of plants and animals. The red-tailed parrot was among them. Worldwide, most people live in coastal areas, and coastal areas normally have the highest density of people living in them per square mile.

Coastal Brazil has been heavily developed for agriculture that provides both domestic and exportable crops and livestock. Many forests have been cut for their lumber, but many have also been cut just to clear the land. Certainly, a nation has the right to use its land for feeding itself, but when complete ecosystems are destroyed in the process, a balance should be struck. Otherwise, species such as the red-tailed parrot can slip almost unnoticed into extinction.

Color distribution

A large Amazon parrot, the red-tailed parrot ranks among the more elegantly colored of its clan. The bird's basic color is dark green. Its wing feathers have yellow edges and tips that scallop the dark green. The outer flight feathers turn from green at the base to blue at the tip. The lore, forehead, and crown are colored deep rose red or lighter red. The bird's face is blue, indigo, mauve, and violet surrounding a bare, white eye ring that sets off the dark-colored eye. The tail is equally colorful. Each individual feather is broadly yellow-tipped. There is a patch of bright red, then an area of deep purplish blue on the outer feathers. The inner tail feathers are green and lack the purplish blue. Its bright colors make the red-tailed parrot a favorite target of bird trappers.

Population concern

The population was estimated at 4,000 to 5,500 birds in 1997, now occurring in an area of no more than 1,926 square miles (3,100 square kilometers). Breeding and roosting areas are

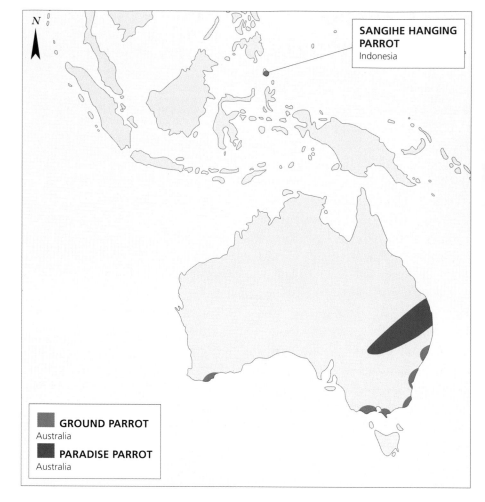

SANGIHE HANGING PARROT
Indonesia

GROUND PARROT
Australia

PARADISE PARROT
Australia

located on small estuarine islands off the coast of São Paulo and Paraná, with a few scattered on the mainland. All these birds migrate every day from island mangrove and littoral forest to feeding areas located in mainland forests. The bird is legally protected under Brazilian law, but this is not locally enforced. Although the parrot occurs within 12 protected areas, none of these reserves entirely safeguards any of the known subpopulations, and the creation of new reserves is hampered by building interests.

The principle threat is now poaching for trade. In one municipality covering about a quarter of the species' range, 356 birds, mostly nestlings, were captured during the 1991–1992 breeding season. Of 47 nests that were monitored between 1990 and 1994, six had suffered natural predation and the other 41 nests were robbed by humans. Some birds are sold on the internal market, but most birds are intermittently trafficked to the U.S. and European countries, particularly Germany. Such trapping also diminishes available nesting cavities since these are almost always destroyed when the nestlings are removed.

These statistics bode badly for the red-tailed parrot. National and international laws on poaching and trade have to be enforced, and the remaining habitat must be protected, or the species will decline from its endangered state to the point of extinction.

Sangihe Hanging Parrot

(Loriculus catamene)

IUCN: Endangered

Length: 4–4½ in. (10.2–11.4 cm)
Clutch size: Probably 2-3 eggs
Diet: Coconut nectar
Habitat: Secondary forest, edges of primary forest, mixed plantations and coconut groves
Range: Sangihe Island, Indonesia

EVERYBODY KNOWS that bats hang from trees and birds perch on top of them. That stereotype fits all but ten birds, known as the hanging parrots. All members of the genus *Loriculus*, the hanging parrots do exactly as their name implies—they hang.

Hanging parrots are also known as elvin birds. When they roost for sleeping, they grasp a twig with their feet, prop their tails against it, and curl into a little ball suspended beneath it. The obvious and inevitable question is why they should assume such a position. No one knows for sure, but a logical guess might be that this practice helps the tiny parrot avoid being noticed by predators. Their coloration suggests that this explanation may be true.

The Sangihe hanging parrot is green overall. It is a slightly darker green above and a more yellow-green below. This is a typical color scheme of leaves. Its forehead and crown are bright red, as are the tips of its green tail feathers. The undertail is more orange, less red. The front edge of the wing is bright yellow-green. Curled into a ball hanging beneath a twig, the tiny parrot looks like just another leaf or maybe a fruit. Either is hardly inviting to the owls and snakes that prey at night on roosting birds. The camouflage works well for a bird in natural habitat, but the habitat on Sangihe is gone.

Once known as Great Sangi Island, Sangihe lies almost exactly halfway between the upturned tip of Sulawesi's northern peninsula and the southern tip of Mindanao in the Philippines. A tiny island, it has been almost completely cut down and replanted with nutmeg and coconut. What little wild vegetation persists is almost entirely the overgrowth of abandoned gardens and small farm plots.

The Sangihe hanging parrot is known to feed on coconut nectar. It may also feed on the pollen, flowers, leaf buds, and small fruit that are the usual fare of other hanging parrots. Whether the species can subsist on coconut and nutmeg blossoms, with a slight mix of other plants, is not known. Being a small island, Sangihe could never have supported a very large population of hanging parrots. Some ornithologists think of the Sangihe birds as a subspecies of the Moluccan hanging parrot (*Loriculus amabilis*), and others see it as a subspecies of the Sulawesi hanging parrot (*Loriculus stigmatus*).

The Sangihe hanging parrot is threatened by habitat loss but it is known to be able to make some use of plantations and groves, although we do not know if it can survive exclusively in such habitats. The remaining population should be monitored closely, and studies of its natural history should be undertaken.

Thick-billed Parrot

(Rhynchopsitta pachyrhyncha)

ESA: Endangered

IUCN: Endangered

Length: 15–16 in. (38.1-40.6 cm)
Clutch size: 2–4 eggs, usually 3
Incubation: Probably about 28 days
Diet: Seeds of cone-bearing trees, especially pines (*Pinus*) and junipers (*Juniperus*); also acorns and buds
Habitat: Montane coniferous and coniferous-hardwood forests and woodlands
Range: Mexico, Arizona, and New Mexico

THE NAME *PARROT* evokes an image of palm trees and warm climates. It is usually assumed that parrots belong in the jungle, but the thick-billed parrot proves that stereotypes and reality often do not coincide.

Living areas

Thick-billed parrots live in dry, montane forests dominated by pines (*Pinus* sp.), but they also descend to foothills and valleys where oaks (*Quercus* sp.) are a conspicuous part of woodland and forest plant communities.

A bright, leaf-green parrot, the thick-billed has a red forehead and forecrown extending over the eye like an eyebrow. A ring of yellow skin surrounds the red eye. Red color also shows at the wing bend and on the lower leg. The thick-billed parrot is a medium-sized and average-looking bird.

Early reports of thick-billed parrots suggested that the species might be a natural wanderer. In some places, in some years, they were quite common, even abundant; in other years they appeared to be completely absent from those same places. By the 1920s the thick-billed parrot ceased wandering into the northern reaches of its historical range. It gradually disappeared from Arizona, New Mexico, northern Chihuahua, and northern Sonora. Three factors probably explain the species' demise in these areas. First, heavy forest cutting to provide logs to the lumber industry destroyed much thick-billed parrot habitat. Some ornithologists believe so much habitat was lost that the parrot will never venture into United States territory again. Second, miners, trappers, ranchers, and settlers all shot the thick-billed parrot for food. Third, trappers caught the birds for the cage bird trade. Trapping probably hurt the thick-billed parrot more as its overall population was waning from habitat loss and shooting.

Pollution control

Since it is nomadic in response to variations in cone abundance, this parrot is difficult to protect in a single reserve. A more suitable system of protected areas has never been created and there are no formally designated protected areas in the thick-billed parrot's range. However, there is a plan in operation at El Carricito, Mexico. Polluters pay the local community not to cut down forest and thus fix carbon rather than cut emissions. This preserves habitat for wildlife.

Protection

Thick-billed parrots are protected by international treaty. They cannot be legally trapped and offered for sale, but people who trade parrots typically do not care so much about the birds as about the rewards. Consequently, there was considerable illegal trade in parrots that continued even into the 1990s. In 1986 wildlife authorities broke a parrot-smuggling ring and confiscated 26 thick-billed parrots. The birds were released in Arizona's Chiricahua Mountains. A few birds were killed, some flew back into Mexico, but several remained in Arizona.

Population estimates for the yellow-shouldered parrot in the late 1980s figured less than 1,000 birds on the coastal islands. The mainland population survives in scattered groups with varying degrees of local abundance.

The powerful beak of the thick-billed parrot is well suited for opening pine cones to extract the seeds, and for shelling acorns.

Two birds, identified as immatures by their light-colored beaks, were seen in 1988. So far these youngsters are the closest proof of wild thick-billed parrots breeding again in the United States. A cooperative program among many zoos has been developed to produce more thick-billed parrots through captive breeding. These reintroduction attempts have had low success rates owing to the proliferation of disease, the inability of captive-bred birds to develop flocking behavior, and predation by raptors.

Extinction

The thick-billed parrot is one of only two parrots that lived in or regularly wandered into the United States. The other, the Carolina parakeet (*Conuropsis carolinensis*), succumbed to extinction in 1918. The last sighting of wild thick-billed parrots in the United States before 1986 occurred in 1935.

Now, with deliberate help from people, the thick-billed parrot is getting a chance the Carolina parakeet never had.

Yellow-eared Parrot
(Ognorhynchus icterotis)

IUCN: Critically endangered

Length: 16–17 in.
(40.6–43.2 cm)
Clutch size: 4 eggs
Diet: Fruit and probably seeds
Habitat: Woodlands of wax palms (*Ceroxylon andicolum*)
Range: Southwest and central Colombia and north and west-central Ecuador

BRIGHT YELLOW, elongated cheek feathers flare out from the yellow-eared parrot's face like shaggy sideburns. The yellow continues across the upper cheek, through the lore, and over the forehead. A ring of bare, whitish skin surrounds the red eye. A dark, leaf green paints the crown, nape, lower cheeks, back, and wing. The throat, breast, and belly are a paler, yellower green. The long tail, green above and dull orangish brown below, tapers to a dull point. Both beak and toe are black. A medium-sized parrot, the yellow-eared is not greatly colorful, but the sideburns do lend it a handsome, aristocratic look.

Disposable

These human interpretations of their appearance mean nothing to a wild creature such as the yellow-eared parrot. They also mean nothing to the developers who see other values present in a tropical forest. To the people who cut down trees and clear forests, birds such as the yellow-eared parrot are just dispensable bystanders.

Rarity

Although formerly common and even abundant in places, the yellow-eared parrot is now rare to the point of extinction. A mere 19 are known to remain in west-central Ecuador, and 61 in the Central Andes of Colombia. Since vast areas of suitable wax palm forest have been cleared within its historic range, habitat destruction must have been an important factor in its decline. However, there are now fewer birds than could be expected, given the extent of available habitat. This suggests that other factors are at work. Since nest-robbing is apparently very uncommon and few birds have been recorded in international trade, direct persecution at communal roost sites seems the most plausible explanation of this bird's current rarity.

Little protection

Until recently, the species has received very little specific protection, and it only occurs sporadically in a number of national parks within its range. This is beginning to change. Land supporting the traditional roost site in Ecuador has now been purchased for reforestation with food plants, and an environmental awareness campaign has targeted human populations in adjacent areas. A similar project has now been instigated in Colombia and was responsible for the discovery of 61 birds in a remote valley in 1999. Certain measures to protect this population are expected to follow.

The yellow-eared parrot has been neglected for too long. If it is to survive, the existing projects in Ecuador and Colombia will have to find sufficient funding to operate effectively. Without such financial resources, this species is destined for extinction.

Yellow-shouldered Parrot

(Amazona barbadensis)

IUCN: Vulnerable

Length: 12–13 in. (30.5–33 cm)
Clutch size: 2–4 eggs
Diet: Fruits, seeds, nectar-rich blossoms and crop plants
Habitat: Dry forests
Range: Coastal Venezuela and near-shore islands, Netherlands Antilles

THE STORY OF the yellow-shouldered parrot is the story of rats, thrashers, and people. Together, they challenge the survival of this particular parrot.

Patterning

The yellow-shouldered parrot is a green bird liberally accented with yellow. The leg, bend of the wing, upper cheek, lore, and midcrown are all bright yellow. The forehead is whitish, fading to cream, then yellow. A pale blue washes over the lower cheek, belly, and outer tail feathers. The flight feathers are dark purple but with a bright red patch that shows when the bird is both in flight and at rest. The head, entire neck, back, breast and belly look scaled because individual feather tips are a dark brownish color. Compared to other Amazon parrots in the genus *Amazona*, the yellow-shouldered parrot is prettier than some but not as beautiful as others. It ranks among the larger members of its group, and it is also becoming one of the most rare.

Pet trade

A bird of dry forests in coastal Venezuela, the yellow-shouldered parrot once inhabited many coastal islands, including Aruba and Bonaire. It was last seen on Aruba in 1955, and ornithologists presume it has vanished from the island. It no longer occurs in large continuous populations along the Venezuelan coast either, but now survives in small, isolated groups.

Some yellow-shouldered parrots are shot as agricultural pests. They are also shot for food and recreation. More disastrously, people raid parrot nests for young birds that can be sold in the largely internal pet trade. There is now evidence that unknown numbers are entering the international market. This trade has harmed the parrot, as have local threats such as tourism on the island of Margarita, and various natural developments, including drought. People are the major, but not the sole threat, to the species.

The pearly-eyed thrasher (*Margarops fuscatus*) has been expanding its range in the Caribbean for many years. An aggressive bird, it competes with other species for cavities in trees where they nest. The pearly-eyed thrasher will harass nesting parrots until they leave the cavity. The thrasher then enters, grasps a parrot egg in its beak, and drops it out of the cavity. The thrasher then moves in. Normally, yellow-shouldered parrots could adjust to this nest predation. However, a reduced population cannot easily endure the disruption of its breeding. Most parrots only attempt to breed once a year, even though many will try again if the first nest is destroyed. However, timing may be critical regarding food supply, and second broods will suffer and die if parent birds cannot find enough food.

Rat threat

Besides thrashers, rats now also threaten the yellow-shouldered parrot. The culprits are probably black rats (*Rattus rattus*) and Norway rats (*Rattus norvegicus*). Black rats are especially known for their ability to climb trees and their taste for eggs and young birds. Just as in the case of the thrasher, the yellow-shouldered parrot could probably endure the rats if the overall parrot population were high and rats were the only problem. In reality the parrots suffer from thrasher, rat, and human predation simultaneously. This combined assault exceeds the parrot's ability to survive. The predictable consequence of predation is a reduced population of a naturally limited species.

Kevin Cook

See also Kakapo and Parakeets.

Bradshaw's Desert Parsley

(Lomatium bradshawii)

IUCN: Endangered

Family: Apiaceae
(Umbelliferae)
Habit: Perennial from a
thickened taproot, 8–25 in.
(20–65 cm) tall, with 1–2 erect
stems
Leaves: 4–16 in. (10–40 cm)
long, pale green, with feathery
segments
Habitat: Seasonally wet
prairies, grasslands, and slough
margins, at 150–500 ft. (45–150
m) elevation
Range: Restricted to the
Willamette Valley of western
Oregon and extreme
southern Washington

BRADSHAW'S DESERT parsley is a
parsleylike perennial related to
carrots and parsnips, and like
many species of the genus
Lomatium it was used as a food
by North American native people. Curiously, most species are
found in very arid regions (and
are called desert parsleys), so it is
unclear why the Bradshaw's
desert parsley is located in the
Willamette Valley of rainy northwest Oregon. Unfortunately,
living in a more hospitable climate has certainly proved no
advantage. The problem is that
the plant only grows in western
Oregon's wet prairie, a vegetation
type originally not unlike the historic tall grass prairies of the

Bradshaw's desert parsley thrives in wet
prairies and grasslands, often in areas
infested with a collection of aggressive
non-native weeds.

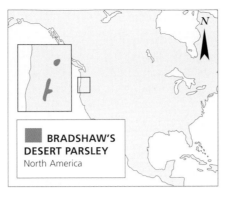

BRADSHAW'S
DESERT PARSLEY
North America

North American Midwest. When
settlers arrived in Oregon in the
1840s and 1850s, the broad
Willamette Valley reminded them
of their homes back east. They set
about making the area more like
home by plowing the fields,
planting orchards, and building
towns. By the turn of the century
little was left of the pristine
grassy heartland of western Oregon, and today it is estimated
that less than 5 percent of the valley has not been drastically
altered. What passes today as the
best habitat for Bradshaw's
desert parsley is often infested
with a collection of aggressive
non-native weeds, such as oat-
grass (*Arrhenatherum elatius*),
velvetgrass (*Holcus lanatus*), and
cats-ear (*Hypochaeris radicata*), a
result of years of agricultural dis-
turbances. Native associates such
as sloughgrass (*Beckmannia syzi-
gachne*) and tufted hairgrass

(*Deschampsia cespitosa*) are in
serious decline, and the rarer
Willamette Valley natives, including Bradshaw's desert parsley, are
particularly susceptible to competition for habitat.

In spite of many difficulties,
fate may have finally turned in
favor of Bradshaw's desert parsley in recent years. Most of the
noteworthy populations of the
species occur in the vicinity of
Eugene, Oregon, a city with an
environmental vision. Utilizing
public funding, efforts are underway by government agencies to
restore and conserve hundreds of
acres of grassy wetlands to their
natural state. This means
improved habitat for desert parsley and some of the other
sensitive native plants.

Conservation measures

Burning prairies is one way used
by local restoration ecologists to
achieve their goals. Another is
stripping an area of weedy plant
communities, then resowing the
site with native seed mass
collected nearby. The work in
progress near Eugene is a model
for wet prairie rehabilitation, and
bodes well for the development of long-term prospects for
Bradshaw's desert parsley.

Robert Meinke

PARTRIDGES

Class: Aves

Order Galliformes

Family: Phasianidae

Partridges mean different things to different people. True partridges are not native to North America, but ruffed grouse (*Bonasa umbellus*) and other grouses are also known as partridges. True partridges are Old World birds that live much as quails do in the Americas. Several partridge species have been released into the United States as game birds.

Partridges have the strong foot and toe structure found in francolins and pheasants, but they lack the foot spur. The flat, blunt claw of each toe serves the ground-dwelling partridges as they scratch among the litter for seeds and invertebrates to eat. Roughly 40 species in the family Phasianidae include *partridge* as part of their English name. Many have suffered habitat loss and population declines, but two species seem particularly threatened. The urgency concerning their welfare stems from the rate of habitat loss and from lack of data about their population status.

Sichuan Partridge

(Arborophila rufipectus)

IUCN: Critically endangered

Length: 11–12 in. (27.9–30.5 cm)

Weight: Males, 14½–17 oz. (410–470 g); females, 12½–13½ oz. (350–380 g)

Clutch size: 5–6 eggs

Diet: Fruits, seeds, invertebrates

Habitat: Forests, bamboo thickets

Range: Sichuan and possibly Yunnan provinces, China

DEEP IN THE HARDWOOD forests of China's mountainous interior lives a small partridge whose exact status is uncertain. Some ornithologists consider it to be a unique species called the Sichuan partridge, and others consider it a well-marked subspecies of the necklaced partridge (*Arborophila torqueola*). This debate over classification may be moot if present human activities continue. The Chinese logging industry threatens to destroy the vast majority of the Sichuan partridge's habitat.

The Sichuan partridge is colored with warm earthen tones, highlighted with white and a trace of black. The habitat of this bird differs from that of the necklaced partridge, which inhabits evergreen coniferous forests, while the Sichuan partridge inhabits deciduous hardwood forests. Typical trees in their habitat include oaks and chestnuts. Even though its Latin name, *Arborophila*, means "lover of trees," the Sichuan partridge is actually a terrestrial bird. The ground cover beneath the trees is as important, if not more so, than the trees themselves. Typical undergrowth in the Sichuan partridge's habitat includes oleasters (*Eleaganus* sp.), berry canes (*Rubus* sp.), and cherries and plums (*Prunus* sp.). The characteristics of evergreen coniferous forests and deciduous hardwood forests are not the same. Spacing of the trees, density of undergrowth and ground cover, and many other factors are different. This habitat difference ultimately may prove important.

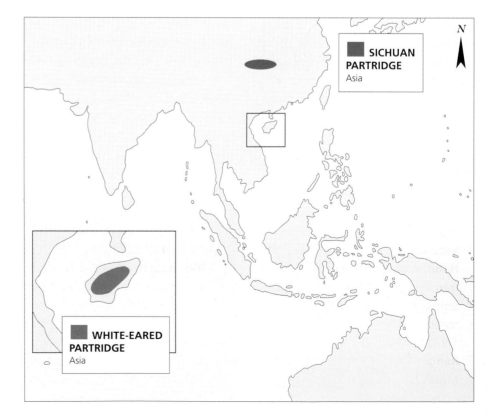

The Chinese government intends to cut the hardwoods for lumber. Traditionally, the forests are then replanted into conifer plantations. Europeans continued this during a three-century period that sorely depleted birds in these forests. The Sichuan partridge appears not to accept conifer plantations over hardwood forests, and the rejection of habitat makes the difference between survival and extinction.

The Sichuan partridge occurs within an area of 3,840 square miles (9,600 square kilometers). Its habitat only covers parts of the area. If one part is not set aside for other purposes besides lumber, the Sichuan partridge will probably not survive. Its relationship to other partridges will then merely be a matter of historical curiosity.

White-eared Partridge
(Arborophila ardens)

IUCN: Endangered

Length: 11 in. (27.9 cm)
Weight: Males, 10¾ oz. (300 g); females, 8½ oz. (237 g)
Diet: Seeds, snails
Habitat: Forests
Range: Hainan Island, China

THE WHITE-EARED partridge is found only on the island of Hainan. If, however, habitat conditions continue to deteriorate on this island, this species of partridge will cease to exist.

Hainan is heavily populated, and to accommodate this mass of people, forests are cut down. The human presence, farming, and the grazing of livestock exert enormous pressure on the remaining forest habitat and the species that live there.

Population decline

The white-eared partridge is shy, sticking close to the undergrowth of forests. Ornithologists rarely see it, but the people of Hainan find it. It is greatly prized both as a cage bird and as table fare. In a dwindling habitat, a species cannot sustain much hunting or collecting pressure before its population declines drastically. It is estimated that the population is now fewer than 10,000 birds. Two nature reserves provide relatively safe habitats in which the white-eared partridge can easily survive.

Kevin Cook

Pauoa
(Ctenitis squamigera)

ESA: Endangered

IUCN: Endangered

Height: Up to 10 in. (25 cm)
Stems: Green
Fronds: Divided, with midrib darker than surrounding leaf tissue
Reproduction: Spores produced during the summer
Habitat: Lowland mesic (requiring a moderate amount of moisture) forests, up to a height of 1,970 ft. (600 m)
Range: Oahu, Lanai, Maui, and Molokai, Hawaiian Islands

PAUOA IS A FERN, a member of the family Aspleniaceae (the wood ferns). It was first discovered in 1947 and it was originally known as *Nephrodium squamigerum*, a name that may still be encountered in some older texts.

The dangers that face *Ctenitis squamigera* are common threats that are typical of any island endemic species, namely competition with non-native species, grazing by animals (chiefly alien species), fire and other natural disasters, and human encroachment on their habitat.

One further problem faced by *Ctenitis squamigera* is the fact that it is present only in small numbers. This will provide a genetic bottleneck that would result in reduced natural variation for the plant to use to react to changes in its environment, and a reduced reproductive vigor (due to incompatibility mechanisms that do not allow closely related individuals to breed). In the past 20 years there have been 10 populations of this plant recorded, totaling some 80 individuals. These populations are spread out over the Waianae Mountains of Oahu and also on Lanai, East

PAUAO
Hawaiian Islands

Pauoa (*Ctenitis squamigera*) lives in lowland mesic forests on four of the islands that form the Hawaiian Islands chain. The small numbers of this plant could mean it is close to extinction.

and West Maui, and Molokai. This spread over several islands is important for continued survival of this species. A diversity of locations means all the remaining individuals are unlikely to be destroyed in a single natural disaster. Also, each of the 10 populations will be genetically different—this will help to maintain overall genetic diversity, although this diversity will be accessible only via artificial breeding programs. All 10 populations are found on land owned or managed by the government, including several military installations. The fern is protected by statute: it is illegal to damage or remove it.

Recovery plans

The U.S. army is currently preparing plans for the recovery and reintroduction of this species within suitable habitat. The recovery plans that are currently in place concentrate on minimizing the impact of military training and activities and the removal of feral animals and alien plants. Some of the areas containing this fern are now in enclosures that exclude animals. The Mount Kaala Natural Area Reserve on Oahu is also being extended to include more suitable habitat. Monitoring and taxonomic and growth experiments are currently being carried out by the Haleakala National Park. This work includes surveying of likely habitats to see if unknown populations are present, as well as monitoring the currently known populations to assess their state of survival. Many suitable habitats are known, so it is hoped that in the near future new populations will be encountered to bolster this species.

The future of this species is very precarious. The best strategy for survival is the protection of the appropriate habitats along with growth and outplanting of new plants.

Gordon Rutter

Green Peafowl
(Pavo muticus)

IUCN: Vulnerable

Class: Aves
Order: Galliformes
Family: Phasianidae
Length: 40–96 in. (101.6–243.8 cm)
Weight: 8½–11 lb. (3.8–5 kg)
Clutch size: 3–6 eggs
Incubation: 26–28 days
Diet: Small fruits, seeds, invertebrates, probably small reptiles
Habitat: Riparian forests, meadows with tall grasses, and dry deciduous forests
Range: India, Chittagong Hills of Bangladesh, southern China, Southeast Asia, and Java in Indonesia

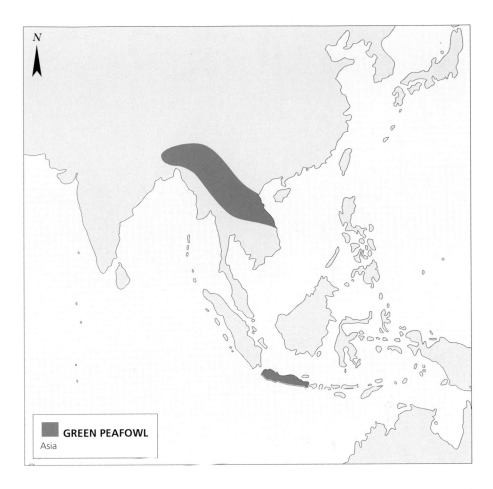

GREEN PEAFOWL
Asia

THE PEACOCK WAS born to strut and display his beautiful plumage. In forest clearings and meadows, he erects and fans his great train of some 200 feathers (like the train of a wedding gown), and then struts about trying to attract females for mating purposes. The train accounts for more than half the peacock's length. From beak to tail, the bird measures about 30 inches (76 centimeters), but his train may extend over another 5 feet (152 centimeters).

The famous peacock tail is really not a tail at all. The train is composed of highly modified feathers from the bird's lower rump. On all birds these feathers are called coverts, because they cover the point where the large tail feathers actually attach to the body. In the peacock, the coverts are elongated and each bears a colorful eyelike disk at the end. The females are more plainly adorned, with a modest train.

The temptation is to call them all peacocks, but many of them are females, more properly called peahens. Together, they make up the group of birds known as peafowl. Ornithologists recognize only three species: the Congo peafowl (*Afropavo congensis*), the Indian peafowl (*Pavo cristatus*) so familiar in captivity, and the green peafowl, now rare and probably still declining.

A large, handsome bird, the green peafowl is green overall as its name implies. It grows a pointed crest of shiny blue-green feathers that accents the bare, yellow cheek and a bare, blue ring about the eye. The neck and upper breast are a bronzed green that shines violet in certain lights.

Fine black tips to the individual feathers give the breast and neck a scalloped or scaled look. The female's train only extends to the tip of her tail. The male green peafowl drops many of his train feathers as the courtship season wanes, and those that remain attached wear quickly.

The green peafowl enjoys a flexible lifestyle and accepts several different habitat types. In some areas it seems to prefer dense riparian forests, but in others it frequently occurs in woodlands. The peafowl readily accepts second growth and small prairies near forests, especially where the grasses grow tall enough to conceal it. The male needs clearings where it can strut during courtship. Despite the species' habitat flexibility, the green peafowl has vanished from large portions of its historic

Green peafowl are large, handsome birds known for their spectacular tail fans. Although growing scarcer, it seems likely that this bird will survive.

range. Not coincidentally, much of the green peafowl's former haunts have been developed and converted to agriculture.

Beginning of trouble

The green peafowl was reported as scarce or declining in the early decades of the 1900s. By 1942 it was considered scarce in western Myanmar, and many accounts cite 1951 as the year it became obvious that it was declining throughout its range. It may be already gone from Assam, India, and Bangladesh. It now occurs in isolated pockets scattered about Thailand, Laos, and Vietnam, and is scarce in Yunnan, China. As many as 200 green peafowls may survive in a small area of

Thailand, but this bird has vanished from Malaysia. A few hundred birds survive in two Javan populations, one on the western end of the island and the other on the eastern end. Around 1,000 birds are known to survive across Java, where the two most important sites are national parks at opposite ends of the island: Ujong Kulon, including the offshore island of Peucang, in the west, and Baluran in the east.

The green peafowl is not a mountain bird, but usually occurs below 4,000 feet (1,220 meters). Lowlands also provide better opportunity for agriculture, and in an area where the human population is high and dense, food production is a concern. Most countries have established national parks or reserves, but administering, managing, and funding them does

not always follow. Hunting the green peafowl has been prohibited in Myanmar, Thailand, Malaysia, and Indonesia. A big bird, however, can feed whole families, and the temptation to shoot or trap it is not easily overcome by the threat of laws.

The green peafowl survives well in captivity, but questions of genetic purity have been raised. Ornithologists classify the green peafowl into three subspecies. Some captive birds represent mixed bloodlines of the three subspecies. This lessens the desirability of using certain captive birds as parent stock for chicks that may be raised in captivity, then released into the wild.

This species is most at risk from poaching, and its ability to survive endangerment mostly depends on preventing poaching.

Kevin Cook

Ginger Pearlfish
(Cynolebias marmoratus)

Opalescent Pearlfish
(Cynolebias opalescens)

Splendid Pearlfish
Cynolebias splendens

IUCN: Vulnerable

Class: Actinopterygii
Order: Atheriniformes
Family: Cyprinodontiformes
Length: 2½ in. (7 cm)
Reproduction: Egg layer
Habitat: Temporary pools filled during rainy season
Range: Just north of Rio de Janeiro, Brazil

IN TERMS OF THEIR worldwide distribution, killifish (of which pearlfish are loosely considered members) have been quite successful, and can be found across the tropical and temperate latitudes of the world. Killifish are capable of tolerating a wide range of environmental conditions, particularly variations in salinity. They can be found in fresh water as well as in water that is even more saline than sea water. Killifish can survive cool conditions, but they also occur in hot springs. Most killifish prefer shallow water that is rich in aquatic vegetation; they use vegetation for cover and as a likely source of aquatic insects, which are their favorite food.

Pearlfish are small and unassuming creatures, with a feathery-finned appearance. Because of their small size, many killifish species are captured and used as bait fish. This type of overexploitation is difficult to combat because of the profit involved. However, educating the general public and those directly engaging in overexploitation of sensitive species may begin to curb these activities.

Drought-resistant

Many species of the family *Aplocheilidae* (including the pearlfish) are known as annual fishes because they have developed the ability to survive for long periods of time without the aid of water. This seemingly impossible feat is achieved by laying drought-resistant eggs in the bottom of ponds and other small basins that dry up during rainless periods.

While the adults fail to survive these waterless intervals, their offspring wait for the rainy season to emerge. They then begin to grow, reproduce, and continue to perpetuate the species.

However, the beautiful pearlfishes of South America are in a predicament: they inhabit a relatively small zone at the base of a range of mountains in Brazil called the Serra do Petrópolis, just north of the city of Rio de Janeiro. Before the city was constructed, their range was open and free. Rio de Janeiro is now a bustling metropolis of well over 10 million people, and as the people move farther north in order to escape the city, they increasingly encroach on the only remaining habitat of several endangered species: the ginger, the opalescent, and the splendid pearlfish.

The pools and ditches that these species use are prime production areas for mosquitoes and other aquatic insects. During the rainy season, these depressions fill and are occupied by the pearlfish, other fish, and mosquitoes. Land developers have resorted to filling these basins to control insects. This has limited mosquito production, but has also limited production of the pearlfishes' preferred food—and destroyed areas crucial to this fish's continued existence.

Striking colors

All pearlfish are spectacular in both color and form. Brilliant blues and reds across the body and fins are accented by a blizzard of white dots that become larger toward the edges of fins or elongate into broken stripes.

The dorsal fin on the back, the anal fin on the belly, the pectoral fins just behind the gills, and the tail fin are long and wide relative to the body and are almost feathery in texture. In contrast, the pelvic fins on the belly are quite short and are nearly nonexistent. The pearlfish breeds at least once

**GINGER PEARLFISH
OPALESCENT PEARLFISH
SPLENDID PEARLFISH**
South America

Pearlfish now find themselves trapped between a mountain range and a booming metropolitan city that is slowly but surely encroaching on their last remaining habitat.

during the rainy season. On average, about 100 fish are produced each cycle, and two or three groups of offspring during a year are not uncommon.

Without a ban on new real estate developments, steps should be taken to move the remaining pearlfish out of this area and to secure its future by locating it in safer tracts of water.

William E. Manci

See also Killifishes.

Chacoan Peccary

(Catagonus wagneri)

IUCN: Endangered

Class: Mammalia
Order: Artiodactyla
Family: Tayassuidae
Weight: 66–99 lb. (30–45 kg)
Shoulder height: 20–27½ in. (50–70 cm)
Diet: Omnivorous
Gestation period: 150 days
Habitat: Dry thorn forest and thick scrub
Range: Northern Argentina, Bolivia, Paraguay

THE PECCARY IS a distant relative of swine—a medium-sized, piglike animal with bristly hair. There are three different types, found from Mexico to southern Brazil and northern Argentina. The most common form, and the one with the widest distribution, is the collared peccary (*Tayassu tajacu*). It is found in a variety of environments from chaparral to tropical forest, and it congregates in fairly large groups. A second variety, the white-lipped peccary (*Tayassu pecari*), is located mainly in the tropical rain forests of Central America. The third is the Chacoan peccary, which was first encountered in 1972 in the dense scrub and cactus bush area known as the Chaco. The Chaco is an area of northern Argentina, southeast Bolivia, and western Paraguay.

A peccary will eat anything it can obtain. Both the Chacoan peccary and the collared peccary like to eat large amounts of cactus. Both males and females are armed with substantial razor-sharp canine teeth—the male's slightly larger than the female's—which they can use to fiercely defend their own family and young. Pecarries are eaten by predators such as jaguars, although groups are never attacked. A jaguar, for example, will only stalk a straggler.

Most peccaries are found in herds of 14 to 50 individuals, but the Chacoan is found in smaller numbers, usually in groups of no more than seven. They have stable territories which they strongly defend, and they mark their territories with dorsal gland secretions, dung piles, and other signs. There is strong group recognition among peccaries, reinforced by their practice of standing side-by-side and rubbing their faces on each other.

The biggest problem for the peccary is its competition with humans. Its habitat is being

CHACOAN PECCARY
South America

Compared to pigs, the Chacoan peccary has a slightly longer body with slender legs. Like pigs, it is omnivorous, preferring to eat a variety of roots, seeds, and fruit.

converted to agricultural lands, and the peccary is regarded as a pest. For instance, it will raid a garden when it finds one. The Chacoan peccary also happens to be a major staple of the dinner table, so intense hunting has reduced its numbers. The animal had nearly disappeared before biologists had a chance to study it. Only 5,000 survive in the Chaco as of 1989. In 1996, 12 animals derived from a captive population of the Chacoan peccary were brought to the Phoenix Zoo. These have reproduced and offspring will be disseminated to other zoos.

Warren D. Thomas

PELICANS

Class: Aves

Order: Pelecaniformes

Family: Pelecanidae

Pelicans are among the world's most recognizable birds. No other bird looks like a pelican. They all have stout, long, and narrow beaks with a hook at the tip. The mouth floor is huge, enlarged into a pouch attached to the throat. They expand the pouch under water and use it like a scoop. Pelicans have an upright posture on small legs and big feet. The feet are unique to the pelican order; all four toes are webbed together. Pelicans are always associated with seawater or fresh water. Ornithologists recognize eight pelican species; two of those are endangered.

Brown Pelican
(Pelecanus occidentalis)

ESA: Endangered

Length: 42–54 in (106.7–137.2 cm)
Weight: 7–8 lb. (3.2–3.6 kg)
Clutch size: 3 eggs
Incubation: 30–32 days
Diet: Fish
Habitat: Ocean coasts
Range: Eastern Pacific Ocean from British Columbia south to Peru; western Atlantic Ocean from New York to northern Brazil, including the Gulf of Mexico and the Caribbean Sea

BROWN PELICANS swoop down within inches of the water and glide over the sea like a squadron of crack aviators. They glide with drill-team precision, riding the air just inches and seconds ahead of breaking waves. This skill is sometimes overshadowed by their comical appearance. To humans, pelicans appear odd. On land, they waddle about on toes and feet that are too large for their short legs. They point their great beaks downward to watch the world, just as someone might tuck their chin down to look over a pair of glasses.

Brown pelicans have gray-brown bodies with darker brownish black bellies. They have white heads and necks, but the foreheads and crowns are usually yellow. During the breeding season, they develop a deep brown or chestnut nape and a bright yellow patch on the lower throat. Their beaks are pale gray in the

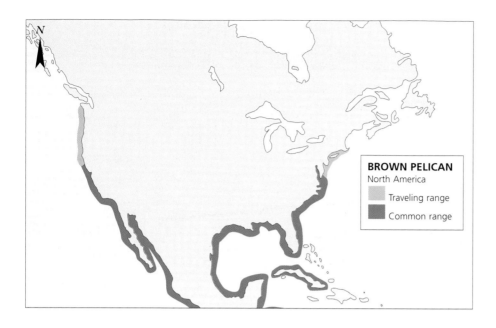

BROWN PELICAN
North America
Traveling range
Common range

breeding season but otherwise they are orangish pink. Their great throat pouches are always gray colored.

Brown pelicans loiter about piers and docks and are a common sight along the seashore. They are more common now than they used to be, but they are not as common as they were a long time ago. Historically they ranged from Maryland south into the Gulf of Mexico and farther down into South American waters. Across the continent they ranged from British Columbia south to Peru, including the Gulf of California. Their breeding areas were more restricted.

Only a few pairs nested as far north as North Carolina, but the species bred by the tens of thousands in Florida and around the Gulf of Mexico. On the Pacific Coast they nested from central California south, with most in the Gulf of California.

Brown pelicans almost always nest low to the ground, or on the ground, just barely above high tide marks. They naturally shift their nesting location around, sometimes from year to year

depending on conditions. They almost always choose islands and islets, probably as security against mammalian predators. But what mammals cannot reach, artificial chemicals can.

With the development of the pesticide known as DDT after World War II, humans introduced a long-lasting toxin into the environment. DDT was effective against mosquitoes and other agricultural pests, but it was so potent that it lingered long after the pests were gone. It persisted in the environment and

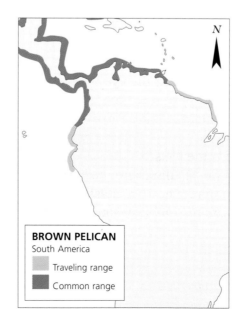

BROWN PELICAN
South America
Traveling range
Common range

could be passed along the food chain when one organism ate another, which is exactly how the brown pelican was eventually affected.

No brown pelicans were directly sprayed with DDT, but the chemical was found in high levels in pelican bodies. Ornithologists discovered that DDT is stored in fat and does not break down. As DDT was used, it was passed from one creature to another. Fish ate contaminated crustaceans, and pelicans ate the contaminated fish. Once inside the pelicans, the DDT interfered with the calcium cycle so much that female pelicans laid thin-shelled eggs. Weak eggshells are vulnerable to breaking during incubation. In some colonies, breakage resulted in total breeding failure. Other pesticides killed pelicans outright.

DDT was banned from general use in 1972. Endrin, another pesticide, was likewise banned. Some 50,000 brown pelicans had nested in coastal Louisiana and Texas before the intense use of DDT during the 1950s and 1960s. By 1960 the brown pelican, Louisiana's state bird, had disappeared as a breeding species in that state. The Texas population nearly followed. California's brown pelicans also declined, as did those living along the Atlantic Coast. In 1970 the U.S. Fish and Wildlife Service designated the brown pelican as endangered. Since then, pesticides have been more strictly regulated, access to nesting islands has been controlled, and the brown pelican has begun to recover. Where it had not been seen for years, the brown pelican is now a regular show stopper once again.

Dalmatian Pelican
(Pelecanus crispus)

IUCN: Vulnerable

Length: 63–71 in. (160–180 cm)
Weight: 23½–29 lb. (10.5–13 kg)
Clutch size: Usually 2–3, rarely 4–6
Incubation: 30-32 days
Diet: Fish
Habitat: Both freshwater and saltwater wetlands, including rivers and lakes, plus the seacoasts
Range: Europe and Asia, from Greece and Albania to Mongolia and China; migratory birds winter in the Middle East, Pakistan, India, and Hong Kong

THE DALMATIAN pelican derives its name from a geographical area. Dalmatia lies east across the Adriatic Sea on the west Balkan peninsula. Sadly, this bird no longer occurs in the land that is its namesake. Actually, the Dalmatian pelican is absent from many parts of its former range.

Appearance

Among the largest flying birds in the world, the Dalmatian pelican cuts an elegant figure when soaring in flocks. Pale gray upperparts contrast modestly with pale blue-gray, nearly white, underparts. A patch of curly feathers extends from the rear of the crown part way down the nape. These feathers become much shaggier and crestlike during the breeding season. A small patch of feathers on the throat are dull yellow. The outer flight feathers are black. Bare skin around the eye turns purple during the breeding season and is yellow the rest of the time.

Space loss

The Dalmation pelican has suffered from a massive loss of suitable habitat since the 19th century. Wetlands have been filled and destroyed whenever people see the land better used for farming and grazing. This has eliminated the species from

The brown pelican may have a comical appearance, but it is a skilled hunter that will swoop down upon its ocean-dwelling prey.

much of its historic range. Such loss has occurred across much of southeastern Europe, eastward through southwestern Asia, and into China and Mongolia. The Dalmatian pelican migrates from its northerly haunts to spend winters in the warmer climates of

1051

The Dalmatian pelican once sustained healthy populations across Eurasia, but today only tiny groups remain.

the eastern Mediterranean Sea, the Black and Caspian Seas, the Middle East, Pakistan, northern India, and Hong Kong.

Persecution

Besides dwindling habitat, the Dalmatian pelican has suffered the wrath of fishermen who destroy birds that catch too many fish. The killing of these pelicans has been severe in some places. In the mid-1800s about a million Dalmatian pelicans swarmed about Romania; only 150 pairs remained in the mid-1990s. Yugoslavia lost nearly all its pelican breeding colonies by 1973, with only one still remaining in 1998. The last strongholds of the pelican are in Greece and in parts of south-central Asia. The total population was estimated to be around 15,000–20,000 individuals in 1998, with 4,000–5,200 breeding pairs. Most of these birds live in small, fragmented groups where some remnants of wetland habitat still endure.

Some wetlands have been protected in national reserves and parks, and legal protection for the pelican has been enacted in many countries.

Conservation measures have been successful in increasing the two main breeding colonies in Greece, but elsewhere legal protection is not enforced, and reserves and parks are not adequately managed. The Dalmatian pelican does not face immediate extinction, but several simultaneous or consecutive catastrophic events could doom the species. It is likely that people will not restore wetland habitat once it has been destroyed, so for the Dalmatian pelican preserving the remaining habitat is crucial.

Kevin Cook

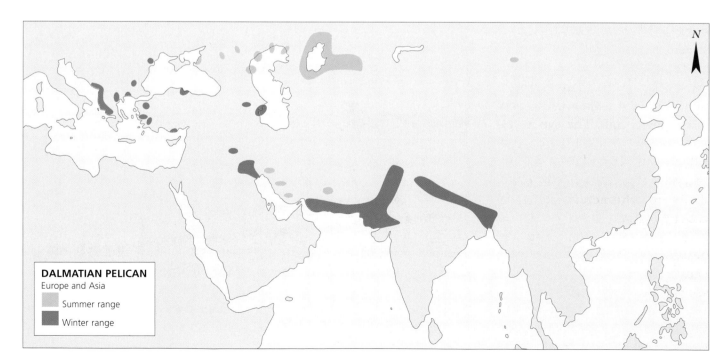

DALMATIAN PELICAN
Europe and Asia

Summer range

Winter range

N

Yellow-eyed Penguin

(Megadyptes antipodes)

IUCN: Vulnerable

Class: Aves
Order: Sphenisciformes
Family: Spheniscidae
Length: 25–30 in. (64–76 cm)
Height: Stands 17¾–21½ in. (45–55 cm) tall
Weight: 11–17 lb. (5–8.5 kg)
Clutch size: 2 eggs, 3–5 days apart
Incubation: Average 42 days
Diet: Squid and small fish
Range: South, Stewart, Auckland, and Campbell Islands of New Zealand

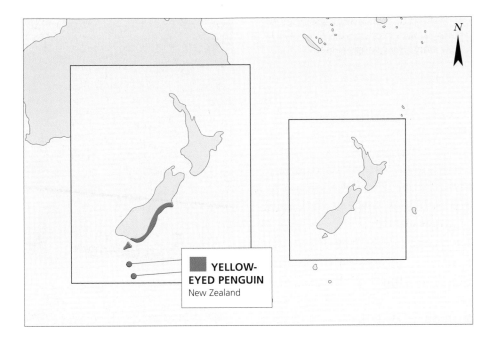

YELLOW-EYED PENGUIN
New Zealand

AN INHABITANT OF New Zealand waters, the yellow-eyed penguin is evenly colored, being gray above and clean white below. The gray also covers the cheek and chin. The crown is crested with gold that extends in an arc from behind each eye, meeting on top of the head in a tuft. The forehead and forecrown have fine streaks of gray. The underwing, foot, and toe are all pink. The thick, stout beak is mostly pink but with a white line on the base of the lower half. The eye is yellow rather than the brown or red color of other penguins. The yellow-eyed penguin has many different characteristics from other penguins.

Yellow-eyed penguins are noticeably plumper than other penguin species. They also stay around their home waters all year. Only a few of the southernmost yellow-eyed penguins migrate northward during the winter months. They nest among vegetation that conceals them from visual contact with neighbors. Because of this they are generally considered solitary nesters. When pairing, yellow-eyed penguins are flexible. Some have remained paired to the same mate for as long as 13 years, but a little over half of them stay paired for only one year. The age of first breeding in males is two to three years, while in females it is three to four years. About two-thirds of the nests of first-time breeders fail, but older birds manage to succeed with more than 90 percent of their nests.

Population changes

As the chicks mature, they leave the nest to form large gatherings. Other species of penguins, but not all, also form such crèches. The chicks become independent at about four months of age, and then they waddle off to sea.

Even seabirds such as the yellow-eyed penguin must nest on land.

Many people assume that penguins live only in frigid climates of the Antarctic regions, but the yellow-eyed penguin is proof that this bird can live in more temperate environments as well.

Loss of habitat has caused a decline in the number of yellow-eyed penguins. Accurate population estimates are not known for all of the penguins' range. Recent estimates of the total population vary between 4,000 and 7,000 individuals and 1,410 to 1,770 breeding pairs. The South Island is estimated at having 507 breeding pairs in 1995. The population on South Island may have declined by 75 percent since the 1940s, while the number of breeding pairs on Campbell Island was 36 percent lower in 1992 than 1988. It is, however, unclear whether these declines are part of a recent overall population trend or due to extreme population fluctuations.

Exotic threat

Humans brought exotic mammals to many of the islands where the penguins nest. House cats (*Felis sylvatica*) were brought largely as pets, but also partly for their ability to catch mice and rats. Ferrets (*Mustella putorius*) and stoats were also brought to the islands in order to control the rat and rabbit (*Oryctolagus cuniculus*) population. Cats and ferrets were not slow to learn how easy nestling penguins were to catch.

Yellow-eyed penguins are plump birds because they have large supplies of body fat to insulate them against cold water. When they come ashore to rest, sleep, or tend their young, they become susceptible to overheating in the sun. They need

good plant cover to shade them while they are ashore and to block visibility between nests, which is a critical factor in successful nesting. People have cleared almost all the native coastal plant communities within the penguin's breeding areas on South Island. What used to be forests and woodlands there are now farms and croplands, which provide no shelter from the sun at all. Being creatures of habit, the penguins return to the same place year after year, but fail to breed successfully and gradually die out.

Ornithologists also know that penguin chicks frequently starve to death. This is a natural phenomenon that may have been intensified by heavy commercial fishing in the waters where penguins normally feed. The yellow-eyed penguin has been the focus of a wide range of ongoing research and monitoring since 1981. The Yellow-eyed Penguin Trust was formed specifically to raise awareness and funds. Many mainland sites have been fenced to minimize trampling by farm stock. Predator trapping is intensive during breeding season at a few South Island sites.

In addition, several programs are in progress that aim to restore scrub and forest to mainland breeding sites.

Kevin Cook

PERRITOS

Class: Actinopterygii
Order: Cyprinodontiformes
Family: Cyprinodontidae

The perritos are similar to the species commonly known as pupfish in the United States, and are located within the country of Mexico. The name perrito refers to a little whelp or pup. These fish are also called cachorritos.

Perritos are part of the rather large and widespread group of fish called killifish (Cyprinodontidae and other families). Representatives of this group are found in temperate and tropical climates throughout most of the world. Killifish are found in North America, South America, Africa, southern Asia, southern Europe, and the East Indies, but they are not native to Australia. Compared to most freshwater fish, killifish are able to inhabit some extreme aquatic environments. They are found in salt water and fresh water, as well as in water with a high mineral content. They also show a tremendous range of temperature tolerance.

Killifish bear a strong resemblance to minnows (family Cyprinidae). In fact, their own family name (Cyprinodontidae) loosely means "toothed carp." Killifish are, however, quite different. The tail is usually rounded, and they have scales on the head.

For the most part, perritos are small and colorful. Most species show a difference in color, markings, or a body form between male and female, which is called sexual dimorphism.

All of the perritos are egg layers, and males often exhibit territorial behavior at breeding time. Most perritos spawn in the spring or early summer, releasing eggs and sperm on or near aquatic vegetation, although some species seem to prefer to lay eggs on gravel or mineral deposits.

Some species have adapted to temporary ponds that contain water only part of the year. Eggs are laid and buried in the pond bottom and are able to survive when the pond has dried up and all adult fish have died. Miraculously, the eggs hatch once the seasonal rains return.

The mouth of most perritos is at the top of their flattened head, and a good percentage of feeding occurs at or near the water surface.

The perritos' small size has allowed them to occupy restricted habitats in significant numbers. They are rarely found with other large predatory fish in their native habitat.

Perrito de Carbonera

(Cyprinodon fontinalis)

IUCN: Endangered

Length: 1½ in. (4 cm)
Reproduction: Egg layer
Habitat: Spring pools and outflows
Range: Guzmán Basin, Chihuahua, Mexico

THE PERRITO DE Carbonera of northern Mexico is in severe danger of extinction. This fish occupies an isolated spring system of the Chihuahuan Desert in a rural area called Guzmán Basin. Water is the key to survival in this region, and that rule holds true for people as well as for fish. Unfortunately, the people who inhabit the area demand that they have priority over fishes such as the perrito de Carbonera.

Given the scarcity of surface water in this desert environment, most of the water used for irrigation and domestic purposes is pumped from a natural underground reservoir called an aquifer. In addition, water from this aquifer supplies artesian springs that support fish such as the perrito de Carbonera. Water use, particularly the pumping of water from the groundwater sources for large-scale agricultural irrigation, is slowly lowering the underground water table and threatening to dry up the springs that are the lifeline of the perrito de Carbonera.

In addition, some of the water that does reach the surface at the fish's spring sites is diverted for human use. Fierce non-native predatory fishes, such as the largemouth bass, have also been stocked into the basin and threaten to wipe out the last populations of perrito de Carbonera. The only hope for the continued survival of this species is to maintain the water table and to exclude predatory fishes.

Appearance

The perrito de Carbonera is protected by large scales over most of its body, but the head and face are nude. It has no defensive spines on the fins. Both sexes are a gray-green color on the back and upper sides, while males may show a brilliant, iridescent blue. The belly is lighter, and the breast and chin are a silvery yellow. The sides are marked by several dark blue vertical bars over a silvery white background. The adult male has a tail fin that is edged in jet black; the female's tail lacks any significant color. Other fins in the male are yellow-orange with some black edging or black at the base. The female's fins are yellowish, with a dorsal fin that carries a prominent dark blotch called an ocellus.

Perritos are often solitary or live with one to three other species of fish. Many are found in closed desert basins, and they often rely on springs or spring-fed environments. Most have evolved in isolated habitats that have been relatively constant for thousands of years. This has allowed evolutionary changes to occur, and over time these isolated fish have become unique species. For many of the perritos, home is like an island of water in a vast desert. Changes in these environments, brought about mainly by human activities, have more often than not had dramatic impacts on these small and curious fish.

Perrito de Potosí

(Cyprinodon alvarezi)

IUCN: Extinct in the wild

Length: 1½ in. (4 cm)
Reproduction: Egg layer
Habitat: Cool spring pond and adjoining waterways
Range: El Potosí, Nuevo Leon, Mexico

THE PERRITO de Potosí has never been an abundant or wide-ranging species. Both historical records and direct observations over the years indicate that it is restricted in range to a small spring system near the town of El Potosí, in the Mexican state of Nuevo Leon. However, this perrito thrived in the spring pond and adjoining waterways until a non-native predatory species, the largemouth bass (*Micropterus salmoides*), was introduced into the spring system. This invader has taken over the primary spring pond, with catastrophic results for the native fish populations.

The perrito de Potosí is small, but brilliantly colored. The body is a solid iridescent blue, with darker patches of blue on the back and sides of some fish, and faint black blotches on the sides that form a horizontal stripe. All fins are clear or faintly blue with the exception of the tail fin. A prominent vertical black bar decorates the very tip of this fin. Like all perritos and cachorritos, the perrito de Potosí has a robust and stout body, a slightly upturned mouth, and jutting lower jaw. The head is small, and the body is well covered with large scales; the head has few scales or is nude.

Reproduction

This fish breeds in the spring of the year, with some color change evident in the male. The dorsal fin on the back becomes somewhat white, and the sides lose much of their blotchiness to display an almost solid blue. Both sexes eat insects and other aquatic invertebrates within the El Potosí spring system.

Currently, only a handful of the perrito de Potosí can be located in the spring pond, and most must survive outside of the pond in much smaller stream

PERRITO DE CARBONERA
North America

PERRITO DE POTOSI
North America

Perritos are extremely vulnerable when larger, more aggressive fish are stocked in their native waters.

pools at the spring pond outlet. Fortunately, largemouth bass have not yet escaped the confines of this water body. The Mexican government has taken steps to protect the perrito de Potosí and other native fish from the ravages of the largemouth bass. A project funded by the Fauna Preservation Society is designed to rid the spring pool of largemouth bass. It has also been recommended that a backup population of this species be established at a separate, secure site until the bass have been eliminated. This perrito has been shown to reproduce in captivity and could be held in artificial systems.

As with other fish that live in arid environments, the pumping of ground water for use in agricultural irrigation poses yet another threat to the perrito de Potosí. Pumping of water at one location often affects the level of the water table in another area. As local farmers use water from this underground source, the water flow to the Potosí spring has decreased.

Water threat

Regardless of efforts to eliminate largemouth bass from the system, if the water table in the area continues to fall, the spring may fail to produce water and the fate of the perrito de Potosí will be finally sealed.

William E. Manci

PETRELS

Class: Aves
Order: Procellariiformes
Family: Procellariidae

Petrels come in many sizes but in only one shape. From giant petrels as big as albatrosses to the small, slight species, they all share certain features: they spend their lives on the sea; they glide on long, slender wings; they produce oily stomach secretions; they lay one egg in the breeding season; and they have tubular nostrils. These characteristics serve them well.

The tubular nostrils are responsible for the common English group name of petrels, shearwaters, and albatrosses—*tubenoses*. The special nostrils probably perform two functions. First, the birds have no access to fresh water, so they either drink sea water or do without. Even without drinking they still take in a lot of saltwater with their food and from preening their feathers. Large salt glands around the eye help extract excess salt from the birds' blood. The salt-rich liquid is then drained through ducts into the nostrils and sneezed away. Second, the tubular nostrils may help the birds detect wind speed and direction vital to sustaining their gliding type of flight.

Tubenoses as a group generally enjoy some of the longest life spans of any birds. They typically require several years to reach breeding maturity, and then concentrate on raising a single chick per breeding season. Under normal circumstances this reproductive technique works very well, as is plainly seen in the vast numbers of sea birds. One chick means fewer trips to and from nesting burrows, and less food that must be captured and carried. Because a petrel spends long hours fasting while incubating its egg, radical weight gains and losses are normal for the various species. These birds compensate with nutrient- and energy-rich stomach oils that can be fed to the chicks. A few species have even developed the stomach oil as a defense. They regurgitate it forcefully onto intruders in order to discourage predation.

Long, narrow wings are perfectly adapted to the air currents that accompany wave formation on the ocean. As the sea water heaves and swells, air is constantly displaced and shuffled around. The tubenoses' wings can catch this air and keep the birds aloft with little waste of energy.

Most petrels nest on islands, and islands—unfortunately—have been badly damaged by people. Most of the world's sea birds have suffered some population decline, and many petrels are among the victims.

Black Petrel

(Procellaria parkinsoni)

IUCN: Vulnerable

Length: 16–17 in. (40.6–43.2 cm)
Diet: Probably squid, crustaceans, and small fish
Habitat: Pelagic; nests on islands
Range: Breeds on Little Barrier and Great Barrier Islands of New Zealand; after breeding wanders to Galapagos Islands and off-coast waters of northwestern South America and Central America

NEW ZEALAND IS split into two large islands, North and South. In historic times, black petrels once bred on North Island and portions of South Island. Now they survive only on two smaller islands: Little Barrier and Great Barrier. Deforestation, conversion of plant communities to agriculture, and other human land uses have worked against the petrels, but the spread of rats (*Rattus* sp.) and house cats (*Felis sylvestris*) across the islands undoubtedly did more to destroy the petrels than anything else.

People recognized the plight of New Zealand birds even in the 1800s. In 1894, an important step was taken when Little Barrier Island was bought by the government and set aside as a nature reserve. The first reserve manager killed a dog and some pigs his first year, and by 1907 cats and Polynesian rats (*Rattus exulans*) were the only exotic predators left. They remain a threat, but they are quite likely to be eradicated sometime in the near future.

Cats capture adult petrels as they return to or emerge from their nesting burrows. They also catch fledgling petrels as they emerge for their first flight to the sea. Headless bird corpses are typical evidence of cat predation. In some years during the 1960s and 1970s, cats killed virtually all the fledgling petrels on Little Barrier Island. Without young birds to sustain the population, the black petrel declined steadily until, in 1977, only six pairs tried to breed on Little Barrier.

Efforts to eradicate cats were sporadic at best. The feline enteritis virus, highly lethal to cats, was introduced into the cat population in 1968. Trapping of cats fluctuated with funding. Great efforts to eradicate cats began in 1977, and the last were destroyed in 1980. The black petrel population on Little Barrier Island has slowly improved.

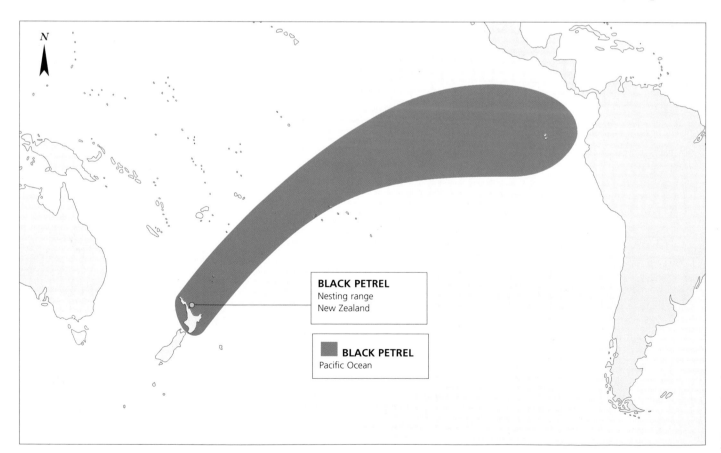

BLACK PETREL
Nesting range
New Zealand

BLACK PETREL
Pacific Ocean

Great Barrier Island also suffers from exotic predators, including rats, cats, and dogs. Black petrels have survived there in healthier, though still reduced, numbers. This may be because cats are at a lower density on Great Barrier Island than on Little Barrier Island. The total black petrel population as of the early 1990s was around 3,000 to 4,000 birds. Cat eradication on Little Barrier saved the species from extinction but the population is only increasing slowly.

The Great Barrier population is thought to be stable, but predation may make an impact. A long-term study, initiated in 1996, should identify the effects predators are having. If work indicates they are causing a decline, predator control will be implemented. Between 1986 and 1990 about 249 fledglings were transferred from Great Barrier to Little Barrier to boost numbers, but the population is slowly increasing on its own.

Chatham Island Petrel

(Pterodroma axillaris)

IUCN: Vulnerable

Length: 11–12 in. (27.9–30.5 cm)
Diet: Crustaceans and small fish
Habitat: Pelagic; nests on land
Range: Nests only on South East Island of the Chatham Islands in the Pacific Ocean

RAISING LIVESTOCK as an occupation makes sense for a lot of people in this world because it can bring commerce to otherwise isolated places. Grazing livestock on islands, however, has never had good consequences for native species that have nowhere else to go. The Chatham Island petrel is such a species.

Although once regarded as a subspecies of the black-winged petrel (*Pterodroma nigripennis*), the Chatham Island petrel now enjoys its status as a full species according to the recommendation of some ornithologists.

It wears a somewhat shrikelike plumage pattern. Sooty brown wings and tail contrast the uniformly pale gray upper parts. The gray continues up the nape, onto the hind cheek, over the crown, and onto the forehead. The lore, front cheek, and chin are clean white and offset the black smudge that circles the eye and the black-colored beak. A pale

PYCROFT'S PETREL
New Zealand

CHATHAM ISLAND PETREL
Chatham Islands

gray band connects shoulder to shoulder across the breast. The Chatham Island petrel differs most notably from the black-winged petrel in that it has black wingpits instead of white.

Distribution

The Chatham Island petrel has never been abundant. Although it is a sea bird and presumably wanders, it has never been seen outside the vicinity of the islands but is presumed to migrate to the North Pacific. The Chathams form an archipelago claimed by New Zealand. Taken all together, the small islands that make up this archipelago cover only 372 square miles (967 square kilometers). The Chatham Island petrel nests only on South East Island, which has an area of about 1 square mile (2 square kilometers). Subfossils show the species also once nested on Chatham and Mangere Island. Exploitation by humans for food, and predation by cats, pigs, and rats (*Rattus* spp.) contributed to the bird's disappearance from these islands.

The New Zealand government acquired South East Island in 1954 and designated it a nature reserve. The last cattle and sheep were removed in 1961. Since that time, the island's vegetation has revived. The livestock undoubtedly crushed many nesting burrows during the preceding 100 years. More importantly, grazing changed the character of the island's plant community. Ornithologists are not certain how this may have affected the petrel. There are now approximately 1.3 million breeding pairs of burrowing seabirds on South East Island, but habitat regeneration due to the end of farming on the island may have an effect on colony distribution.

Ornithologists originally expected that the Chatham Island petrel would recover once grazing was halted. South East Island has no other exotic mammals that could prey upon eggs, nestlings, or fledglings. The recovery never happened. Research indicates that intense competition for burrows from the abundant Broad-billed prion, (*Pachyptila vittata*), including lethal attacks on chicks and eggs, and occasionally adults, is the primary threat to the species. Such competition may be the cause of the observed low breeding success and high rates of pair bond disruption. As a consequence of competition with the Broad-billed prion, the Chatham Island Petrel has become one of the most threatened bird species in New Zealand. The total population of the bird is estimated at 800–1,000 birds, and this number is declining.

DEFILIPPE'S PETREL
Nesting range
South America

DEFILIPPE'S PETREL
Pacific Ocean

Defilippe's Petrel
(Pterodroma defilippiana)

IUCN: Vulnerable

Length: 11–12 in. (27.9–30.5 cm)
Diet: Crustaceans and small fish
Habitat: Pelagic; nests on islands
Range: Juan Fernandez and Desventuradas Islands, off the coast of South America

OUT IN THE eastern Pacific Ocean, south of the equator, two tiny islands and a handful of rocky islets define the Juan Fernandez Islands. They form a natural archipelago 417 miles (667 kilometers) off the Chilean coast. Defilippe's petrels were among the island natives that kept the buccaneer Alexander Selkirk company from 1704 to 1708. Selkirk had quarreled with his captain, demanded to be put ashore, and was abandoned on Mas Afuera, which is situated off the coast of Chile.

In 1712 the book *The Life and Adventures of Alexander Selkirk* appeared. Popular opinion credits Selkirk with inspiring Daniel Defoe's *Robinson Crusoe*. Fact or fiction, the tale moved the Chilean government to rename the Juan Fernandez Islands. The more distant island, Mas Afuera, was dubbed Isla Alejandro Selkirk, and the nearer island, Mas a Tierra, became Isla Robinson Crusoe.

Defilippe's petrels, first described in 1869, have been considered both a discrete species and a subspecies of the Cook's petrel (*Pterodroma cooki*). They nest in burrows excavated

Defilippe's petrels inhabit several islands off the coast of South America. They eat small fish and crustaceans.

into the soils of mountain forests on both the Juan Fernandez and the Desventuradas Islands. Both island groups have been radically altered by the actions of people during the last three centuries.

Goats (*Capra hircus*) were released on the Juan Fernandez Islands in the late 1500s. Sailors often did this as a way to ensure fresh meat on future voyages. Goats were the usual animal chosen because they survived well aboard ships and they survived even better when left unattended on islands with no natural enemies. In fact, goats survived well enough to overpopulate and consequently overgraze most of the islands on which they were released. Other exotic mammals, such as European rabbits (*Oryctolagus cuniculus*), feral cats, and coatis (*Nasua nasua*), have been introduced to the islands and harmed native animals and plants, as have exotic brambles

Rats, house cats, and short-tailed weasels (*Mustela erminea*) have created the worst problems for native birds in New Zealand. Pycroft's petrels have not altogether escaped these exotic predators.

(*Rubus ulmifolius*) and eucalyptus (*Eucalyptus* sp.). Although Santa Clara and San Ambrosio appear to be predator-free, feral cats and coatis are blamed for the possible extinction of Defilippe's petrel on Robinson Crusoe island, and cats have caused extensive mortality on San Félix.

Special protection

The Chilean government has declared the Juan Fernandez Islands a national park, and have shown international cooperation in designating the islands an International Biosphere Reserve. Some effort has been made to trap cats and rats, but not to the extent necessary to protect the petrels. The species has possibly

been extirpated from Robinson Crusoe Island but still survives on Santa Clara, where there are thought to be from 100 to 200 individuals. On the Desventurada Islands the population is restricted to San Ambrosio, where there were 10,000 or more birds in 1970, and San Félix, where there were from 150 to 200 pairs in 1970. Such figures are too indefinite to motivate recovery plans and actions.

Basic natural history research is needed to distinguish the Defilippe's petrel's needs from the better-known Cook's petrel's needs. When the life story of Defilippe's petrel is better understood, more can be done for it.

Pycroft's Petrel
(Pterodroma pycrofti)

IUCN: Vulnerable

Length: 10½–11½ in. (26.7–29.2 cm)
Weight: 6¾ oz. (187.5 g)
Clutch size: 1 egg
Incubation: Possibly 45 days
Diet: Probably crustaceans and small fish
Habitat: Pelagic; nests on islands
Range: Nests only on Poor Knights, Hen and Chickens, and Red Mercury islands, New Zealand

IN 1933 the Pycroft's petrel was described as being a separate species distinct from the Cook's petrel (*Pterodroma cooki*). Sixty years later, ornithologists still know little more about the bird than when it was first discovered.

The Pycroft's petrel is smaller than the Cook's petrel. Its coloration is also darker. The Pycroft's plumage is gray from the crown down the nape and across the back to the central tail feathers. The white forehead continues through the lore and across the lower cheek. From chin to undertail, the underparts are white. The underwing is silvery with a little dark gray showing on the leading edge.

Living spaces

Pycroft's petrel nests in burrows, often far inland from the sea and on mountain slopes, but at much lower elevations than the Cook's petrels. It always excavates its burrows in dense, heavy forest. Presumably, the forest cover helps it elude predators. Under natural circumstances, the Pycroft's petrel could rely on dense forests and nocturnal behavior to escape predation by natural enemies such as the skua (*Catharacta* sp.) and the morepork (*Ninox novaeseelandiae*). However, people brought predatory mammals to the New Zealand islands, and the petrel cannot easily avoid them. Some clearing of forests has damaged petrel nesting habitat. At the same time the exotic predators have thrived. In 1990 ornithologists estimated that the Pycroft's petrel population was under 1,000 pairs.

Programs to eradicate cats from New Zealand's smaller coastal islands have been undertaken. Even on islands where eradication is not a priority, some trapping is done just to control cat and rat populations. Success on islands such as Little Barrier prove the value of eradication programs. More of them will eventually result in better conditions for birds such as the Pycroft's petrel.

Kevin Cook

See also Albatrosses, and Shearwaters.

PHEASANTS

Class: Aves

Order: Galliformes

Family: Phasianidae

Pheasants, francolins, partridges, junglefowls, and peafowls all belong to a fascinating family of birds. All the pheasants are smaller than peafowls, but many of them sport extravagant plumages that surpass those of the peafowls for sheer elegance. The pheasants also have bright red wattles that are more or less developed according to species. The elaborate comb and jowls of the domestic rooster illustrate how far such wattles can be developed. Male pheasants also grow a spur on the back of the foot. The spur is a separate growth and unrelated to any toe. Some species may grow two or three spurs on each foot. They may be quite large and sharply pointed.

Some pheasants form pair bonds with a single mate. They defend territories, and both parents help with rearing the young. In these species the males lack extravagant plumage. The more elaborately dressed pheasants defend territories in which they display their fine plumage to attract females and to intimidate other males. Intimidation does not always work, however, and the pheasants often are driven to battle. The wattles about the face become engorged with blood, making them much larger than usual. The birds square off, often pumping their tails, then leap into the air, rear back, and slash at each other with their spurs. The winner keeps the territory. Victorious males typically mate with several females within their territories.

The pheasants have many enemies. Their eggs and young are vulnerable to snakes, rodents, and weasels. Young pheasants are also easy prey for various predatory birds. Hawks and owls present a very real threat to adult birds, as do wild cats and foxes. Pheasants typically first defend themselves by crouching among the plants to escape detection. When discovered, they explode into flight on short, rounded, and cupped wings that beat furiously, giving them instant speed.

Pheasants probably developed in Southeast Asia. That region's exploding human population now threatens the habitat of many species. Hungry people also find pheasants worthwhile to hunt and trap. Pheasant populations squeezed by habitat loss and excessive shooting and trapping cannot help but decline. The pheasants' elegant beauty has attracted human interest for centuries. People have successfully kept many species, and the knowledge gained may help keep some species alive. Keeping species in aviaries, however, is no substitute for preserving the species in the wild.

Brown Eared-pheasant
(Crossoptilon mantchuricum)

ESA: Endangered

IUCN: Vulnerable

Length: 40 in. (101.6 cm)
Weight: Males, 3⅔–5½ lb. (1.7–2.5 kg); females, 3–4½ lb. (1.5–2 kg)
Clutch size: Normally 4–14 eggs; reports of 22 eggs
Incubation: 26–27 days
Diet: Plant materials including roots, tubers, bulbs, leaves, shoots, fruits, and seeds; animal material including insects and earthworms
Habitat: Montane woodlands
Range: Shanxi and Hebei Provinces, China

THE BROWN EARED-pheasant could pass as an ornamental chicken. It possesses the same fountainlike spray of tail feathers as the common barnyard rooster, is approximately the same size as a chicken, and has a similar overall physique. Pheasants and chickens both have spurs on their feet, but there the similarities end.

Domestic chickens originated from the red junglefowl (*Gallus gallus*), which is native to southern Asia from Pakistan to Southeast Asia, Malaysia, and western Indonesia. The brown eared-pheasant is one of three eared-pheasant (*Crossoptilon*) species that evolved in central China.

A mountain bird, the brown eared-pheasant lives in habitat with a mixture of oaks, birches, and pines.

The brown eared-pheasant has a black crown below, with a large oval of bare red skin that surrounds the eye and includes the lores and upper cheek. A narrow band of white feathers originates on the chin and sweeps backward across the cheek. Elongated cheek feathers extend beyond the back of the head in wispy tufts. The black neck fades to a brown back, wing, breast, and belly. The silvery white color of the rump extends onto the tail. The tips of the tail feathers are shaded dark brown, with a purplish or blue sheen. Females do not differ from males. The brown eared-pheasant grows a loose, hairlike plumage unlike the feathers seen on a chicken.

High living

Generally, the brown eared-pheasant ranges between 4,300 and 11,500 feet (1,300–3,500 meters). At high altitudes, harsh environmental conditions stunt tree growth so that forests give way to dense woodlands of dwarf trees. The brown eared-pheasant works the ground beneath these trees. When searching for food, the brown eared-pheasant also moves to forest and woodland edges, even into meadows. It digs up roots and tubers and scratches among the litter for large seeds and acorns. It also readily eats large insects and other invertebrates that it uncovers while scratching. After feeding, the pheasant returns to the protective shelter of the trees.

The brown eared-pheasant appears to form pair bonds. Males defend territories and attract other females by displaying their plumage. They then mate with any females that enter their display areas. The brown eared-pheasant, however, may remain paired all year, despite mating with a variety of females. Even in winter, when two or three dozen birds may huddle together for warmth and protection, the bonds between males and females are apparent.

Most of the brown eared-pheasant's former habitat has already been cut down. The Chinese have cleared nearly all the useful timber. The pheasant survives in three reserves and possibly in remnants of dwarf forest that are not valuable for lumber products. Population estimates are nonexistent, so the exact status of the species is unknown. The species does appear to be healthy in at least one of the reserves.

Cheer Pheasant
(Catreus wallichi)

ESA: Endangered

IUCN: Vulnerable

Length: 38–40 in. (96.5–101.6 cm)
Weight: 2¾–3¾ lb. (1.2–1.7 kg)
Clutch size: 9–14 eggs, usually 9–10
Incubation: 26 days
Diet: Leaves, roots, tubers, small fruits, seeds, and invertebrates
Range: Northern Pakistan and India into western Nepal

PHEASANTS MAKE good eating, and for a hungry person a pheasant is worth hunting whether it is rare or abundant. The cheer pheasant, so named for its call, has been hunted for centuries by the people of the western Himalayas. Hunting is just one of several factors now pressuring the cheer pheasant.

Color patterning

An attractive bird, patterned in earth tones of brown, buff, tan, gray, black, and white, the cheer pheasant is well camouflaged for life in the tall grass. Its most distinctive feature is a long, thin crest that projects from the back of the head. The crown is deep brown, and the bare skin around the eye is bright red. The chin, throat, and neck are all gray or dingy white. The breast is gray-white, boldly barred with black, yielding to a more golden belly with a central black patch. The undertail is golden red. The back is dark buff and gray, strongly marked with black bars. The rump is golden copper with black bars. The long, pointed inner tail feathers are mostly a dingy white, crossed by gray-brown bars patterned with black. Orangish brown bars replace the gray-brown bars on the shorter outer tail feathers. Females resemble the males in pattern, but their colors are slightly duller and the tail is much shorter.

Distribution

Historically the cheer pheasant occurred along the western slopes of the Himalaya Mountains from extreme northeastern Afghanistan through Pakistan, northern India, and into Nepal. It inhabited dense grassy areas on steep slopes with rocky outcroppings. It was typically found

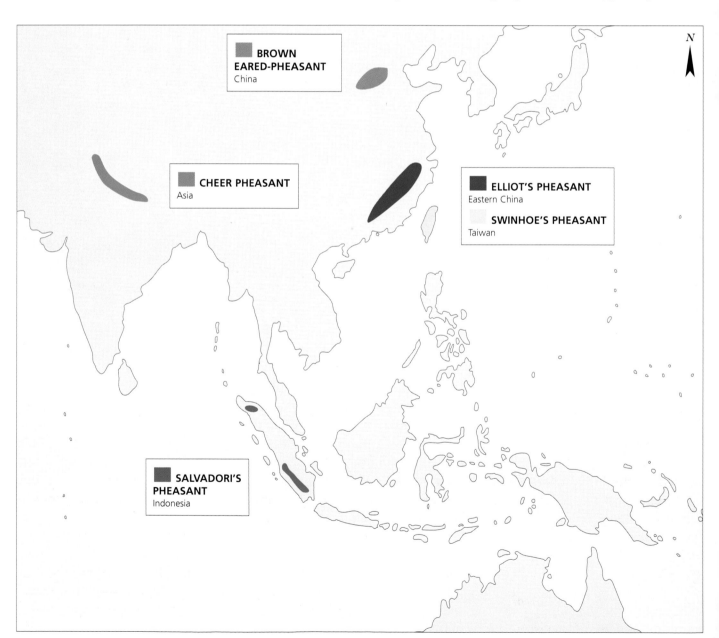

between 4,000 and 9,800 feet (1,200–3,000 meters) elevation. Cheer pheasants in Nepal are found at 5,900–10,000 feet (1,800–3,050 meters). It seems that everywhere the cheer pheasant lives, it has encountered competition from people.

Habitat loss

Heavy livestock grazing changes the character of grassy habitats needed by the bird. It forages in open grassy places, retreating to the dense vegetation of shrub land to gain protection at night. Grazing keeps the grass short. People also cut the grass to use for hay. When a bird species such as this pheasant loses enough of its habitat, its population declines to a level that is compatible with the amount of habitat available.

Population problems

Ornithologists once thought the cheer pheasant had already disappeared from Pakistan because no sightings had been recorded in that area in many years. However, a small population of scattered birds has been discovered. Pakistan has tried to reestablish the cheer pheasant since the late 1970s, but the species has not responded. Although the cheer pheasant has been reported from northeastern Afghanistan, nothing has been reliably recorded about the bird in that country for decades. The

Historically, the cheer pheasant occurred along the western slopes of the Himalaya Mountains from extreme northeastern Afghanistan through Pakistan, northern India, and into Nepal.

cheer pheasant does live in a few reserves in India and still survives in Nepal. Good estimates have not been compiled, but the cheer pheasant's total population probably numbers in the low thousands. The survival of this bird will depend upon controlling livestock grazing, grass cutting for hay, and hunting.

Sightings from Nepal indicate that the cheer pheasant will use second growth, but no habitat will be usable or safe as long as people continue overhunting this bird.

Elliot's Pheasant

(Syrmaticus ellioti)

ESA: Endangered

IUCN: Vulnerable

Length: 20–24 in. (50.8–61 cm)
Weight: 2–3 lb. (1–1.3 kg)
Diet: Leaves, fruits, and seeds; very little invertebrate food
Habitat: Shrub lands, broad-leaved evergreen forest, and coniferous undergrowth
Range: Eastern China

THE ELLIOT'S PHEASANT lives well in captivity. In fact, almost everything known about the Elliot's pheasant is based on observations of captive birds. The bird's ability to thrive in captivity may be vital to its future. It is disappearing in the wild, and the combination of factors now pressuring it may be irreversible.

The Elliot's pheasant is just one of five species known as the long-tailed pheasants. The copper pheasant (*Syrmaticus soemm-erringi*) lives in Japan, but the others are residents of China. The Elliot's pheasant is a distinctive bird of eastern China, south of the Yangtze River.

Appearance

The male sports a large, bright red, patchlike wattle that covers most of the face, including the lores and cheek and the area surrounding the eye. The dark brown crown has no crest. The

Little research has been done on Elliot's pheasant in the wild. Information about this bird comes primarily from captive populations.

gray-brown below the cheek wattle fades to grayish white on the side of the neck and darker gray on the nape. The chin and throat are black, in sharp contrast to the deep coppery brown back and breast. The long, pointed tail shows pale gray bands, separated by chestnut bars and irregular black lines. The female is smaller and lacks the bright red facial wattle. She has a much shorter tail, and wears more muted colors in a pattern similar to that decorating the male.

Bamboo thickets and shrubby areas mingled with pine (*Pinus* sp.) woodlands are used by the

Elliot's pheasant, although it also inhabits forests. This pheasant is terrestrial, searching the ground and scratching among the litter for seeds, small fruit, and probably insects. Very little research has been done on the Elliot's pheasant, so details of its life in the wild are unknown.

Habitat crisis

Eastern China has been home to the Elliot's pheasant, but the same area now supports an enormous human population with resultant clearing of land for human needs. Without habitat to accommodate them, releasing captive birds into the wild is senseless, and many of China's remaining forests are not protected from further cutting.

Salvadori's Pheasant

(Lophura inornata)

IUCN: Vulnerable

Length: 18–23 in. (45.7–58.4 cm)

Clutch size: In captivity, 2 eggs

Incubation: In captivity, 22 days

Diet: Fallen fruit

Habitat: Lower montane forests

Range: Sumatra in the Greater Sunda Islands of Indonesia

THE SALVADORI'S pheasant lives on only one island in Indonesia. Sumatra is the second largest island of Indonesia, with an area of about 182,900 square miles (473,600 square kilometers). Sumatra also ranks among the largest islands in the world, but

still may not be able to accommodate both people and pheasants in the 21st century.

Since the 1960s, the Indonesian government has pursued a policy called transmigration. The government permanently relocates people from areas of high population density to areas with a low population density. The transmigration policy has created enormous political friction inside the nation, and has accelerated the rate of land development. Sumatra and the Salvadori's pheasant have both been affected by this policy.

Forest destruction

Sumatra's primary forests have been heavily cut, and the lumber products are marketed internationally. The former forest land is then typically converted to growing plantation crops such as rubber. The expanding human population on Sumatra has also been the cause of much forest and woodland loss, particularly at lower elevations. Salvadori's pheasants usually occupy primary forests between 2,600 and 8,000 feet (800–2,500 meters). So little is known about this bird that no one is sure whether the species adapts to secondary

Elliot's pheasant lives in the coniferous woodlands of Eastern China.

growth or to plantations. Considering the extent of forest destruction on Sumatra, however, the Salvadori's pheasant is most likely in jeopardy.

Coloring

A dark bird with a tail much shorter than that of most pheasants, the male Salvadori's pheasant has black feathers with blue edges across the upperparts, breast, and sides. The only other color is a bright red face wattle that encircles the eye, including the lores and most of the cheek. The female wears a much browner plumage. Her individual feathers bear a central buff streak that is spotted with black, broadly bordered on either side by a deep reddish brown color. She has a similar short, dark tail and bright red face wattle as the male of the species.

Little is known of their reprodutive habits in the wild. A few breeders have been successful rearing this species in both Europe and America. In all cases, the clutch size has been very small; it is usually just two very small eggs. Incubation lasts for around 22 days.

Preservation

It has been estimated that fewer than 20,000 birds survive. The last specimen was collected in 1937, and records of sightings in the wild are quite scarce. Until extensive natural history studies are undertaken by scientists, no specific action can be undertaken on the bird's behalf. A general commitment to preserve portions of habitat within its known range would help to protect the Salvadori's pheasant long enough to learn more about it.

Swinhoe's Pheasant

(Lophura swinhoii)

ESA: Endangered

IUCN: Lower risk

Length: 20–32 in. (50.8–81.3 cm)
Weight: 2½ lb. (1.1 kg)
Range: Taiwan

LIKE SO MANY of its kin, the Swinhoe's pheasant boasts gaudy plumage. In the male, a great red wattle covers the face, drooping below the jaw line and extending above the forehead like fleshy horns. A white crest sweeps back from the deep blue crown. The upper nape, sides of the neck, chin, throat, breast, sides, lower back, and rump are all adorned with black feathers broadly edged in shiny blue. The belly and outer tail feathers are dull dusky black, as are the outer flight feathers of the wing. The lower nape and upper back are covered with a single continuous white patch. The white is repeated in the long, arching central tail feathers. A chestnut band sweeps from shoulder to shoulder, separating white upper back from blue lower back. The uppermost small feathers of the wing are bordered in

As Taiwan's human population and economy have grown, much of the native landscape has been radically altered, and this has reduced populations of Swinhoe's pheasant.

shiny green. The legs and feet are pink. The female has a bare red patch around the eye, and her plumage is mottled with buff, tan, brown, gray, and black.

Distribution and habitat
The only place to find a Swinhoe's pheasant is in Taiwan. Taiwan is an island nation due north of the Philippines and at the end of the Ryukyu Islands that sweep southwest of Japan. It has survived the political turmoil with mainland China by a policy

of aggressive industrialization. Taiwan competes actively in the global market for electronic appliances and other manufactured goods. As Taiwan's human population and economy have grown, much of the country's landscape has been radically altered.

Living spaces
The Swinhoe's pheasant inhabits Taiwan's primary forests between 5,904 and 7,544 feet (1,800 and 2,300 meters). These forests contain a mixture of evergreen hardwoods. Because they are true forests, only dappled sunlight penetrates the canopy and reaches the ground. The shaded ground has scattered ferns, shrubs, and plants suited to little sunlight. Swinhoe's pheasants are not known to scratch among the

litter in the way that other pheasant species behave, but they do dig. They consume various plant parts from a broad variety of plant species. They also readily eat invertebrates such as insects and earthworms.

It is not known whether the male Swinhoe's pheasant pairs with a single female or mates with more than one. Nor are ornithologists clear about when and where the species nests. Presumably, this pheasant nests mostly on the ground, but evidence indicates that some of the birds choose nest sites well above ground on stumps and other solid supports.

Population variation
Knowledge of the Swinhoe's pheasant's population status is also uncertain. Swinhoe's

pheasant lives well in captivity and has been bred successfully, but a species needs habitat to live in the wild. Throughout the 1970s, at least, several thousand pheasants still occupied available habitat scattered about the island. In 1974 a 9,200-acre (3,680-hectare) sanctuary was est- ablished for Swinhoe's pheasant and other species of pheasant. Unfortunately, primary forests were cleared through the 1980s, and Swinhoe's pheasant is not known to use mature secondary forest. In the 1990s conservationists estimated that the population was around 6,500 in Yushan National Park, which is one of the several sites where a population still survives.

Kevin Cook

See Francolins, Partridges, and Green Peafowl.

PICATHARTES

Class: Aves
Order: Passeriformes
Family: Muscicapidae
Subfamily: Picathartinae

The picathartes looks like no other bird, which is why it has caused ornithologists lots of problems. For years it was believed to be related to the jays (Corvidae). A traditional system puts them in the Old World flycatcher family (Muscicapidae). Recently they classified in their own family s(Picathartidae). Traditionally, the picathartes was treated as a single species represented by two subspecies. Recently, the subspecies have been thought to be separate species. In any case, the picathartes faces an uncertain future.

Gray-necked Picathartes
(Picathartes oreas)

IUCN: Vulnerable

Length: 11–12 in. (27.9–30.5 cm)
Clutch size: 2 eggs
Habitat: Dense forests
Range: Southeastern Nigeria, Cameroon, northern Gabon

DEEP IN THE mountain country of western Africa, where rocky cliffs interrupt the dark forests of tall trees, lives a strange bird. This bird—the gray-necked picathartes—is seldom seen. It measures slightly larger than a blue jay (*Cyanocitta cristata*) but is smaller than a black-billed

magpie (*Pica pica*)—both common species in the United States. Its beak, as stout as a magpie's, is black, thick, and decurved. The legs and feet are strongly built to suit a bird that spends much of its life on the ground.

The gray-necked picathartes inhabits dense, damp forests, where it hops among the lower tree branches with graceful ease, much as a jay would do. The hopping does not stop in the trees. Dropping to the ground, the gray-necked picathartes moves about in great hops. It searches the ground carefully for earthworms, crickets, spiders, and other invertebrates. This hopping is a distinctive behavioral characteristic of the picathartes.

The few people who have been privileged to see gray-necked picathartes in the wild

White-necked Picathartes
(Picathartes gymnocephalus)

IUCN: Vulnerable

Length: 11–12 in. (27.9–30.5 cm)
Weight: 6–8 oz. (166–226 g)
Clutch size: 2 eggs
Incubation: 21–23 days (in captivity)
Diet: Crustaceans, insects, and snails
Habitat: Montane forests with rock cliffs or outcroppings
Range: Ghana, Ivory Coast, Liberia, Sierra Leone, and Guinea

THE WHITE-NECKED picathartes does not appear in standard books about Africa. Most books about African wildlife focus on the big, easy-to-see animals. Elephants, zebras, giraffes, vultures, and ostriches fill the pages. But

report with equal regularity that the bird moves around either singly or in small groups. Both observations are probably true. The gray-necked picathartes nests in colonies, so a sighting of a small troupe of the birds feeding together would not be particularly surprising.

The picathartes nests either in caves or within deep recesses beneath overhanging rocks in cliffs. Individual birds build mud nests, shaped like a quarter of a cantaloupe, which they fasten to a vertical rock surface. This cave-nesting behavior initially seems unusual, but cliff swallows (*Hirundo pyrrhonota*) of North America nest on cliffs in much the same way.

The gray-necked picathartes hunts in dense forests. While caves remain intact, the forests

The head of the gray-necked picathartes may be its most remarkable feature, for it is completely bald and has three distinct color regions. The face, including the lore, the cheek, and around the eye, is black; the forehead and crown are bright blue; and the back of the head is rose red.

are being cut down. Ornithologists have feared that cutting the forests would cause the number of gray-necked picathartes to decline. Surveys in the 1980s find picathartes colonies yielded many previously unknown nesting localities, but the discovery of more colonies does not necessarily mean that the species is secure. Forest cutting continues in the picathartes' homeland. Unless some habitat is left intact, this bird could quickly change from a vulnerable to an endangered status.

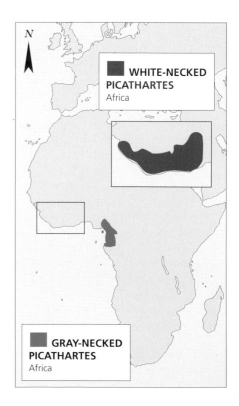

Africa also supports another class of interesting wildlife that is small and hard to find.

Africa hosts many different bird species, and one of its least well-known is the white-necked picathartes. One of two species in the genus *Picathartes*, it is an example of a species for which the Latin name has been adopted as the common English name.

Appearance

A long, slender perching bird, the white-necked picathartes measures decidedly larger than the American robin (*Turdus migratorius*) and is closer to the boat-tailed grackle (*Quiscalus major*) in size. The similarity stops there. The white-necked picathartes has a much stouter beak that is thick and black. The tail is somewhat rounded because the outer feathers arc slightly shorter than the inner feathers.

The white-necked picathartes uses its strong legs to hop agilely about the forest floor, searching for earthworms and insects. It may hunt for food alone or in small flocks of just a few birds. When not on the ground, the white-necked picathartes is either in the trees or in caves. This bird can hop through the trees with ease, but it nests in caves. Typically, several pairs will build individual mud nests that they attach directly to vertical rock. They especially favor caves for nesting, but they also use the deeper recesses of cliffs where overhanging rock offers shelter.

Some sources claim the white-necked picathartes has been heavily trapped, but the species is nowhere common in zoos. The San Antonio Zoological Gardens is the only zoo in North America to have a white-necked picathartes on display. Local people do trap and hunt the bird for food, but its biggest threat comes from lost habitat. Forest cutting in western Africa has been very heavy for years. Not only are the people there running out of trees, but the birds are also running out of habitat. No one has estimated the white-necked picathartes' population size; but considering the extent of forest destruction within its range, the species must be severely reduced from its historic populations.

Kevin Cook

The upper half of the white-necked picathartes' beak is noticeably decurved. Its head is entirely bare and mostly dull straw-colored, except for two large, sooty brown patches—one on each side toward the back of the head. The neck, including nape, sides, chin, and throat are pure white, as are the breast, belly, sides, and undertail.

PIGEONS

Class: Aves
Order: Columbiformes
Family: Columbidae

Pigeons are among the most easily recognized of all birds. With more than 250 species in this family, one species or another lives in almost every mild or tropical climate. Some occupy remote oceanic islands. One species, the passenger pigeon (*Ectopistes migratorius*), was once the most abundant land bird in the world. Passenger pigeons were so common that people believed they could never kill them all. However, the passenger pigeon became extinct.

No special anatomy or behavior distinguishes pigeons from doves. Their common names reflect this fact. For example, birds in *Columba* are known as pigeons; those in *Ptilinopus* are called fruit-doves; and imperial-pigeons belong to *Ducula*. Although pigeons and doves closely resemble each other, they also differ from other birds.

Pigeons drink by keeping their heads down, immersing their beaks, and sucking up the water. Usually birds drink by scooping water into the beak, raising the head, tilting it back, and swallowing. Pigeons also feed their young in an unusual way. The parents produce a thick, nutrient-rich lining in their crops. Nestlings reach their own beaks into their parents' open mouths and take this nutrient as their first food. However, it is not true milk. Many pigeons also bask in the sun by fluffing up their feathers, elevating a wing, and rolling over on to one side. They often bathe in the rain in a similar manner.

Pigeons have become important to people in several different ways. They have been both hunted and raised as food. They have carried messages in times of war, and they have been hunted for sport. Pigeons have been captured as pets and destroyed as nuisances. While the rock dove (*Columba livia*) has proliferated in urban areas, other species have faltered. The future of many pigeon species depends mostly on how quickly people act to preserve their habitats.

Pink Pigeon
(Columba mayeri)

ESA: Endangered

IUCN: Critically endangered

Length: 11½–12½ in. (29.2–31.8 cm)
Weight: Male, 8½–14 oz. (240–410 g); female, 7½–13 oz. (213–369 g)
Diet: Plant shoots, leaves, fruits, and seeds
Habitat: Primary forests and woodlands, some secondary forests and woods, shrub lands
Range: Mauritius Island, lying east of Madagascar in the Indian Ocean

THE PINK PIGEON'S entire native habitat has been subject to destruction or severe degradation as a result of human colonization and exploitation. The pink pigeon lives on Mauritius, second largest of the three Mascarene Islands. Covering 747 square miles (2,046 square kilometers), Mauritius lies 600 miles (960 kilometers) east of Madagascar and just north of the Tropic of Capricorn. Portuguese sailors discovered the island in 1507, but it was generally ignored because it was not within usual navigation routes.

Dutch sailors claimed the island in 1598. The Dutch brought agriculture to an island never before inhabited by people. Agriculture meant the clearing of forests and woodlands, and the settlers also introduced livestock and crab-eating macaques (*Macaca fascicularis*) to Mauritius. Macaques are large monkeys that were probably pets that got loose or were released. Black rats (*Rattus rattus*) also found their way to the island, probably as stowaways in ships' cargo.

French settlers, and eventually British settlers followed the Dutch. All of these colonists intensified the changes to the island's natural landscape. Ebony trees (*Diospyros tesselaria*) were heavily cut for their valuable wood. Other woodlands, forests, and shrub lands were cleared to make way for growing sugarcane, and tea, and for pine plantations. Local people imported the Timor deer (*Cervus timorensis*) to the island for the purpose of recreational hunting.

During the five centuries of human occupation on Mauritius, at least 27 bird species have become extinct. The first to disappear was the dodo (*Raphus cucullatus*), which became extinct in the 1680s. Extinction has not yet ended. Another dozen bird species unique to Mauritius are imperiled. Among them is the pink pigeon.

This pigeon takes its name from the soft pink wash that

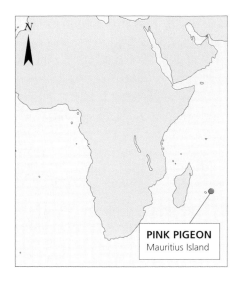

PINK PIGEON
Mauritius Island

covers its head, neck, and breast. The cheek, lore, and forehead are more white than pink. The upper back is a darker, more brownish pink. The wing is dark brown, as is a thin band across the middle back. The bluish white rump yields to a reddish brown tail. This fades to a pinkish buff belly, and the bird stands on a dull red foot and toe. The long, slender beak is mostly yellow, a little reddish at the base, and slightly hooked at the tip.

Pink pigeons undoubtedly inhabited most of Mauritius before human settlement began. Because they eat plant materials almost exclusively, they wander through diverse plant communities to get all the food they need. Once people settled, plant communities began to change. Birds accustomed to tropical, broadleaved hardwoods could not survive in very large plantations of crops. Rats and macaques ate eggs and nestlings. Feral house cats (*Felis sylvestris*) killed adult pink pigeons that settled on the ground to pick up grit and

A program to breed the pink pigeon in captivity has succeeded in improving its total numbers.

seeds. Habitat loss, combined with exotic species, dramatically reduced the population of pink pigeons.

Early trouble

The species was already endangered in the early 1900s. By the 1950s, the pink pigeon occurred only in the southwestern part of the island, with a population totaling somewhere between 40 and 60 birds. Dramatic population declines in subsequent decades reflect a tragic consequence of habitat loss. Powerful cyclones in 1960, 1975, and 1980 killed more pink pigeons. By destroying the pink pigeon's

habitat, people diminished the pigeon's ability to find vital shelter during these damaging storms. The pink pigeon population dropped to just 25 birds in 1960, recovered somewhat in the next decade, then fell to around 20 birds again in 1975. After Cyclone Claudette in 1980, the population may have plummeted. In 1991 it had declined to its lowest numbers of just ten individuals. Since then the population has recovered as a result of intensive management by the Mauritius Wildlife Foundation. Between 1987 and 1992, about 50 captive-bred birds were released into the wild, and there

was a further release program on the predator-free *Ile aux Aigrettes* in 1994. By 1997 the known population had increased to 330 individuals. The pink pigeon population recovered to no more than 20 wild birds by 1990.

Special protection

Pink pigeons are legally protected on the island of Mauritius, and much of its remaining habitat is protected in the Black River National Park. Some plots of native vegetation are subject to a special program of rehabilitation. However, other habitat destruction has continued.

Destruction of nature

The extraordinary collection of unique plants, birds, tortoises, and lizards on Mauritius is a vital laboratory for studying how life evolved on earth. It has also become a classroom for studying habitat destruction and species extinction. The pink pigeon, just one of nature's many victims on Mauritius, may not survive for long in the wild.

Puerto Rican Plain Pigeon
(Columba inornata)

ESA: Endangered

IUCN: Endangered

Length: 14–15 in. (35.6–38.1 cm)
Clutch size: 1 egg, rarely two
Incubation: 14 days
Diet: Fruits and seeds
Habitat: Primary forests, woodlands, coffee plantations
Range: Puerto Rico

IN PUERTO RICO, a few cents can buy a pigeon for dinner. The pigeons hanging in the markets may look like any other pigeons to the average person; however, these birds are sometimes among the last of the Puerto Rican plain pigeons.

Once common and widely distributed across Puerto Rico, the plain pigeon began disappearing from the island late in the 1800s. It is a large pigeon and easily recognized by its two-tone plumage. The back, wing, rump, and tail are dark to bluish gray; but the head, neck, and breast are a purplish red or sometimes wine-colored. In flight, the spread wing shows thin white edges on the outer flight feathers. The foot and toe are dark red, and the dark beak is long and slender for a pigeon. The Puerto Rican plain pigeon looks like any other urbanized pigeon to the casual observer. For the hunter looking to earn a few pennies, it is just another edible bird.

As a species, the plain pigeon occurs on all the Greater Antilles islands of the Caribbean. The subspecies *Columba inornata inornata* lives on the Isle of Pines, Cuba, and Hispaniola; *Columba inornata exigua* lives on Jamaica; and *Columba inornata wetmorei* lives only on Puerto Rico. Modern settlement of Puerto Rico pushed the plain pigeon into near extinction.

Spanish invasion

When Spanish colonists claimed Puerto Rico in 1509, the Carib people inhabited the island. No one knows what the pigeon population was at that time, but presumably it was still flourishing. The Spaniards sought gold, but settled for wealth derived from agriculture. They began cultivating sugar cane in 1515. Pineapples, tobacco, bananas, and coffee plantations followed. The people on Puerto Rico steadily cleared more and more land for plantations. The island was once nearly covered from shore to shore in woodlands and forests. By 1910 only 20 percent of the island's primary forests

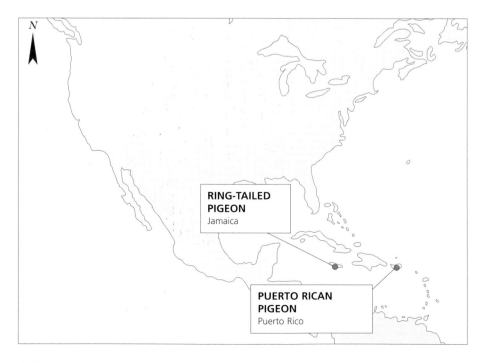

RING-TAILED PIGEON
Jamaica

PUERTO RICAN PIGEON
Puerto Rico

and native woodlands remained uncut. Only one percent of forest remained intact by 1920.

Besides destructive agricultural practices, people brought black rats (*Rattus rattus*) and house cats (*Felis sylvestris*) to Puerto Rico. Black rats eat birds' eggs and nestlings. Cats catch pigeons that settle on the ground to eat seeds and grit, or to drink and bathe. These pigeons were thus preyed upon by exotic predators and also hunted by people. Because the Puerto Rican plain pigeon lays a single egg in every clutch, any hunting or predation of the already weakened population will have dangerous consequences for the bird. Although hunting within the range of this pigeon is illegal, there is evidence that such practices continue.

Ornithologists believed the Puerto Rican plain pigeon slipped into extinction sometime in the late 1920s, because the bird was not seen or reported for more than three decades. In the early 1960s, however, some plain pigeons began showing up for sale in town markets. A population estimate in the late 1970s put the plain pigeon population on Puerto Rico at less than 100 birds. By 1996, a combination of improved census techniques and a genuine recovery resulted in a revised population estimate of about 700 birds.

A captive-breeding program was initiated in the early 1980s, and birds have been released to bolster the single population on Puerto Rico. A special foundation has been established solely to conserve this pigeon, and has run environmental awareness campaigns to promote its survival. This is the key to preventing its extinction. No matter how many birds are captive-bred, this pigeon will disappear if hunting continues, and hunting will continue unless there is an overall change in people's attitudes.

Ring-tailed Pigeon

(Columba caribaea)

IUCN: Critically endangered

Length: 16 in. (40.6 cm)
Clutch size: Probably 1 egg
Incubation: Probably 18–20 days
Diet: Fruits, seeds
Habitat: Montane forests and woodlands
Range: Jamaica

HIGH UP THE Jamaican mountain slopes, where trees stand watch over the Caribbean Sea, pigeons fly about the forests and woodlands. Some settle themselves on the ground. With typical pigeonlike behavior, they strut and peck. Other pigeons settle in the treetops. Clinging to the outermost twigs, they peck at the fruits growing there.

The pigeons on the ground are ruddy quail-doves (*Geotrygon montana*), and those in the treetops are ring-tailed pigeons. Their separate lifestyles indicate a lot about how plants and animals interact to create natural landscapes. Ruddy quail-doves eat many different foods, and they gather it all from the ground. Ring-tailed pigeons probably consume fewer different kinds of foods than the quail-doves, but they find their food in the trees. Whereas ruddy quail-doves are quite terrestrial, ring-tailed pigeons are decidedly arboreal. The ruddy quail-dove occurs throughout the Greater Antilles, and in Central America from Mexico into northwestern South America. The ring-tailed pigeon occurs only on Jamaica, and it has declined severely.

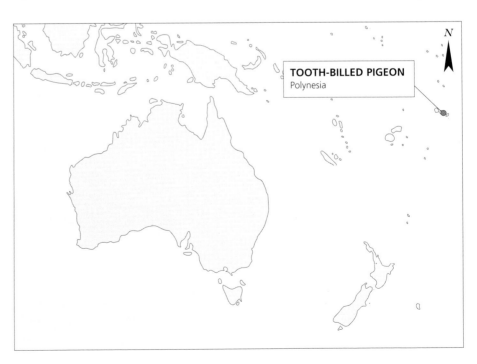

TOOTH-BILLED PIGEON
Polynesia

N

Jamaica ranks third in size among the Caribbean islands. Most of its 4,227 square miles (10,991 square kilometers) are mountainous, and the mountain slopes and foothills are a blend of forest and woodland. Approximately 2.5 million people now live on the island. They mine bauxite and gypsum, grow many different agricultural crops for both export and domestic use, and work in diversified industries. All this activity carries a price, and the price paid has been the loss of Jamaica's native forests and woodlands. Habitat loss is compounded by illegal year-round hunting, owing to the bird's tasty flesh. Hunting has a particularly heavy impact on this species' population.

Interesting behavior

Ruddy quail-doves live in many different places. Habitat loss on Jamaica only moderately affects them as a species. By contrast, the ring-tailed pigeon has no other populations in other places. What happens to this bird in Jamaica has an effect on the entire species.

The ring-tailed pigeon is the only one of nine pigeon species on Jamaica with a two-toned tail. The tail is overall dingy gray, with a distinct black band across the middle. The back is bluish gray, and the wing is dark. A collar of shiny feathers looks greenish golden in some lights and pinkish in others. The head, throat, and breast are pinkish gray, with a purplish cast. The chin and undertail are pale grayish white. The beak is black, but the foot and toe are dull red.

The ring-tailed pigeon feeds on the fruits of a number of trees, including those of the Jamaican sweetwood tree (*Nectandra antillana*). Like the pigeon, the tree occurs nowhere else except on Jamaica. One team of researchers has suggested that a unique bird which eats the fruits of a unique tree quite possibly has a close relationship with the life of the tree. This relationship is known as mutualism: each species depends on the other for life. In this case, the tree provides fruit for the pigeon to eat, and by eating it, the pigeon helps disperse the tree's seeds. Loss of the ring-tailed pigeon, then, could eventually affect the distribution and abundance of Jamaican sweetwood on the island. This theory has not been studied in detail, but it is a plausible one.

No population size has been estimated, but ornithologists consider that the ring-tailed pigeon has become very rare. Despite legal protection and designated protected areas within its range, none of these laws are effectively enforced. Until they are, this species will continue to decline toward extinction.

Tooth-billed Pigeon
(Didunculus strigirostris)

IUCN: Vulnerable

Length: 11–12 in. (27.9–30.5 cm)
Clutch size: Probably 2
Diet: Fruits, seeds
Habitat: Primary forest
Range: Savaii and Upolu Islands of Western Samoa

BIRDS DO NOT grow true teeth, and the tooth-billed pigeon is no exception. A chunky, short-tailed bird, the tooth-billed pigeon has a peculiar beak. It is thick from top to bottom, and the upper half curves down past the tip of the lower half, making this pigeon's beak looks more like that of a hawk or a parrot. Near the tip of the lower half of the beak, three

The isolated mountainous regions in which the tooth-billed pigeon makes its home may be the only protection for this severely threatened bird.

small points are defined by two prominent notches. These points are the teeth that give the tooth-billed pigeon its name.

The pigeon is a dark bird. Its entire head and neck, upper back, breast, belly, and outer wing feathers are a deep dark green color. Feathers on the nape and sides of the neck have a slightly silvery, almost bluish, sheen to them. The middle and lower back, rump, and small feathers of the wing are brick red. The short tail is cinnamon in color. The leg, foot, and toe are red. The beak has a black tip, yellow in the middle, and red at the base. The red extends through the bare lore and includes a thin eye ring. The points on the lower half of the beak are visible only at close range and are clearly distinguishable when the bird is in hand. However, these teeth are not the only thing unique about the tooth-billed pigeon.

Distinguishing behavior

The tooth-billed is one of only two species of pigeon that use their toes to hold food while pulling the food apart with their beaks. Also, other pigeons drink by keeping their heads down and their beaks immersed while sucking. The tooth-billed pigeon does not drink with its head down. These distinct behaviors have prompted some ornithologists to place the tooth-billed pigeon in its own family, *Didunculidae*. This classification has never met wide acceptance, but some ornithologists concede it as a subfamily.

The tooth-billed pigeon now faces severe threats to its survival. It naturally occurs on just two islands, Savaii and Upolu, in the Western Samoa group. Savaii

The blue-crowned pigeon (*Goura cristata*) sports exotic feathers on its head. This bird inhabits Indonesia, and is classified by IUCN as vulnerable.

covers only 670 square miles (1,742 square kilometers) and Upolu only 429 square miles (1,115 square kilometers). Both islands are very mountainous, which may be the only factor that has saved this pigeon. The only good habitat for tooth-billed pigeons exists in small patches in remote mountain valleys.

Human threat

Many Samoans hunt the pigeons for sport and for food. They also cut trees for firewood and exportable lumber, and clear forests for banana, coconut, and coffee plantations.

The pigeon does not live as well in secondary forests, and not at all in plantations of exotic trees. As primary forests are cut down, the tooth-billed pigeon approaches endangerment more rapidly. As the available hab-

itat declines, the pigeons become more vulnerable to predation by pet cats and by feral house cats (*Felis sylvestris*).

The tooth-billed pigeon has recently been chosen as a flagship species that is used to promote conservation awareness in Western Samoa. It is protected by the law, but some birds may still be captured in the seasonal harvest of unprotected pigeon species. This pigeon occurs in some proposed areas and a few existing protected areas, but these have suffered cyclone damage and forests remain threatened by logging and cattle farming.

Kevin Cook

See also Doves.

PIGS

Class: Mammalia

Order: Artiodactyla

Family: Suidae

Wild pigs or hogs are medium-sized mammals with short, stout bodies. Certainly the most distinguishing feature of these animals is their mobile snout. The tip of the snout is a cartilage disk that can be used in conjunction with the pigs' tusks to dig for roots, fruit, small reptiles, and eggs.

Although wild pigs originated in Eurasia more than 38 million years ago, humans later helped spread at least one species (*Sus scrofa*) to other parts of the world, including North America. Domestic pigs are derived from this species. While pigs for livestock are raised in pens, wild pigs are normally found in forests, woodlands, and grasslands.

The taxonomy for wild pigs has undergone extensive revision, and several new species have been described, especially in the Southeast Asian area.

Javan (Bawean) Warty Pig

(Sus verrucosus)

IUCN: Endangered

Weight: 176–331 lb. (80–150 kg)

Shoulder height: 14–35½ in. (35–90 cm)

Gestation period: Probably 120 days

Longevity: 15–20 years

Habitat: Rain forest, both primary and secondary growth

Range: Islands of Java and Bawean

WARTY PIGS are found on Java and Bawean, which are islands of Indonesia. They no longer survive on Madura, which has been deforested.

These pigs get their name from the large growths on the sides of their elongated face and jowls. Only the males tend to develop these growths, and they only become apparent with advanced age. Old males can look grotesque with these enlarged growths, which are commonly known as warts. Females and juveniles lack these warty growths. The male pigs are at least twice the size of females.

The warty pig is found in primary and secondary growth in rain forests, and in dense vegetation. It tends to be fairly shy and retiring; however, when cornered, it can put up a considerable battle. Like most swine, the warty pig is omnivorous and is known as an opportunistic feeder—it will eat almost anything that it can catch, as well as any vegetation that happens to be available.

Pigs are generally social by nature and can be found in fairly large groups. In Indonesia, some seasonal animal migrations appear to have some connection with the monsoon season.

The warty pig's predators used to include the tiger and the leopard; however, most of these animals have been killed and have virtually disappeared from Java. Human beings have become the warty pig's primary predators. Java is one of the most densely populated islands on earth, so there is barely enough space to support a substantial population of warty pigs, especially when hunting is a common

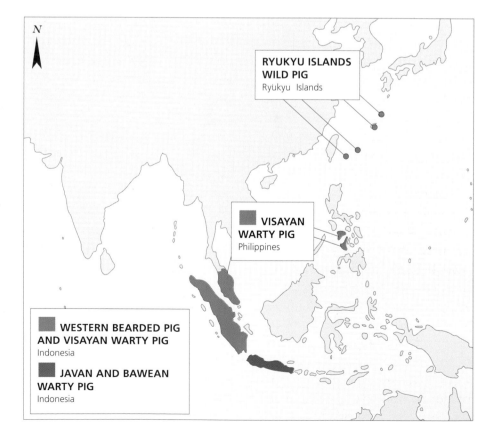

activity. The warty pig is also known to interbreed with the wild boar, which dilutes the purebred pig population and threatens its survival.

There are several sizable populations of warty pigs breeding in captivity. One is in the Surabaya Zoo and another lives in a zoo in Jakarta. There have been very few warty pigs taken out of Southeast Asia to captivity in Europe and North America.

Visayan Warty Pig

(Sus cebifrons)

IUCN: Critically endangered

Western Bearded Pig

(Sus barbatus oi)

IUCN: Lower risk

Weight: 331–606 lb.
(150–275 kg)
Shoulder height: 27½–33½ in.
(70–85 cm)
Diet: Omnivorous
Gestation period: 120 days
Longevity: 10–15 years
Habitat: Rain forest, both primary and secondary growth
Range: Visayan Islands, western Malaysia, and Sumatra

THE WESTERN bearded pig is one of three subspecies that occupy a rather extensive range. The western form is found in Malaysia and Sumatra; another is from Borneo, and the third is found in parts of the Philippines. None of them are at severe risk at this time, but populations are declining and becoming rare. There is a growing captive population of the Bornean form which was recently established in a few North America zoos. The western bearded pig is a dark brown-gray animal with a white beard on its cheeks. It also has facial warts, and the longest head and slimmest torso of all the pigs.

The bearded pig is large, with traits much like the common Asiatic boar. It prefers tropical and secondary forest. The bearded pig digs for roots and eats all types of vegetation, but will also eat small mammals and birds if it can catch them, and even carrion if it is available. In some areas these pigs are preyed upon by tigers and leopards, but mostly they are preyed on by people.

Both pigs prefer the same habitat and share the same traits. The Visayan warty pig gets its name from the obvious substantial growths on its face. A substantial amount of facial hair is characteristic of the male, especially during the breeding season. The western bearded pig is typical of the bearded pig group, with extensive amounts of hair over the snout, muzzle, and jowls. This hair tends to have an almost yellowish appearance, which makes it highly visible. This pig was, until very recently, considered to be part of the bearded pig group. Now it is given full species recognition. It is found in the Visayan Island region of the Philippines.

When the female gives birth, litters of up to eight are not uncommon. These animals have been given some protection, but basically are still being poached heavily. Their biggest problem is the destruction of habitat caused by rain forest clearance. The Visayan pig is extinct over 98 percent of its former range in the Central Philippines, and now only survives in small, fragmented populations on the island of Negros and in a single population on Panay.

A captive population of Visayan pigs has recently been established on its home range, and it is expanding.

The bearded pig, showing the characteristic white beard on its cheeks, inhabits Malaysia, the Philippines, and adjacent islands. It is considered to be at lower risk.

Ryukyu Islands Wild Pig

(Sus scrofa riukiuanus)

IUCN: Vulnerable

Weight: 331–705 lb.
(150–320 kg)
Shoulder height: 29½–47 in.
(75–120 cm)
Diet: Omnivorous
Gestation period: 115 days
Longevity: 15–20 years
Habitat: Open forest
Range: Ryukyu Islands, Japan

THE RYUKYU ISLAND wild pig is a subspecies of *Sus scrofa*, or the European wild boar. This pig is found all over Eurasia from Spain to Japan, and there are at least 17 different types of subspecies. The island pigs from Sardinia and Ryukyu are the smallest; however, their traits are much the same as those of their mainland cousins.

This wild pig's preferred habitat is thick bush or dense forest with good cover. It will come out and feed in the open, but it much prefers the security of cover. Wild pigs are often found in groups of eight to ten. Sometimes these groups will assemble into much larger groups. They are diurnal, but are particularly active at dusk. Old boars tend to be solitary, but the sows stay together, and the younger pigs stay with them until the males start to mature. They are then driven away from the group. The breeding season brings out more aggressive behavior in the male.

The wild pig's diet is varied. A pig will eat a lot of vegetation, but it is an opportunistic animal: it will also eat insects, small mammals, fish, reptiles, and even carrion.

Vulnerable

This Japanese population is vulnerable mainly because it occupies a tiny area that is suffering as the human population expands. The Ryukyu Islands wild pig is protected and is considered vulnerable, but stable. Small captive populations are being maintained in a few Japanese zoos.

Warren D. Thomas

Kozlov's Pika

(Ochotona koslowi)

IUCN: Endangered

Class: Mammalia
Order: Lagomorpha
Family: Ochotonidae
Weight: 3½–14 oz. (100–400 g)
Length: 5–10 in. (12–25 cm)
Diet: Mostly grasses
Habitat: Rocky terrain
Range: Guldsha Valley Pass, on the border between Tibet and China

LITTLE IS KNOWN of Kozlov's pika. The original specimens of this animal were collected by Przewalski in 1884. It was around 100 years before additional specimens were collected.

Pikas are known to be lagomorphs, which makes them small relatives of rabbits and hares. This particular species is uniformly pale, with a whitish buff upper coat and a white underbelly. The ears are rounded and yellow in color, with white tips. There is no externally visible tail.

Kozlov's pika has many of the characteristics of all the other pikas (there are 21 different

KOZLOV'S PIKA
Asia

species). Highly vocal, they communicate with each other through a series of whistles and calls. These calls are so distinctive that they help distinguish individuals (and their territories) from one another. Alarm calls are sent immediately upon sight or smell of a predator, passing from male to male, but females also use such calls to signal territory. Because of this vocal ability, pikas are also known in Asia as whistling hares, or piping hares.

Pikas are social animals, living in family units that are grouped together to form a larger social unit or colony. The size of each family unit is unknown, but it is believed to be between six and eight animals. Their sociability does not extend to other pikas outside their family group, however, and in some species intruders are chased away and even killed. In certain pika species, the sexes also live apart except for periods of mating.

Kozlov's pika lives in the tundra grasses of a high mountain pass bordering Tibet and China. A pika will burrow, but it is not really suited to the task because of its short limbs; it prefers to live among the rocks on the side of the mountains. Moving in short jumps or hops, Kozlov's pika cannot run well and depends upon the rocks for concealment. Caught in the open, it will become easy prey for predators such as foxes.

In the summer and late fall, this pika will stack piles of grasses and other foods in a few places in its range. This behavior has prompted locals to call this animal the "haystacker." In winter the pika will burrow from stack to stack under the snow to get to

The Kozlov's pikas display a preference for terrain with broken rock cover, and this has earned them the nickname *rock conies*.

its stored food. But the material in these little stacks is not large, so pikas probably continue foraging year-round.

Livestock left to graze in the winter will often raid these haystacks if they find them, and this growing intrusion may be a factor in the decline of the pika population. Human campaigns to curtail other vertebrates within the range of Kozlov's pika have probably had an adverse effect on the pika as well.

Lack of data
Because of its rarity, there is little natural history information about this animal. Without more data, conservation efforts are liable to be inadequate. At the present time, there are no population figures available, and due to its present narrow range, the Kozlov's pika must be presumed to be a highly endangered animal that is in need of immediate protection.

George H. Jenkins

See Hares and Rabbits.

Pindu
(Stomatepia pindu)

IUCN: Critically endangered

Class: Actinopterygii
Order: Perciformes
Family: Cichlidae
Length: 4⅓ in. (11 cm)
Reproduction: Egg layer
Habitat: Inshore areas among wood and rock
Range: Lake Barombi-Mbo, Cameroon

CICHLIDS ARE such a varied group of fish that, judging from appearances, it seems remarkable that they all belong to the same family. The pindu and other members of the genus *Stomatepia* are slightly different from other cichlids in that they tend to be more streamlined. While most cichlids have an extremely long gut for digesting food, the pindu and other *Stomatepia* have a shorter gut. It is used less to digest plant material than to digest small animals such as insects and other invertebrates.

Threatened habitat
Barombi-Mbo is a lake in Cameroon, in west Africa. It is home to a number of cichlids which are threatened by overfishing. This freshwater lake is the main source of food for a nearby village, so it is not surprising that the lake population has begun to feel the strain. At least ten other species of cichlid are either threatened or endangered in this isolated habitat.

A distinctive characteristic of the pindu is the long, spiny dorsal fin on the back that can extend from just behind the head all the way to the tail section; the dorsal fin segment near the tail is usually longer than the segment near the head. In many cichlids, the part of the fin near the tail carries a dark blotch called a tilapia mark. In an adult pindu, the dorsal fin does not carry a tilapia mark, though it does in a juvenile.

This species is much darker in color than some of its other close relatives such as the mongo (*Stomatepia mongo*), which lives in deeper water and has a more robust body. Most likely the pindu's dark gray to black overall color is useful in reducing the fish's visibility from the surface, a deterrent to shoreline predators such as birds. A further deterrent is that the pindu can rapidly lighten its color as camoflage against a light background.

Similar to other *Stomatepia*, the pindu has a prominent bony ridge across the snout just below the eyes. The pectoral fins (just behind the gills) and the anal fin are unusually long, for more efficient swimming in tight places, and the body is well scaled to protect against abrasion. The face is partially scaled around the eyes, and the gill covers are protected as well.

The pindu produces relatively few young, only about 20 per female per breeding cycle. It is believed that the pindu, like other cichlids, is probably a mouth brooder. After large eggs are laid and fertilized, one or both of the mouth-brooding parents picks up the eggs and protects them within its mouth for a week to ten days. This parental care continues even after the eggs hatch and the juvenile fish are swimming about. When danger appears, the parent opens up its mouth and the newly hatched fish scurry inside, safe from attack. This type of parental care is one significant way to keep such a low birth rate from jeopardizing the species.

The fish and fauna of Lake Barombi-Mbo now face a variety of threats. The forests along the edge of the lake are being cut down, which could lead to soil erosion and, in turn, to siltation. The local Barombi fishermen used to live in harmony with the lake, but improved fishing techniques now threaten various species. The use of chemicals in

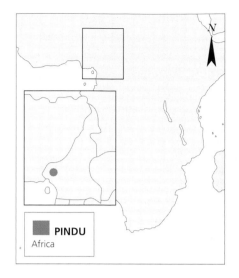

PINDU
Africa

agriculture is also a threat, since there is a risk that they could leak from the soil into the lake. Overfishing, due to increased demand from the nearby town of Kumba, adds to these problems.

William E. Manci

See also Myakamyaka and Otjikota tilapia.

PINES

Phylum: Pinophyta (conifers)

Family: Pinaceae

Pines make up the largest group of cone-bearing plants, with about 110 species. Ecologically highly versatile, they are found from the edge of the Arctic tundra to tropical, coastal savannas. Most pines are tall trees with a single trunk, though some are multi-stemmed shrubs with needlelike leaves. They are mainly plants of the northern hemisphere, with the greatest concentration of species in Mexico and the United States, although eastern Asia is also rich. Although many species are common, some have tiny natural distributions now threatened by such disasters as clear felling or forest fire.

Krempf's Pine

(Pinus krempfii)

IUCN: Endangered

Phylum: Pinophyta (conifers)
Family: Pinaceae
Size: Up to 180 ft. (55 m) tall, with domed crown and trunk up to 6½ ft. (2 m) thick
Habitat: Emergent tree in evergreen monsoon forest on steep slopes at 3,900–6,600 ft. (1,200–2,000 m)
Range: North of Nha Trang and between Da Lat and Nha Trang in southern Vietnam

KREMPF'S PINE is one of the most unusual species of pine because of its flattened, narrow, bladelike leaves. Unlike other pines, the leaves are not needle-shaped. The moist, subtropical forest habitat of Krempf's pine is also unique: other subtropical pines grow in dry areas.

It is an extremely rare tree, known only from a few places between Da Lat and Nha Trang, and also north of Nha Trang, in southern Vietnam, principally near Bi Doup Mountain. These magnificent pines grow as emergent trees that rise above the evergreen monsoon forest canopy. They grow on very steep slopes at altitudes of 3,900–6,600 feet (1,200–2,000 meters). The Vietnamese people are said to be very proud of the few trees that are left in the wild, and they are very eager to conserve the forest habitat and maintain the pine's numbers. Because of the high level of protection that surrounds the pine, it is nowadays difficult to gain permission to visit the sites where it grows.

Krempf's pine is, of course, merely a translation of the Latin name given to it by the French botanist Paul Henri Lecomte (1856–1934), who formally described the species in 1921. The Vietnamese names are *thông lá det* and *ngo rí*, while the indigenous Indochinese names are *sral* or *sri*.

Distribution

Although extremely rare on a global scale, Krempf's pine may be quite prolific in the immediate areas where it grows. For instance, there are some 200 trees at one of the sites. Often they grow mixed with other coniferous trees, for example: the Da Lat pine, *Pinus dalatensis*, also known only in Vietnam; *Fokienia hodginsii*, which is a member of the cypress family (*Cupressaceae*) from southern China, Laos, and Vietnam; and *Dacrydium elatum*, a member of the podocarp family (*Podocarpaceae*) from Indochina and Sumatra. There may also be broad-leaved trees such as *Exbucklandia populnea* and *Rhodoleia championii*, both members of the witch-hazel family (*Hamamelidaceae*).

Krempf's pine has certain adaptations enabling it to survive in dense forest in a moist, subtropical climate. These features have not yet evolved in other pines, which are much more recent immigrants to subtropical areas and are currently restricted to drier habitats.

At higher altitudes than the Krempf's pine zone, the landscape is covered by forest of the

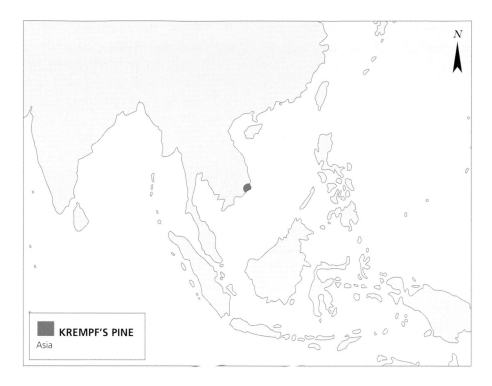

KREMPF'S PINE
Asia

Khasia pine, *Pinus kesiya*, which has quite a wide range from India and China to the Philippines. Below the Krempf's pine zone, tropical rain forest prevails.

Krempf's pine can become a large tree, growing up to 180 feet (55 meters) tall, with a single trunk up to 6½ feet (2 meters) thick. The trunk is often buttressed at the base. It has a domed crown with many large branches. The silvery gray bark is scaly and flaky, peeling off into irregular fragments, while the soft, light wood is slightly resinous. The leaves are narrowly bladelike and slightly curved, 1¼–2¾ inches (3–7 centimeters) long and 2–5 millimeters wide on adult trees, but much larger on young trees.

The male cones, which make the pollen, are relatively small, but the egg-shaped female cones, which carry the seeds, may reach 3½ inches (9 centimeters) long when mature, borne on a downward-curved cone stalk. They are glossy orange-brown in color

when freshly ripe, each with 12 to 20 seed-bearing woody scales. Each seed is 4–5 millimeters long. The wings are 10–15 millimeters long.

Habitat conservation

The continued existence of Krempf's pine depends heavily on the conservation of its natural habitat. Two nature reserves, Nui Ba and Dao Ngoan Muc, contain stands of the pine. The trees often grow on deep, humus-rich soils along streams. Apparently, the rate of natural regeneration from seeds is very low. Germination and establishment of seedlings can occur under the heavy shade of the forest canopy on deep, humus-rich soils, but germination is more successful in open situations. The natural life cycle and reproductive biology of the pine needs to be studied in much more detail so that the remaining wild trees can be conserved in an effective way.

It may not be enough simply to protect the natural habitat;

there may be natural processes upon which the pine depends for its survival. If conservationists do not take into account these processes when managing nature reserves, protection efforts may fail to maintain a healthy population of pines.

Botanical solution

An additional measure could be to grow seeds in botanical gardens to provide a backup in the event that a natural or human-induced disaster, such as a fire, occurs in the wild. So far, this pine has not been established in botanical gardens.

Martinez Piñon

(Pinus maximartinezii)

IUCN: Endangered

Phylum: Pinophyta (conifers)
Family: Pinaceae
Size: Tree height up to 52½ ft. (16 m), with a single trunk up to 15¾ in. (40 cm) thick
Leaves: Needlelike, 2½ in. (6–12 cm) long and about 1 mm wide
Cones: Massive, cylindrical to egg-shaped, 5½–9¾ in. (14–25 cm) long
Habitat: Montane dry forest
Range: Near Juchipila in the Sierra de Morones, Mexico

THE MARTINEZ piñon is matched only by the Coulter pine *(Pinus coulteri)* of California in bearing the heaviest pine cones in the world. These enormous seed-bearing structures may grow to 9¾ inches (25 centimeters) long and 4¾ inches (12 centimeters) wide, and weigh up to 4½ pounds (2 kilograms) while they are still green. The edible seeds contained in the cones are correspondingly large, and are the biggest known of any pine, at up to 1 inch (2.5 centimeters) long. This remarkable pine is also one of the world's rarest: estimates of the total number of naturally growing Martinez piñons vary from as low as 2,000 to as many as 10,000. The trees grow in scattered stands in dry montane forests on limestone and gypsum soils at altitudes from 5,250–8,370 feet (1,600–2,550 meters). They occur within a highly restricted area of only 1½–4 square miles (4–10 square kilometers) on high, barely accessible slopes of the Sierra de Morones, near Juchipila in the southern part of the state of Zacatecas, Mexico.

Discovery

Professor Jerzy Rzedowski, a botanist from Mexico, discovered the Martinez piñon in Zacatecas in 1963. He formally described it the following year, naming it after Mexican botanist Dr Maximino Martinez (1888–1964).

The total world population of the Martinez piñon consists of two main stands of trees separated by a summit ridge. One group is on an east-facing slope; the other is on a southwest-facing slope. On the eastern slope, the trees grow mainly in small groups of three to five, but there are also widely scattered, solitary trees. This patchy distribution is probably because of past felling, grazing, and fire. On the southwestern slope, the pines are fewer in total number but grow closer together, with some groups containing 10–30 trees. The finest individuals grow at higher altitudes. These trees bear the largest cones, whereas those growing at lower altitudes are stunted because of drought, and bear smaller cones.

Features

The Martinez piñon grows into a tree up to 52½ feet (16 meters) tall, with a trunk up to 15¾ inches (40 centimeters) thick. The bark is thinly scaled and gray-brown on mature trees, and the crown is broad and irregularly branched. The leaves are needlelike, blue-green, and arranged in bunches of five.

The female seed-bearing cones, as already noted, are huge and very heavy, hanging down on incongruously slender cone stalks. Each cone is cylindrical and egg-shaped, 5½–9¾ inches (14–25 centimeters) long and 4–4¾ inches (10–12 centimeters) wide, initially green but ripening to a pale brown color. The woody, seed-bearing scales are large, 1½–2 inches (3.5–5 centimeters) wide and about ¾ inch (2 centimeters) thick, each one bearing a single, large, orange-buff seed, with a long, tiny wing that remains attached to the scale when the seed is removed. The helicopter blade wing of many

MARTINEZ PIÑON
North America

pine seeds allows effective dispersal by the wind. However, the seeds of the Martinez piñon do not naturally drop out of the cones and are, instead, picked out and dispersed by birds, so that the wing is unnecessary.

Seeds and germination

The cones ripen in August, about two years and 3–4 months after pollination, which is an unusually long period for pines. The seedlings possess up to 24 seed leaves (cotyledons) at germination. This is yet another record: the largest number of cotyledons of any plant.

The surviving Martinez piñons grow on privately owned land. Natural regeneration is said to be rather poor. This may be partly because the edible seeds are collected by the local people for food, tempted by pine nuts over ¾ inch (2 centimeters) long. The owners of the land value the trees as a source of these huge pine nuts, and try to conserve the mature trees, but obviously such a practice cannot continue indefinitely because eventually the old trees will die and there will be none to replace them.

Young seedlings are eaten by cattle, which may also cause longer term damage by breaking up the vegetation cover that protects the soil and allowing erosion to set in. There is also a very serious threat to trees of all ages from fire: the bark is thin and gives little protection to the actively growing cambium layer beneath, and even old trees can be killed. On top of all these factors, the Martinez piñon grows extremely slowly, so recovery from disasters such as fire can take very many years.

During this time the saplings have to contend with several possible hazards.

Conservation

Immediate conservation measures must be put in place to create just the right conditions for the pines to regenerate. A genetic conservation project has already been started at North Carolina State University, and the Centro de Genética Forestal in Chapingo, Mexico. In addition, seeds have been collected throughout the Martinez piñon's tiny range, and conservation plantings and research trials are now planned in Mexico and other countries.

Nick Turland

River Pipefish
(Syngnathus watermayeri)

IUCN: Critically endangered

Class: Actinopterygii
Order: Syngnathiformes
Family: Syngnathidae
Length: 5½ in. (14 cm)
Reproduction: Egg layer
Habitat: Estuaries and coastal inshore areas
Range: Eastern Cape of South Africa

THE RIVER pipefish belongs to one of the most unusual families in the world, Syngnathidae, which also includes sea horses. Most people are familiar with seahorses and their upright posture, finless prehensile (or grasping) tail, and 90-degree bend in the head. Pipefish are long and slender like sea horses, but swim in a horizontal position and lack both the bend in the head and the prehensile tail (the tip actually has a small fin).

Unusual shape

As the name implies, the river pipefish is extraordinarily long and slender. It has a long and tubular snout, and ringlike plates surround the body.

Pipefish and sea horses display reproductive behavior that is quite different from other fish. After eggs are laid by the female and fertilized by the male, the male protects the eggs in a marsupial-like brood pouch on his belly. Males of other species are known to protect eggs in a nest, or even within their mouths, but the pouch adaptation is rare.

The river pipefish has a dorsal fin located mid-body on the back, and the pectoral fins are positioned just behind the gills. Like all pipefish, it lacks pelvic fins on the belly.

The river pipefish can be found in the coastal rivers and

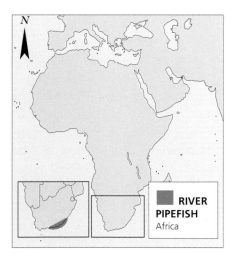

RIVER PIPEFISH
Africa

southern coastline of South Africa. One threat to this fish is the deterioration of its river and coastal habitats by chemical pollution. Another is the result of South Africa's cultivation of land for farming. Millions of tons of sediment have washed into waterways due to deforestation. Polluted habitat spells trouble for any species.

William E. Manci

Although the pipefish does not look very much like a sea horse, they are related. Both are part of the family Syngnathidae.

Sokoke Pipit
(Anthus sokokensis)

IUCN: Vulnerable

Class: Aves
Order: Passeriformes
Family: Motacillidae
Length: 5½–6 in. (13.9–15.2 cm)
Clutch size: Probably 2–3 eggs
Incubation: Probably 14–15 days
Diet: Insects and other invertebrates
Habitat: Forest, woodland
Range: Small area of coastal Kenya

MORE GREAT mammals, such as lions, tigers, and elephants, have survived in Africa than on any other continent. Yet Africa has its share of small mammals and birds too. While wildlife enthusiasts focus their attention on the plight of Africa's gorillas, elephants, and cheetahs, smaller species are dwindling away equally fast, if not faster. The Sokoke pipit is one example.

The Sokoke pipit belongs to a family of 54 wagtail and pipit species. Two of these species, the American pipit (*Anthus spinoletta*) and the Sprague's pipit (*Anthus spragueii*), are permanent residents of North America. Several others irregularly visit North America from Asia and Europe. The Sokoke pipit does not share the broad distribution enjoyed by some of its relatives. It occupies a small area along Africa's coast on the Indian Ocean. Its homeland is the Sokoke Forest.

This forest is a reserve of 160 square miles (400 square kilometers) that covers the distance between the villages of Sokoke on the southwest and Arabuko on the northeast. Some refer to this area as the Arabuko-Sokoke Forest. The Sokoke Forest is actually a tract of land where four major plant communities mingle. The forest and woodland portion has been badly damaged. Much of the soil is poor, but people have cleared the land for farming anyway. Many trees have been cut for lumber, and in some places no commercially valuable trees

remain. Farmland and secondary growth shrub lands have replaced the forests and woodlands. Portions of the reserve have also been cut to make space for plantations of more commercially desirable trees, all exotic species. Much of the Sokoke Forest is sparse, with a thin forest canopy or no canopy at all. Because plenty of sunlight reaches the ground, a thick undergrowth of shrubs and grass covers the ground like a quilt.

Forest habitat
The Sokoke pipit is a small, terrestrial songbird, amply striped in black, brown, buff, and tan. It has the long, thin beak of a bird that eats insects. Ornithologists long presumed the Sokoke pipit occupied forest edges and sparser woodlands. Researchers in the 1970s, however, found it was common inside the forests, not just on the edges. By the late 1980s the Sokoke pipit was no longer common, and its abundance was in doubt. The same clearing activities that have destroyed much of the forest and

woodlands outside the reserve have been occurring inside the reserve as well.

Historical change

In the mid-1970s, the pipit's population was estimated at between 3,000 and 5,000 birds. No recent population estimates are available. The Sokoke pipit historically occurred in very similar habitat located across the Kenyan border in Tanzania. It was known from the Pugu Hills and another region near the town of Moa. Forest and woodland clearing in these localities has been extremely steady and thorough.

No recent reports of Sokoke pipits have originated from either of these particular places.

Ornithologists suspect that the bird's habitat in Tanzania may have been completely eliminated.

Without specific field work to verify the status of Sokoke pipits, ornithologists can only speculate on its population levels.

So much habitat has been destroyed that concerns for the Sokoke pipit's welfare are more than justified.

Bleak future

At least three sawmills closed many years ago as the trees in the forest were used up. Now, the sawmills and the jobs that they provided are gone. The people of the area have no remaining trees, and there is little left of the wildlife that once completely depended on those trees. Mean-

SOKOKE PIPIT
Africa

while, a small nature reserve inside the Sokoke Forest is supposedly protected from tree cutting. Living there may prove to be the last chance for the Sokoke pipit bird.

Kevin Cook

PITCHER PLANTS

Class: Magnoliopsida

Order: Nepenthales

Family: Sarraceniaceae

The North American pitcher plants are insectivorous plants that have a modified tubular leaf with a hooded top. Insects and other animals are attracted to nectar just below the hood. They enter and fall into the pitcher where they are prevented from climbing out by hairs that point downward. Once in the pitcher, the prey is broken down by enzymes and micro-organisms, which release nutrients to the plant and supplement its nitrogen supply. *Sarracenia* species live in boggy areas which are deficient in nutrients. Some plants are used in flower arranging, and it is this illegal collection which is threatening the group.

Alabama Canebrake Pitcher Plant

(Sarracenia rubra alabamensis)

ESA: Endangered

IUCN: Vulnerable

Leaves: Erect, tubular
Flowers: Nodding flowers, petals are maroon outside and greenish within
Habitat: Fall-line acidic seepage bogs over shallow hardpans
Range: Autaga, Chilton, and Elmore Counties, central Alabama

THE ALABAMA canebrake pitcher plant (*S. alabamensis*), is also known simply as the canebrake pitcher plant. It is a perennial herbaceous evergreen that pro-

duces tufts of insect-trapping leaves from a much-branched, stout, creeping rhizome at or just below the surface. The spring leaves, produced at the same time as the flowers, are erect, tubular pitchers gradually tapering from a narrow base to a mouth ¼–1 inch (0.7–3 centimeters) wide, greenish, covered with fine soft hairs, and from 3–19½ inches (8–50 centimeters) tall. At their top, partially covering the open mouth is a heart-shaped, sub-erect hood up to 3 inches (8 centimeters) long and 2 inches (6 centimeters) broad, pale-green in color but with a network of reddish veins. Later in the season the pitchers are larger, and are a yellowish-green color, somewhat winged on the lower surface, and with a more pointed hood that is faintly whitish and opaque just above the pitcher mouth. In late autumn to winter the plant produces persistent phyllodia, which means shorter, spreading, sickle-shaped, flattened leaves that do not have an insect trapping function. These consist of an expanded version of the wing produced by the summer pitchers. In some plants two flower stalks may be produced, which is a very unusual feature in the genus.

Flower features

The unusual nodding flowers are typical of the genus. At the tip of the flower stalk is a sheath of three small, firm, recurved triangular bracts. These are followed by the five ovate, inwardly bent, reddish sepals, ½–1 inch (1.7–2.6 centimeters) long. The five petals are larger, up to 2 inches (4.5 centimeters) long, and they have a very distinctive shape, with a narrowed middle rather like a violin body. The petals are maroon on the outside and greenish within. They hang down around the broadened style apex, which looks like an inverted umbrella. It measures 1¼–1½ inches (3.5–4.2 centimeters) across. Shielded beneath the apex are many stamens with deep yellow anthers, and five stigmas. The whole structure sits on top of the warty, nearly circular, five-chambered ovary.

This pitcher plant is limited to three counties in central Alabama, where it is now only known from 11 sites, all of which are privately owned and most of which are very small. The species only occurs in wet pine-barrens, the swampy, treeless, so-called islands in the dominant dry pine forest. These sites have been destroyed by railroad, pond building, and other industrial

construction activity. Incompatible land-use practices, such as intensive livestock grazing, drainage and afforestation, gravel mining, and prevention of the fires that maintain the required open habitats, continue to threaten this rare plant's existence. As with all carnivorous plants, poaching, or unauthorized digging up of plants from the wild, and the resulting damage to their fragile habitats, is a constant problem.

Future survival

The Alabama canebrake pitcher plant represents one geographically isolated group within a larger complex of closely related taxa, currently recognized as subspecies of the sweet pitcher (*Sarracenia rubra*). Many of these distinctive local variants are threatened, and are listed as endangered by the U.S. Fish and Wildlife Service. Their commercial trading is strictly regulated under CITES. Among the most threatened of these North American pitchers, the Alabama canebrake has been lost from at least 20 sites. A census taken in the period between 1994 and 1996 found only 3,572 plants, 60 percent of which were

The leaves of the Alabama pitcher plant are a tubular shape, and they are covered with a network of reddish veins. The plant is only found on privately owned land.

at a single site. Most worryingly only three sites were thought to contain populations that were viable in the long term. In spite of the great reduction in range and abundance, the few plant populations that remain have comparatively high levels of genetic diversity, and if suitable management and *ex situ* propagation can be used, as suggested in the 1992 recovery plan issued by the United States Fish and Wildlife Service, then the plant may be saved.

The Alabama canebrook pitcher plant is currently grown only by a limited range of carnivorous plant enthusiasts and a few botanic gardens. The plants are rarely commercially available.

ALABAMA PITCHER PLANT
North America

Green Pitcher Plant

(Sarracenia oreophila)

ESA: Endangered

IUCN: Vulnerable

Leaves: Short and flat, except for modified leaves that form the pitchers. These can be up to 30 in. (75 cm) long and may be colored with purple spots or veins

Flowers: Yellowish or greenish

Stems: Essentially stalks to which leaves and flowers are attached

Flowering season: April to June

Pollination: By insects

Height: Up to 3 ft. (1 m)

Habitat: Woodlands and bogs with acidic soils

Range: Alabama, Georgia

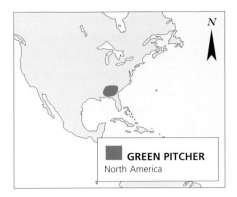

GREEN PITCHER
North America

THE GREEN PITCHER plant is an insectivorous species. It is always found in areas where nitrogen is in low supply (the insectivorous habit is an adaptation to supplement low nitrogen supplies in the soil). These areas are generally acidic boglands. A relatively constant supply of water is required for the survival of these plants. The plant produces its stems, leaves, and flowers from underground rhizomes. These structures enable the plant to survive during the winter.

These plants are characterized by flowers up to 29½ inches (75 centimeters) long that hang from leafless stems. The flowers are also unusual in that they hang upside down.

Historically this plant was widespread and the populations were stable. This seemed to provide a good base for the plant. Because populations were widespread, they were protected from habitat destruction, and because there were a large number of populations the genetic diversity was high. Unfortunately the green pitcher plant is now known only in three areas, which represent 26 colonies. This may sound like a large number but some of these colonies are represented by a single individual. The largest colony has 1,000 plants, and it is restricted to northeastern Alabama.

The two main threats to the continued survival of the green pitcher plant are habitat loss, fertilizer application, and herbicide application. The habitat loss is brought about by a lowering of the water table. This allows the bog to dry out, which kills the plant. Herbicides and fertilizers that are applied to adjacent agricultural land can enter the water table and alter chemical balance, which in turn makes the land less suitable in compostition for the green pitcher plant.

Conservation of this plant can occur through habitat preservation. To do this, first the water table must be maintained in suitable areas. This means that bogs must not be drained or filled in. Second, agricultural runoff must be controlled. Reduced application of fertilizers and herbicides will reduce the amount of these substances in the water. All these chemicals are applied during the drier times of the year. This ensures that excess herbicide and

The green pitcher plant is characterized by very long flowers that hang upside down from leafless stems. It prefers to grow in acidic bogland soil.

fertilizer is not instantly washed off into the water supply.

Management of habitats will also be necessary in the short-term. As environmental succession proceeds, the natural tendency of the land is to become woodland. This encroachment of trees into areas previously inhabited by the green pitcher plant will irrevocably destroy the habitat of this plant. Insectivorous plants are a particularly unusual group of organisms. Because of this they are popular, and many are bought and sold, particularly from illegal wild collections. To further protect these plants, collecting must also be halted.

Conservation strategy

When appropriate areas of land have been identified, long-term management strategies must be devised. These areas will also need to be fenced off. Once these safeguards are in place, reintroduction of the plant can be attempted. This can take place from nursery stocks following successful cultivation. In the short-term, transplantation between colonies is the only way to maintain viable populations with sufficient population density and genetic variability.

One other problem facing the survival of this species is its ability to hybridize. The green pitcher plant is capable of producing fertile hybrids with other members of the *Sarracenia* genus. The eventual outcome of this would be to lose all species of *Sarracenia* and to be left with only one species that is intermediate between the parental types. To overcome this, reserves of pure genetic stock must be set aside.

Mountain Sweet Pitcher Plant
(Sarracenia rubra jonesii)

ESA: Endangered

IUCN: Endangered

Leaves: Waxy green, some modified into trumpet shaped pitchers with purple veining
Flowers: Red to purple
Stems: Simple, erect stalks that bear the flowers
Flowering season: April to May and June
Pollination: Insects
Height: 30 in. (75 cm)
Habitat: Streams and mountain bogs
Range: North and South Carolina

THE MOUNTAIN sweet pitcher plant grows in streams and bogs in mountains. It is produced from an underground storage organ called a rhizome. It is the rhizome that overwinters. Once flowering has started the plant is very distinctive. Large, attractive flowers are produced. These are generally a red to purple color. They grow individually, hanging upside down from a leafless stem. They are characteristically fragrant, which is an unusual feature of this genus. The pitcher, which is used to catch insects to supplement the nitrogen intake of the plant, is hooded and green in color. On this structure there is a network of purple veins that, along with the smell produced by the pitcher, serves to attract insects. The mountain sweet pitcher plant grows in mountain bogs and along streambeds.

The mountain sweet pitcher plant grows in the wet, shady areas found in habitats such as stream beds and mountain bogs.

These two habitat types provide the required conditions of wetness and shade. The main threats to this plant are habitat loss and alteration, and collection by humans. Many populations have been destroyed in the past 20 or so years by human activities. These include drainage of habitats, flooding of habitats caused by the construction of dams, agricultural development, and construction of golf courses. There are no known figures for current population sizes but the mountain sweet pitcher plant is known only from 10 populations spread between North and South Carolina. It is known that these populations are small and that their distribution is also limited within these areas. Collectors of

MOUNTAIN SWEET PITCHER
North America

these plants have been known to remove entire populations to sell and they have taken seeds from other populations. Pitcher plants are protected by federal and state laws, but due to the locations of the habitats these laws are difficult to enforce.

Habitat preservation

To conserve these plants one of the most important first steps is habitat preservation. This is a two-fold process. First the habitat must be identified and further development, such as building and drainage, must be stopped. Damage to this sort of habitat can occur over vast distances. The construction of a dam or golf course many miles away can have a profound effect. Once habitat preservation has been carried out, the area then needs to be managed for the benefit of the mountain sweet pitcher plant.

Conservation of species such as this plant is not simply a case of avoiding damaging activities. Active site management must be carried out to ensure the survival of the habitat. The tendency is for areas to change into woodland, and a woodland habitat is not suitable for this plant. Periodic fires or cutting would stop the areas from being encroached upon by trees. Eight of the ten known populations are found on private land and some of these landowners do not employ preservation methods. Of the remaining two public land sites, one site is managed by the wildlife department, which gives some protection. The second site is part of the parks department, where the plant is threatened by increased recreational usage.

Biological threat

There is also a biological problem associated with this plant. In common with other members of the genus *Sarracenia*, it is able to produce fertile hybrids. This can lead to the possible future loss of pure, discrete species.

Fred Rumsey

Gurney's Pitta

(Pitta gurneyi)

IUCN: Critically endangered

Class: Aves
Order: Passeriformes
Family: Pittidae
Length: 8–9 in. (20.3–22.9 cm)
Clutch size: 3–4 eggs
Diet: Earthworms, snails, insects, spiders, small frogs
Habitat: Primary forest
Range: Extreme southern Myanmar and Thailand

A PILE OF BROKEN snail shells lying beside a rock could indicate the presence of a pitta nearby. Pittas are large, short-tailed, and usually colorful birds. Being terrestrial, they often find snails in the debris on the forest floor where they search for food. Lacking a specialized beak to extract the snail from its shell, some pittas bash the snails against small rocks until the shells break. Favorite stones are used again and again, leaving a telltale pile of broken shells.

The Gurney's pitta inhabits dense primary forests of the

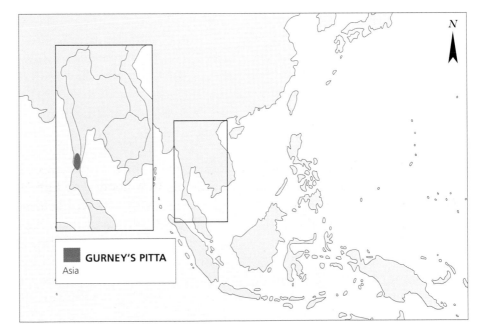

GURNEY'S PITTA
Asia

Pittas are shy, secretive birds. They often sing from dense cover and rarely are seen out in the open.

northern Malay Peninsula. Its behavior and habitat makes the Gurney's pitta extraordinarily difficult to study. This pitta has short, rounded wings, a trait common to most forest-dwelling birds. The leg, foot, and toe are well adapted for life on the ground, and it escapes danger by running through the undergrowth. The undergrowth in this part of the world can be immensely thick. Gurney's pitta has the short neck, large head, stout beak, and stubby, turquoise tail typical of this genus. A patch of bright, shiny blue covers the hindcrown and nape. The forecrown, forehead, lores, and cheek are deep black, which continues behind the eye, down the side of

the neck, and from the shoulder down to the lower breast and belly. The chin is dull yellow, but the throat and upper breast are brilliant yellow in a biblike patch. The sides are bright yellow, with thin, dark brown stripes. The back and wing are cinnamon, and, unlike other pittas, the wing has no white. The female Gurney's pitta has a blue tail, but her head patch is brown. Her underparts are dull yellowish white and are heavily patterned with thin black bars.

A caged species

In the past the Gurney's pitta was highly regarded as a cage bird and many were taken from the wild for this purpose. Today there is no hard evidence of any trade in this species but there is always the fear that it may begin again in the future.

The Gurney's pitta has not been sighted in Myanmar since 1914, and until 1986 no ornithologist has reported seeing a live Gurney's pitta in the wild for fully 50 years. Still, occasional reports of Gurney's pittas have been noted. In 1986, following reports of Gurney's pittas still appearing in illegal trade, some ornithologists located the regions in Thailand where trappers caught these endangered birds.

Valuable data

After two years of field work, these ornithologists had tallied 16 pairs. They gathered the first information of nesting and the first details of calls and songs. They also gathered valuable information about feeding habits and natural predators. Such information is essential for devising good plans to preserve endangered species. Two points are worth noting. A friendly trapper helped the ICBP ornithologists to find the Gurney's pitta, and the Thai government has responded favorably to the Gurney's Pitta Action Plan that was proposed.

Illegal cutting

Thailand's forests have been severely depleted by timber cutting. Many reserves and national parks have been established to protect sensitive areas and primary forests, but an extremely well coordinated group of timber cutters continues to operate illegally. Also, farmers continue to cut primary forests to open up more land for crops. The Gurney's pitta prefers mature, dense primary forests that are well supplied with undergrowth.

Kevin Cook

Cape Platanna

(Xenopus gilli)

IUCN: Vulnerable

Class: Amphibia
Order: Pipidae
Suborder: Aglossa
Family: Salientia
Length: 2 in. (5 cm)
Diet: Crustacea, small fish, aquatic insects, and larvae
Habitat: Fresh water with dense vegetation
Range: Forelands around Cape Town, South Africa

THE PLATANNA got its common English name from a Dutch word, *plathander*, which means flat-handed creature. It is also known as the clawed or tongueless frog. Frogs with claws can be found nowhere else in the world except in tropical and southern parts of the African continent. The platanna's claws are found on only three of the amphibian's toes and none of its fingers. This unusual feature is how the platanna got its generic name *Xenopus*, which means "strange foot." These claws are probably used to rake up mud or sand to use as camouflage when danger is encountered. They may also be used to burrow into soil.

The suborder to which this species belongs is Anglossa, or tongueless frogs, and this is another feature that distinguishes platannas from other frogs. Most frogs use their long, sticky tongues to catch prey. Since platannas have no tongues, they use long, sharp, forklike fingers to pick up food. A jerking motion brings the fingers together to hold a worm or other prey, while the frog seizes it by the middle with its mouth.

The platanna is known for its preference for the aquatic life. This amphibian's pointed head, upturned eye, tapering body, powerful hindlimbs, and broadly webbed feet are all adaptations that suit it perfectly for life in the water. While the platanna is quick and agile in water, on land it is rather awkward, moving in a succession of flopping motions. The platanna is perhaps the only frog that is capable of jumping backward and can do so on land or in water.

Reduced numbers

The most common platanna is the *Xenopus laevis*, and for many years scientists believed it was the only species of the genus to occur on the Cape Peninsula, or perhaps in all of South Africa. In 1926, however, a second and much rarer species was found: *Xenopus gilli*, the Cape platanna. This species is restricted to the forelands around Cape Town in South Africa, although its former distribution was probably larger. It seems that the *Xenopus gilli* was the original inhabitant of the Cape Peninsula, but the common platanna was a larger, stronger, cannibalistic form that was more capable of migration when conditions were unfavorable for its survival. Consequently, the common platanna is displacing the smaller Cape platanna, which is now found only in very small, sporadic colonies. The Cape platanna displays a yellow undersurface marked with small, dark spots. It is less aquatic and more easily captured than its relative and is also more agile on land.

The Cape platanna has diminished in number largely because of the arrival of its more aggressive relative. However, many of this amphibian's original localities had been developed for residential use by 1970, reducing the Cape platanna's already small range. Because the species is not as adept at migration as the common platanna, it had nowhere to go when humans encroached upon its habitat.

For many years, the platanna has been collected and used by medical laboratories in a convenient test for human pregnancy. This probably has not significantly affected the wild populations of Cape platannas, because the frogs used for this test are often bred for that particular purpose.

Safety alert

The most important measure in protecting the Cape platanna is to alert local authorities to the precarious nature of this amphibian's tiny habitat. Any large-scale drainage schemes or development in the area should take into account the occurrence of this rare amphibian.

Elizabeth Sirimarco

See also Frogs.

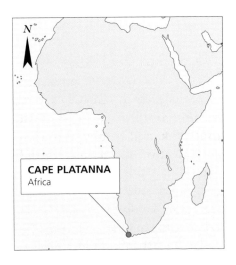

CAPE PLATANNA
Africa

PLATYFISH

Class: Actinopterygii
Order: Cyprinodontiformes
Family: Poeciliidae

Fish in the genus *Xiphophorus* are commonly called platyfish and swordtails. These names are very familiar to aquarium hobbyists. These colorful and fascinating fishes are prized for their interesting appearance, manageable size, ease of care, high reproductive rate, and mode of reproduction. A side benefit of their adaptability to aquariums has been their contribution to the sciences of endocrinology (hormonal systems), genetics, embryology (developmental biology), and cytology (cellular biology).

Like all fish of the family *Poeciliidae*, platyfish are known for their ability to give birth to live young. The most familiar member of this family is the guppy (*Poecilia reticulata*), a common aquarium fish. Platyfish distinguish themselves with their nearly uniform habitat preference for dense vegetation and a specific taste for adult and larval mosquitoes. This characteristic has made platyfish and other poeciliids—notably the mosquitofish (*Gambusia affinis*)—popular in many regions around the world that have problems with mosquitoes. Even though the mosquitofish sometimes wreaks havoc on the habitat of less aggressive native fish, it is often used to aid the fight against malaria and other mosquito-born diseases. But in almost all cases, native poeciliids (such as platyfish) are usually available to do the same job, and the stocking of mosquitofish should be avoided.

Platyfish, as well as other live-bearing poeciliids, do not lay eggs like most fish. Rather, they hold the eggs within their body. Males are therefore required to fertilize eggs while they are still within the female. Male platyfishes use a penislike structure, called a gonopodium, to insert a sperm filled sac (*spermatophore*) into the female. Interestingly, the female is not required to utilize the sperm immediately, because the sperm sac may be carried for a period of up to around ten months.

As the eggs mature and become ready for fertilization, the female releases sperm from the sac to fertilize the eggs. After several weeks the eggs hatch and the young emerge from the mother's abdomen. This fascinating process of reproduction is called ovovivipary, which literally means "live birth from eggs."

Other characteristic physical features of platyfish include an upturned mouth to facilitate feeding at the surface, large scales on the body, a dorsal fin that is positioned back toward the tail, and a tail fin that is rounded instead of forked. These features probably result from the preference of the platyfish for inhabiting still waters. Unfortunately, none of the fins carry spines as protection from the animal's predators.

Platy Cuatro Ciénegas

(Xiphophorus gordoni)

IUCN: Endangered

Length: 1¼ in. (3 cm)
Reproduction: Live bearer
Habitat: Spring pools and waterways in dense vegetation
Range: Cuatro Ciénegas Basin, Coahuila, Mexico

SOUTH OF THE United States-Mexican border, near the geographic center of the Mexican state of Coahuila, is a basin called Cuatro Ciénegas (meaning "four marshes"). This unusual area was formed as a result of the uplifting of surrounding mountain ranges. This isolated the basin and its animals from neighboring river drainages, creating a natural laboratory for the study of animals and plants, and their evoluiion. The Cuatro Ciénegas Basin is a unique place on earth.

Unfortunately, the Cuatro Ciénegas Basin and its marvelous diversity of wildlife are under attack from farmers and ranchers who are eager to use the basin's water resources. Quite a few canals have been constructed to divert water from Cuatro Ciénegas to nearby fields and ranches for irrigation and livestock watering. As more water is diverted from the area, shallow marshes and pools will continue to dry out, and resident fish and other animals will be forced to concentrate in tracts that are smaller and smaller. Competition for space and food has increased, and alterations in the population of the platy Cuatro Ciénegas and other organisms have already been noticed.

Nearby towns also demand water from the Cuatro Ciénegas region for domestic and commercial purposes. The relatively small amount of water that is returned from these towns contains sewage and other pollutants. Overall, reduced water levels in the Cuatro Ciénegas streams and marshes increase average temperatures and destroy fast-flowing stream riffles and other critical habitat. All this spells trouble for the creatures of this basin.

Appearance

The platy Cuatro Ciénegas is short compared to other members of this genus. It lacks the usually pronounced swordlike projection at the base of the tail. However, this trait is not unusual for an isolated species.

This platy displays the typical upturned mouth of a poeciliid, and a rounded, swordless tail. The overall color of this species is olive-brown and yellow. The upper half of the fish is blotchy and darker, while the lower half is much lighter and has few spots or patches of dark pigment. A prominent, dark horizontal stripe marks each side. The base of the dorsal fin on the back also has

spots that suggest banding, and the lower edge of the tail fin displays a solid dark stripe of color.

As with most poeciliids, the platy Cuatro Ciénegas actively seeks mosquitoes and other surface-film insects as its primary food source. This fish is fairly opportunistic and will consume other similarly-sized food when plentiful. This fish breeds from the spring onward and probably continues throughout the warmer months of summer.

Efforts are underway to declare the Cuatro Ciénegas Basin a national park, a move that would curtail water use for outside purposes. Additionally, conservationists hope to acquire funds for continued biological research of the unique plants and animals that occupy the region.

Platy Monterrey
(Xiphophorus couchianus)

IUCN: Critically endangered

Length: 1¼ in. (3 cm)
Reproduction: Live bearer
Habitat: Spring and stream pools over mud
Range: Rio Santa Catarina, Nuevo Leon, Mexico

GIVEN ITS STRICT requirement for very clean spring or river water, and the small size of its home range, it is not surprising that the platy Monterrey is in danger of extinction. This fish is found only in the Rio Santa Catarina Basin near Monterrey in the Mexican state of Nuevo Leon. Situated in the Chihuahuan Desert, both the Rio Santa Catarina and the platy Monterrey are under heavy pressure from the surrounding human population. Both fish and people are competing for the available water. The principal demands on the river's water are for agricultural and domestic use. Competing non-native fish and direct destruction of river habitat by cattle and people also take their toll on this species.

Problems such as these certainly are not unique to the platy Monterrey. Many endangered species suffer from similar assaults on their habitat. A saving grace for this species may be the interest and demand of aquarium hobbyists. The platy Monterrey adapts well to aquarium life and will reproduce readily in that environment. The aquarium may be the last refuge of the platy

PLATY CUATRO CIÉNEGAS
PLATY DE MUZQUIZ
North America

PLATY MONTERREY
North America

The platy Monterrey has been put in the position of competing with non-native fishes for its habitat and food.

Monterrey until natural habitats can be restored and managed.

This species is shorter in length than other members of its genus. In addition the platy Monterrey has no swordlike projection at the base of the tail, a common feature of poeciliids. This would add to its overall length. The overall coloration of this species is silvery brown; the upper half of the fish is quite blotchy and dark, while the lower half is somewhat lighter and has a few spots or patches of dark pigment. The tail section of the body carries several dark spots in three rows that suggest horizontal bands. The base of the dorsal fin on the back also has spots that suggest banding.

Nutrition

The platy Monterrey eats mosquitoes and other surface insects, but will eat many other types of foods if they are plentiful. Its situation in the wild, however, is not likely to remain stable if the remaining water of its habitat is pumped away. Unfortunately, given the political and economic problems of this country, the needs of wildlife go unnoticed in Mexico's struggle to improve the living conditions of its people.

Platy de Muzquiz

(Xiphophorus meyeri)

IUCN: Endangered

Length: 1¼ in. (3 cm)
Reproduction: Live bearer
Habitat: Spring outflow pools near bank vegetation
Range: Melchor Múzquiz, Coahuila, Mexico

THE PLATY DE MÚZQUIZ is the northernmost species of the endangered Mexican platyfish. At home in northern Mexico's desert region, this fish resides in adjoining outflow pools of a spring near the town of Melchor Múzquiz. Unfortunately for this fish, the springs and the surrounding area have been significantly altered to satisfy human needs, and the outflow pools are used for swimming.

Other fish occupy the spring pools in addition to the platy de Múzquiz. The shortfin molly (*Poecilia mexicana*), the mojarra (*Cichlasoma* sp.), the guayacón (*Gambusia* sp.), and an undetermined species of catfish share the limited habitat of this site. These other species are more aggressive and may be a threat by outcompeting the platy de Múzquiz for dwindling resources.

Color and structure

Like the other platys, the platy de Múzquiz lacks the swordlike extension at the base of the tail. The overall coloration is silvery brown; the upper half of the fish is blotchy and dark, while the lower half is lighter and has a few spots or patches of dark pigment. The tail section has several dark spots arranged in rows.

The platy de Múzquiz has the same diet as the other platys, namely mosquitoes and other water surface insects.

The diversion of water from its spring for agricultural irrigation threatens to destroy the only home this platyfish has known. In addition, pumping from nearby wells that tap the same supply as the spring is lowering the local water table, and could cause the spring to fail.

Unless steps are taken to provide a protected home for the platy de Múzquiz fish, its survival is in doubt.

William E. Manci

PLOVERS

Class: Aves
Order: Charadriiformes
Family: Charadriidae

Plovers look like sandpipers, but the groups differ in subtle, yet visible, ways. Plovers tend to have shorter legs and necks, making them look squat and stubby. They peck for food, while sandpipers probe, bobbing their heads up and down. Pipers walk as they probe. Plovers have a walk-and-stop habit of feeding. They walk a few steps, stop to look around, then peck at what might be food.

The plover family contains 64 species, some of which inhabit dry land. The mountain plover (*Charadrius montanus*) lives on dry plains and is one of the few bird species in which the female lays a clutch of eggs for the male to raise, as well as a clutch for herself to raise. The killdeer (*Charadrius vociferus*) is the most familiar of U.S. plovers. It enjoys the broadest distribution and occurs in fields, pastures, park lawns, and other places. People know it for its broken-wing act when distracting attention from eggs or chicks, a trick used by many other birds as well.

Many plover species are found near water. They inhabit ocean beaches or rocky seacoasts, or they live inland along lakes, rivers, and marshes. Unfortunately, this tendency has caused many plover species to decline as wetlands are destroyed by humans. Habitat loss has severely affected one plover in North America, and a New Zealand species has suffered more from the degradation of its habitat than from the problems caused by the existence of exotic species.

Piping Plover
(Charadrius melodus)

ESA: Endangered

IUCN: Vulnerable

Length: 6½–7¼ in. (16.5–18.4 cm)
Weight: 1½–2¼ oz. (46.4–63.7 g)
Clutch size: 4 eggs
Incubation: 30 days
Diet: Crustaceans, insects, mollusks
Habitat: Sandy or gravelly seacoasts, lake shores, riverbanks, and river flats
Range: Eastern North America

THE SUN BAKES the sandy river flats of the Great Plains dry during the summer. Drained by irrigation, the rivers sometimes barely carry enough water for gravity to pull them toward the sea. Flies and dragonflies move around, and a few cicadas drone from the cottonwoods scattered along the banks. Every so often, there is the cheerful, whistling call of the piping plover.

Sandy gray above and pure white below, the piping plover blends perfectly with the bleached sands of plains waterways. Only when the plover moves does it betray itself. In breeding plumage it wears a black shoulder patch that connects across the breast in some birds. It also has a narrow black forecrown line that separates its white forehead from a sandy gray crown. The piping plover's only bright color is the orange base of its black-tipped beak and its orange leg, foot, and toe. When the bird molts after breeding, it loses the black shoulder patches and forecrown line for the winter. Its coloration makes it almost invisible when it stands still.

This camouflage defense helps protect the piping plover from its natural enemies, and it has plenty. Snakes, rodents, weasels, skunks, and foxes all steal eggs and can easily take

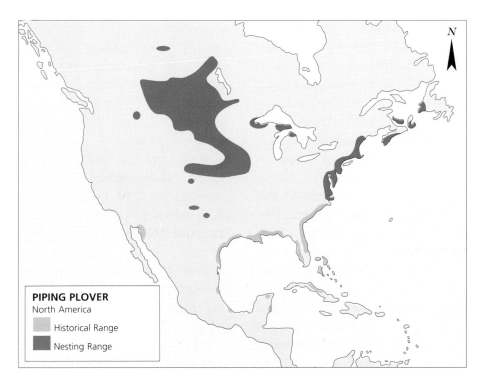

PIPING PLOVER
North America

    Historical Range

    Nesting Range

The subtle coloring of the piping plover acts as camouflage. In addition, it has a high-pitched call that helps obscure the bird's location—only another plover is likely to find its secret hiding place.

nestlings. Hawks, falcons, night-herons, and many mammals also prey on adult plovers. Camouflage coloration and quiet bird calls, however, cannot protect the plover from unnatural enemies.

Wetland destruction

Commercial hunters shot many piping plovers for market in the late 1800s. The piping plover population entered the 20th century already depleted. The early and middle decades of the 1900s witnessed an extraordinary human assault on wetlands all over North America. Originally viewed as useless wastelands, these areas were drained and filled to make way for farming and building. Those areas not completely destroyed were developed for recreation. If croplands or housing development did not drive the plovers away, boaters and campers on the beaches did.

Off-road vehicles have proved especially disruptive to nesting plovers. People who drive such vehicles are often motivated to travel in the most remote places they can find. Piping plovers look for the same kinds of places in which to build their nests. Many historic nesting grounds of the piping plover were inundated by huge reservoirs, but some reservoirs created habitat where none existed before. The balance, however, has clearly been a net loss of nesting habitat for piping plovers. In some cases, the loss was created merely by cementing river channels, thereby eliminating river flats and islands suitable for nesting. This species has been affected across its entire range.

Distribution

Piping plovers naturally occurred across much of Canada, including southeastern Alberta, southern Saskatchewan, and Manitoba, into extreme southwestern and southeastern Ontario, plus coastal New Brunswick, the Gaspé Peninsula of Quebec, and the southwestern tip of Newfoundland. In the United States, plovers occurred in northeastern Montana, across most of North Dakota, the northern half of Minnesota, around the Great Lakes of Wisconsin, Illinois, Michigan, and New York, as well as the Atlantic Coast from Maine to North Carolina. This was the plover's main summer nesting area, with very small isolated populations found in South Dakota, Nebraska, and eastern Colorado. In winter, piping plovers traditionally inhabit the Atlantic Coast from North Carolina to Florida, and all around the Gulf Coast beyond Texas into Mexico. A few birds move to the Bahamas, Barbados, Bermuda, Cuba, Jamaica, Puerto Rico, and the Virgin Islands.

Deserting its range

Piping plovers have disappeared completely from many areas where they used to nest. Fewer than 2,500 pairs remained in 1991. The Great Lakes population had fallen to a mere 16 pairs and the larger numbers breeding on the Great Plains were declining at a rate of more than 7 percent each year. However, the piping plover is no longer declining across its range. The Atlantic coast population increased from 800 pairs in 1986 to 1,150 pairs in 1994. Although this is encouraging, it does not remedy the large historical declines in range and population. Even known wintering areas have been converted to human uses, which further works against the species. Attempts to conserve these birds is compounded by the 40–86 percent of breeding birds that are unaccounted for on the wintering grounds.

Some measures have been taken to help surviving populations. For example, known nesting areas have been fenced to exclude motor vehicles and pedestrians. Predators have been monitored, and some trapping has been done to keep piping plover populations from growing too large. Some beaches on public land have been closed during the nesting season, and a public education campaign has been implemented. The U.S. Fish and Wildlife Service has also maintained long-term monitoring of the plover population.

Uncertain future

Much has been accomplished, but a lot of piping plover habitat has been irretrievably lost. Despite protection and preservation work, some populations continue to decline. This may reflect conditions in the wintering grounds and migration routes, as much as the condition and availability of nesting grounds. Ultimately, the future of the piping plover in the 21st century depends on what people have done to the continent's remaining wetlands at the end of the 1990s.

Shore Plover
(Thinornis novaeseelandiae)

ESA: Endangered

IUCN: Endangered

Length: 8 in. (20 cm)
Clutch size: 3 eggs
Incubation: Probably 28–30 days
Diet: Crustaceans, mollusks, small fish
Habitat: Rocky seashores
Range: South East Island of the Chatham Islands, east of New Zealand

A PRETTY shorebird lives in a naturally violent land. Its last home lies in a strip around a volcanic island. There, where tides and surf erode solid stone, the shore plover searches for its prey, builds its nests, and raises its young. Despite the natural hazards of its chosen landscape, the bird has survived for thousands of years. What the shore plover could not survive was human threat.

Warm, earthy brown colors the shore plover's back, wing, and tail. The underparts, from breast to undertail, are white. The brown crown matches the back but does not connect with it in continuous color. Instead, a thin white ring circles the head. A thin black line crosses the nape and expands to cover the entire cheek, lore, forehead, chin, and throat. A thin red ring of bare skin defines the eye in the black mask. The leg, foot, and toe are orange-pink. The two-tone beak is bright orange-red at the base and black at the tip. The female's mask is more brown, less black, and her beak is more black than orange. The pattern makes the shore plover especially attractive in a clan known for its drab brown, gray, and white birds.

Feeding habits

Shore plovers spend the day foraging in search of food. Unlike the usual walk-and-stop plover behavior, shore plovers walk and pick, a little more like sandpipers. Also unlike typical plovers, they occasionally feed in shallow

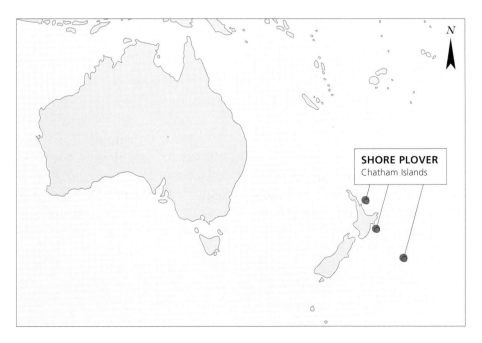

SHORE PLOVER
Chatham Islands

Shore plovers inhabit a narrow habitat belt between the water and the line where island plant life becomes too thick for them to walk around.

water, plunging their heads completely under the water in order to grab small fish and crustaceans.

Nesting

When not feeding, shore plovers seek shelter in protected areas. They may rest in the hollow beneath a shrub or in the recesses excavated by lapping waves. They also select protected sites for nesting. Most plovers nest in the open, but the shore plover lives where open nests would surely fail. Skuas (*Catharacta* sp.), petrels, and other sea birds patrol the islands. Eggs and plover chicks would be vulnerable to their hungry eyes and ceaseless appetites. For nesting safety, the shore plover uses abandoned petrel burrows and rock over-hangs—anywhere out of view from predators. Such places were secure until people arrived.

When the Maoris, the first set-tlers, arrived in New Zealand between C.E. 900 and 1000, the only terrestrial mammals were seals and bats. The humans bought with them the Polynesian rat (*Rattus exulans*) and a foxlike dog (*Canis familiaris*), both of which preyed on the naive and defenseless bird fauna. The Maoris also hunted the birds for food, clothing, and ceremony. The result of this first human set-tlement was the extinction of at least 32 species of the birds that were most vulnerable to change.

Animal hazards

British colonists came in the late 1700s, and brought with them a variety of livestock and animals for recreational hunting. Rabbits were released but became a pest of pastoral farming. In an attempt to control them, weasels, stoats, and ferrets (*Mustela* spp.) were released, but quickly turned on the native fauna. Pigs became wild and took eggs and chicks and trampled nests. Feral cats were also a dangerous predator. Another nine species became extinct in the next 200 years.

The shore plover, which was once widespread throughout most coastal areas on New Zealand and Chatham Island, was eventually devastated by nest predators against which they had no defense. Cats and brown rats are believed to be the main rea-son for their disappearance.

Island change

By 1990 perhaps as many as 120 shore plovers survived on South East Island in the Chatham Island group. Shore plovers probably occupied all the Chatham Islands at one time, but rats and cats eventually dis-covered those islands as well. South East Island has no animals such as cats, weasels, ferrets, or rats. But these predatory pests could eventually become est-ablished on South East Island.

The government declared this island to be a nature reserve many years ago, but the waters around the Chatham Islands are prized for their lobsters. Although fishers and other boaters are legally prohibited from landing on South East Island, they do so with some reg-ularity. Enforcing the ban would be a formidable task. The biggest danger is that humans landing on the island might release rats or cats, since both of these mam-mals can easily stow away and escape undetected.

Dangerous games

The shore plover is just one of many birds that has been devastated by humans meddling with the earth's wildlife. The same problem could spread to South East Island, even by accident. If this does occur, the shore plover will have no remaining refuge.

Kevin Cook

POCHARDS

Class: Aves
Order: Anseriformes
Family: Anatidae

Pochards are ducks, and it is interesting to watch their activities. When courting, male pochards (usually pronounced POE-churds) become quite animated. They throw their heads back between their shoulders, inflate their wind-pipes to puff out their chests, and pump their heads to impress females and intimidate other males. When they take flight, they patter across the water to gain enough speed to become airborne. All this makes them quite interesting to watch.

The pochards are a group of 15 species distributed over every continent except Antarctica. Many of them have done well under professional waterfowl management. Some of them continue to decline despite management.

Baer's Pochard

(Aythya baeri)

IUCN: Vulnerable

Length: 16–18 in. (40.6–45.7 cm)
Weight: Males, 1¾–2 lb. (0.8–0.9 kg); females, 1¼–1½ lb. (0.6–0.7 kg)
Clutch size: 6 to 10 eggs
Incubation: 27 days (in captivity)
Habitat: Nests around small freshwater lakes; winters on large lakes, rivers, coastal marshes
Range: Nests in northeastern China and extreme southeastern Siberia; winters in east-central China south of the Yangtze River to northern Vietnam, Thailand, coastal Myanmar, Bangladesh, and northeastern India

THE BAER'S POCHARD is a plain, medium-sized duck. It is not nearly as well known as the mallard (*Anas platyrhynchos*). Hunters do not seek the bird for its meat because its flesh is nearly inedible. It is not remarkably beautiful, so does not attract the attention of collectors.

Ducks may be the world's most familiar, beloved, and sought-after group of birds. They have been domesticated for their eggs and their flesh. They are popular among hunters who, in developed countries, pay considerable fees for the privilege of shooting them. In undeveloped countries they are hunted and trapped, not for recreation, but for food. They have been plucked for their downy feathers, which are used to fill blankets and winter clothing. They helped develop wildlife management as a profession when their populations declined and public interest demanded solutions. Some ducks have benefited from all this attention. A few species, such as the American wood duck (*Aix sponsa*), have even expanded their ranges and populations. But this is not the case with the Baer's pochard.

The Baer's pochard has a blackish head that shines green in good light. The white eye shows clearly in the dark face. The black neck loses the green sheen and changes into a dark brown back and a chestnut breast. The breast fades to plain brown on the sides. The belly is white, extending onto the sides. The tail is black. The wing has a long white wingbar and is mostly white on the underside. The beak is a steely blue, with a black nail at the tip.

Some collectors only want rare species, because rarity restricts the number of people

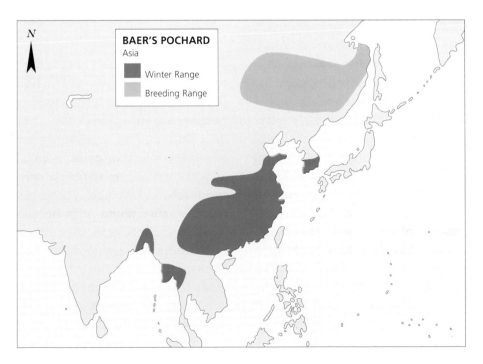

BAER'S POCHARD
Asia
Winter Range
Breeding Range

Birds such as the Baer's pochard do not usually interest collectors, who are attracted to good colors, elegant plumes, and bright patterns. However, its rarity has made it a popular bird among collectors.

who will own members of the species. As of the early 1990s, collecting was not the problem facing the Baer's pochard. Habitat loss was the main issue.

Small lakes with good aquatic vegetation around the edges seem to appeal most to nesting Baer's pochards. Just exactly what these lakes offer the pochards that other waters do not remains a mystery. Unlike some ducks that have been studied in great detail, Baer's pochards are virtually unresearched, but a few general traits are understood. Pochards are divers, obtaining their food from under the water. This makes them uncomfortable on land, so they nest amid shoreline vegetation at the waterline, or on floating nests that are anchored to the vegetation.

In the late 1980s, some experts believed this bird was not as rare as many people thought. On the other hand, some researchers believe the declining numbers of pochard specimens from wintering grounds are indicators of a troubled species. Worldwide destruction of wetlands has threatened many species, and the Baer's pochard is not likely to be an exception, considering the amount of wetland in Siberia and Manchuria being converted to agriculture.

Although it is believed to be vulnerable, the exact status of the Baer's pochard cannot be known until population surveys have been completed.

Madagascar Pochard
(Aythya innotata)

ESA: Endangered

IUCN: Critically endangered

Length: 16–18 in. (40.6–45.7 cm)
Incubation: 26–28 days (in captivity)
Habitat: Lakes and marshes
Range: Northeastern Madagascar

MORE THAN 30 years have elapsed since anyone has reported seeing a Madagascar pochard. A single bird was seen in 1970, and that observation came ten years after ornithologists recognized that the bird was headed for extinction. An organized effort made to find the Madagascar pochard in the last half of the 1980s failed to locate even a single bird. Ornithologists view the situation with mixed emotions. The species appears to have vanished, but those who searched for it caution against presuming the worst. The Madagascar pochard may yet survive in the places that people cannot reach. Those places, however, are shrinking.

This pochard inhabits a single, large wetland complex around Lake Alaotra in northeastern Madagascar. The lake area varies between 78 square miles (203 square kilometers) in the dry season and 137 square miles (356 square kilometers) in the wet season. Depth varies from 6½ feet (2 meters) to 13 feet (4 meters), and also by season. Vast tracts of seasonal and permanent marshes border the lake. The marshes are mostly grown in papyrus (*Cyperus madagascariensis* and *Cyperus imeriniensis*) and reeds (*Phragmites australis*). Water lilies (*Nymphus* sp.) and water chestnuts (*Eichornia crassipes*) are also common, or once were. In this setting the Madagascar pochard evolved as a unique species, as did the Alaotra grebe (*Tachybaptus rufolavatus*). Both species have been affected by human activities.

A dark chestnut brown colors this bird's head, neck, and breast. The back, wing, tail, and sides are lighter brown. The inner flight feathers form a white patch in the wing. The belly is also white. The eye is white and the beak is black. In posture and physique it is a typical pochard. Almost nothing is known about the Madagascar pochard apart from its appearance and home. Various collectors and zoos kept it successfully in captivity before World War II, but it died out and was never replaced. Now, it is too late to reestablish it in captivity.

People have cut down the trees around Lake Alaotra. Without the trees and associated undergrowth, the soil has no protection against rain. Erosion has carried enormous loads of soil into Lake Alaotra. People have also burned the marshlands and converted them into grazing lands and rice paddies. From 1926, people released various exotic fish into Lake Alaotra. These fish quickly took to eating the lake's native plants and

The Madagascar pochard's habitat is difficult for people to negotiate, and some places are virtually impossible for people to reach. This bird may yet survive in some of the more remote areas of the island.

greatly reduced their abundance. When the plant community changed, the entire web of life in the lake changed.

Of course, wherever fish are available, people learn to catch them. Traditional nets, traps, and spears posed little threat to the pochards and other aquatic birds. Eventually, however, fishers in Lake Alaotra acquired nylon gill nets that greatly increased their success. Not only did they catch more fish, but they also caught birds, including the diving Madagascar pochard.

Human threat

Killing pochards did not begin with fishing nets. French colonists introduced recreational hunting to Madagascar, and pochards were a favorite prey. The Madagascar people have never adopted duck hunting as a recreational sport, but they have trapped ducks and collected their eggs as food for centuries.

With all these factors operating over the same few decades, the Madagascar pochard was almost certainly doomed. The

MADAGASCAR
POCHARD
Madagascar

pochard is a specialized bird that adapted to a unique environment, and it is confined to a small area of only one island. It has nowhere else to go. Some reaches of the Lake's marsh (plus adjoining small lakes connected by wetlands) are impossible for humans to traverse. Thus, some hope remains that a few Madagascar pochards survive where ornithologists cannot find them.

Protective measures

Many recommendations have been proposed to support the wetland system at Lake Alaotra. Specifically, the surrounding countryside needs to be replanted so that a forest can develop again. No further burning of the marsh or conversion to rice paddies should be allowed. No new exotic fish should be introduced, and existing exotics should be discouraged or eradicated. Laws that protect birds need to be enforced, but even if all these actions were implemented in good faith, the Madagascar pochard may not survive long enough to benefit from them.

Kevin Cook

See also Ducks and Grebes.

Pahrump Poolfish

(Empetrichthys latos latos)

ESA: Endangered

Class: Actinopterygii
Order: Cypriniformes
Family: Cyprinodontidae
Length: 2 in. (5 cm)
Reproduction: Egg layer
Habitat: Small spring ponds
Range: Corn Creek and Shoshone Ponds, Nevada

ONCE FAIRLY abundant in the Pahrump Valley of southern Nevada, the Pahrump poolfish (previously called the Pahrump killifish) has been totally eliminated from its natural range. This valley was once occupied by other closely related killifish: the Pahrump Ranch poolfish (*Empetrichthys latos pahrump*) and the Raycraft Ranch poolfish (*Empetrichthys latos concavus*). Today, both subspecies are extinct. In nearby Ash Meadows another closely related species, the Ash Meadows poolfish (*Empetrichthys merriami*), has also succumbed to the pressures of extinction. The Pahrump poolfish is the only remaining member of the genus *Empetrichthys*. If not for the work of biologists, the Pahrump poolfish would have become extinct too. Rather than risk leaving all of the fish in the Pahrump Valley, most survivors were captured and cared for.

These dramatic changes to the Pahrump Valley and the efforts to save the Pahrump poolfish were made necessary by a single activity: the pumping of ground water within the valley for agricultural irrigation. As more water was pumped from beneath the surface, artesian springs that sustained the poolfish and other wildlife began to fail.

In general, poolfish and other killifish have been very successful; they can be found across the tropical and temperate latitudes of the world. As a group, killifish are capable of tolerating a wide range of environmental conditions, including variations in salinity (the salt content of water). They can be found in fresh water as well as in water that is more saline than sea water, and can survive cool conditions or hot springs. Most killifish prefer shallow water rich in aquatic vegetation. The vegetation is used for cover and as a source of aquatic insect food.

Aquarium life

Killifish are popular with aquarium owners because of their diverse color patterns, relative tolerance of aquarium conditions, and ease of spawning in captivity. Successful spawning has made it possible to hold and maintain Pahrump poolfish in artificial systems. In some cases, demand by aquarium lovers has been at least partly responsible for the threatened or endangered status of some killifish. Because of their size, many species are captured and used as bait. These types of overexploitation are difficult to combat because of the profits involved.

All killifish display a fairly uniform pattern of physical characteristics. Almost without exception, they are less than four inches (10 centimeters) long, with an elongated, robust body and a plump belly. The rounded and fan-shaped fins are never large and lack spines for protection. An upturned mouth, jutting lower jaw, and eyes that are set high on the head help them capture insects at the surface.

Killifish distinguish themselves when it comes to color. Without a doubt, they are some of the most spectacularly colored fish in the world.

The Pahrump poolfish has a typical killifish body form that is robust and chunky. It displays the usual upturned mouth and rounded fins. The sexes vary in color and size. The male is larger and has green-brown blotchy shading. The more petite female is silver-blue in color.

The future of the Pahrump Valley's water supply is unclear, but as long as landowners continue to demand water for their own purposes, the Pahrump poolfish is forced to survive outside its natural home range. The Parhump poolfish was previously listed by IUCN as endangered, but was not evaluated by 1996, when the Red List was compiled. Until more information is available, the species is included with other endangered taxa, because it may still be at risk.

William E. Manci

See also Killifish.

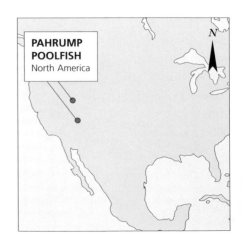

PAHRUMP POOLFISH
North America

Poouli
(Melamprosops phaeosoma)

ESA: Endangered

IUCN: Critically endangered

Class: Aves
Order: Passeriformes
Family: Drepanididae
Subfamily: Psittirostrinae
Length: 5–5½ in. (13–14 cm)
Diet: Snails, insects
Habitat: Dense forest with thick undergrowth
Range: Maui in the Hawaiian Islands

The poouli is tiny—just five inches (13 centimeters) in length.

IN 1773 A GOOD ornithologist could go out in the field and discover many new birds. By 1873, ornithologists had to go farther afield and explore more remote places, because the bird life close to home had already been well documented. By 1973, the era of discovery in ornithology had drawn to a close. It was assumed that almost all the birds had been found. Then the poouli appeared.

While conducting field surveys for Hawaii's endangered forest birds, some ornithologists discovered an unfamiliar bird. In 1974 the bird was officially described as representing a new species in a new genus, *Melamprosops phaeosoma*—the poouli.

At just five inches (13 centimeters), the poouli is a small bird. Its crown and upperparts are uniformly brown. It has a black mask around the eyes, and on the chin and forehead. A dingy white band runs across the throat. The buff-colored breast fades to more rufous sides, belly, and undertail. The very short tail and leg make the poouli look short and stubby.

These colors and patterns help the poouli hide in the shadows as it works the forest canopy, finding tree-dwelling snails and various insects for food. Besides its dark color and forest canopy habitat, the poouli is relatively quiet and fairly calm. Together, these traits explain how a bird could go undetected for so long.

Another factor might also be responsible. All the ornithologists who scoured the islands probably missed the poouli because it was never abundant. It could be a species that is just emerging—or one that is fading away. Human presence on Maui has so radically disturbed the island's plants and animals that interpreting a bird's status before human disturbance is nearly impossible.

Polynesian immigrants were the first to change Hawaii's habitat. They discovered the islands sometime around C.E. 500 to C.E. 800 and cleared lowland forest. Europeans settled in the late 1700s, bringing a number of exotic species. Many birds were harmed by these.

As many native Hawaiian birds disappear, their own unique roles in the islands' ecosystems vanish. Their absence may be felt in the failure of plants to disperse seeds, or of insects to be curtailed. Despite all this, however, the poouli has survived.

In the early 1980s, as many as 140 to 150 pooulis survived. They were known to inhabit more than 1½ square miles (4 square kilometers) of dense ohia (*Metrosideros polymorpha*) forest north and east of Haleakala. Despite conservation measures, in 1999 only three were known to survive; the total population was thought to be less than 10.

Various Hawaiian conservation organizations have tried to preserve habitat by fencing forest parcels and eradicating livestock within these, as well as removing exotic plants and regenerating native forest. The conservation organizations intend to capture one bird and release it within the range of an individual of the opposite sex. Even with these efforts, prospects for the poouli's survival are slim unless a number of birds remain undetected.

Kevin Cook

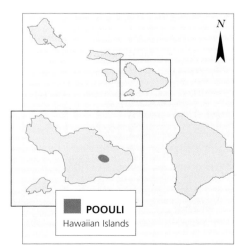

POOULI
Hawaiian Islands

Harbor Porpoise (Vaquita)

(Phocoena sinus)

IUCN: Critically endangered

Class: Mammalia
Order: Cetacea
Family: Phocoenidae
Weight: 110 lb. (50 kg)
Length: 5 ft. (1.5 m)
Diet: Fish, squid
Gestation period: Possibly 300–330 days
Longevity: 6–10 years
Habitat: Saltwater coastal areas
Range: Gulf of California

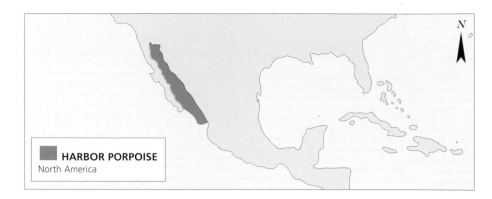

HARBOR PORPOISE
North America

THE GULF OF California porpoise, also known in Spanish as the vaquita or cochito, belongs to a small group of mainly oceanic, toothed whales called porpoises. It is usually easy to differentiate between a porpoise and a dolphin, despite the similarities between these two small cetaceans. For example, dolphins are usually much larger, frequently up to 10 feet (3 meters) long, while porpoises are usually only 5 to 6 feet (1.5 to 2 meters) in length. Also, most dolphins have a noticeable rostrum, or beak, while porpoise heads are much more rounded, with little or no evidence of a beak.

Another difference between dolphins and porpoises is that dolphins have sharp, cone-shaped teeth, while porpoises have small, peg-shaped teeth. There are other internal differences as well, such as in the structure of the skull, but these differences are not obvious to the casual observer.

There are three species of porpoises in the genus *Phocoena*. All three species are coastal animals, frequently found near shore, in bays, and occasionally even in the mouths of rivers. The best known species is the harbor porpoise (*Phocoena phocoena*) of the North Atlantic and Pacific oceans. Although common over much of its range, many populations of the species have declined drastically due to incidental drowning in gill nets, hunting, and pollution. The second species, the black or Burmeister's porpoise (*Phocoena spinipinnis*) of South America, is also threatened by hunting and net entanglement.

A new species

The Gulf of California porpoise, or vaquita, was first brought to the attention of scientists in 1958. A single skull was described, and enough structural differences were found to allow the naming of a new species. Some scientists now think that this porpoise is more closely related to the black or Burmeister's porpoise than to the harbor porpoise, despite the fact that the harbor porpoise's range almost reaches the Gulf of California.

This species is one of the smallest of cetaceans. It is a dull gray or brown in color, gradually lightening toward the underside, to appear almost white on the belly area. A dark line runs from the eye to the pectoral fin. It has a short, triangular dorsal fin, which is common to the genus *Phocoena* and also helps to differentiate it from most species of dolphins. Like other members of the genus, the Gulf of California porpoise is rarely found in deep waters, tending to spend its time near the shore.

The vaquita may have the most limited distribution of any ocean-going cetacean. Its original range was apparently limited to an area only about 900 miles (1,500 kilometers) in length within the Gulf of California. The Gulf is the part of the Pacific Ocean that slips between mainland Mexico to the east and Baja California to the west. While once thought to occur as far south as the Tres Marias Islands, at present the vaquita appears to be found only in the upper reaches of the Gulf. Here it wanders alone, in pairs, or in small groups in search of fish, squid, and possibly small crustaceans. It is shy, rarely following ships or allowing close encounters.

According to fishers in the area, the vaquita was once extremely common in the Gulf of California. However, the development of large commercial fisheries in the area in the 1940s spelled trouble for porpoises. Nets laid down for sea bass and other marine life killed large numbers of them. For an animal with a small initial population within a limited area, this type of fishing proved disastrous. As many as ten vaquitas drowned in gill nets every day, and by the time the Mexican government halted sea bass fishing in 1975, the vaquita had almost vanished. Continued use of gill net fishing for other fish species, with the resulting capture and drowning of porpoises, still threatens to push the vaquita population from endangerment to extinction.

While the vaquita has been given a measure of protection from direct persecution, it is now facing more subtle threats from human activity. The damming of the Colorado River, which is the major freshwater source for the Gulf of California, threatens to disrupt the ecology of the Gulf by changing water, nutrient, and salinity levels. The reduction in water flow also puts stress on the coastal marshlands at the mouth of the Colorado that are important to the economic productivity of the entire Gulf.

Heavy pesticide use in the agricultural areas bordering the Colorado River and the Gulf is also affecting aquatic life. Runoff brings the pesticides into the Gulf, and then into the food chain. As with other coastal animals, the vaquita must face the influx of these contaminants. Since it is an animal that lives near the top of the food chain, the vaquita is likely to develop higher concentrations of these chemicals in its body tissues (because it will consume more animals that already have the chemical in their bodies).

As is true with so many rare species, one of the greatest problems facing the vaquita is human ignorance. While there is no question that the vaquita population has declined drastically in the past 50 years, no actual numbers are available to determine exactly how large the threat is to this porpoise. The basic biological and ecological requirements of the vaquita are still mostly a mystery. Therefore the reasons for its limited range also remain a mystery. These issues, as well as the problems caused by gill nets, pollution, and habitat destruction, must be addressed if the survival of this porpoise is to be secured.

Peter Zahler

Leadbeater's Possum

(Gymnobelideus leadbeateri)

ESA: Endangered

IUCN: Endangered

Class: Mammalia
Order: Marsupialia
Family: Petauridae
Weight: 3½–5¾ oz. (100–166 g)
Head-body length: 5¾–6½ in. (15–17 cm)
Diet: Plant sap, insect secretions, arthropods
Gestation period: 15–17 days
Longevity: Around 3–4 years
Habitat: Mature, wet montane forest
Range: East-central Victoria, Australia

KNOWN ONLY from five specimens collected between the years 1867 and 1909, Leadbeater's possum was long believed to be extinct. In 1961, however, Australian naturalists found the first of what was later determined to be several widely scattered colonies. Considering its nocturnal and arboreal nature, it is no surprise that this possum remained unobserved for so long. Fears of extinction are beginning to surface again, because this species has a relatively small range. In addition, it has very specific nesting requirements that are threatened by the Australian timber industry, and this is an even more serious threat.

The soft fur of Leadbeater's possum is a dull brownish gray on its back and sides, with a dark stripe running from the middle of

the forehead down the spine to the base of the tail. The ventral surface—or chest and belly region—as well as the inner surface of the legs, is a creamy yellow to pale gray color. In addition to the stripe in the middle of this possum's forehead, there are stripes running from the base of each ear, through each eye, to the

The female Leadbeater's possum, which is about the same size as the male, is the more territorial sex in this species. This behavior is uncommon in female mammals, having been observed in only five other species.

nose. These facial markings are similar to, although less distinct than, those of another member of the family Petauridae, the sugar glider (*Petaurus breviceps*).

While Leadbeater's possum resembles the sugar glider, it lacks one key characteristic of the glider: the membrane between the legs that allows all gliders to travel by air. In addition, Leadbeater's possum also lacks the prehensile tail often found on arboreal marsupials, and seems to use its tail mainly for balance while climbing. This possum's digits are wide, and they have strong, short claws. But individuals seem to rely more on the grip supplied by their fleshy toe pads as they move around in the woody vegetation.

While this species obtains most of its protein requirements from eating just about any arthropod it can catch (insects, spiders, and centipedes), it also harvests the honeydew which leaks from the bodies of aphids as they feed on plant sap. In addition, Leadbeater's possum cuts wounds directly into the bark of woody plants in order to obtain the plant saps and gums that it relies on as its main source of carbohydrate.

Mother runs the nest

Colonies of this species have been found to den from 30 to 100 feet (10 to 30 meters) above the ground within a hollow mountain ash tree (*Eucalyptus regnans*). The nest is usually lined with shredded bark, which helps the possum meet its energy conservation needs during the winter months, when both temperature and food supplies drop. Colonies consist of one breeding pair and one or more generations of that pair's offspring. In addition, there are usually several other unrelated adult males in residence.

Births seem to occur almost year-round, with distinct peaks in fall (April to June) and spring (October to December). Even though litters are small (1 or 2 young), the potential reproductive capacity of this species is high due to the short (15- to 17-day) gestation period. Also, females can, and do, give birth within 30 days following the loss of a litter. Captive females have even been observed giving birth with a previous generation of young still in the pouch. The young remain in the pouch for three months following birth, then spend another 5 to 40 days in the nest.

The female, which is about the same size as the male, is the more territorial gender in this species. While females allow unfamiliar males to enter their colony, they drive out any intruding females. Juvenile female offspring are also harassed by their mothers and, to a certain extent, their fathers. This is believed to be the reason why females disperse from their birth territories sooner (7 to 14 months) than their brothers (11 to 26 months). In addition to dispersing earlier, females disperse farther and die younger on average than males.

Will old homes be cut?

The apparent abundance of nest sites may not continue. Mountain ash trees must be well over 100 years old to provide a hollow large enough for a colony of Leadbeater's possums. As of the late 1980s, the timber extraction policy in Victoria called for a 40- to 80-year rotation cycle. This does not allow for the regeneration of suitable nest trees. In addition, the shrubs and saplings under trees that are so vital to the possum may not fare well under current timber plans.

Since Leadbeater's possum is evenly spread over numerous areas, studies could be designed to determine the effect of different timber harvesting methods on nesting. Perhaps by leaving a few large trees for den sites—as well as some trees that provide sap, gum, and insects, we can protect this species from extinction due to timber harvesting. While Leadbeater's possum is protected from direct killing by Australian game and wildlife acts, it is essential that conservation and timbering communities work together to determine its habitat needs before it is too late.

Terry Tompkins

Attwater's Greater Prairie-chicken

(Tympanuchus cupido attwateri)

ESA: Endangered

Class: Aves
Order: Galliformes
Family: Phasianidae
Subfamily: Tetraoninae
Length: 16–18 in. (40.6–45.7 cm)
Clutch size: Usually 12 eggs
Incubation: 23–25 days
Diet: Plant sprouts, buds, seeds, and insects
Habitat: Coastal prairie
Range: Around the Gulf of Mexico

BEFORE THE dawn, a weird *wooing* sound rises from the coastal prairie of Texas. Voice after voice joins the cacophony, punctuated by crazy cackling. As the rising sun fires the eastern sky, the voices trail away. By the time morning comes, the sounds have ceased for another day. These natural noises have celebrated spring on the North American prairies for a million years or longer. They are the sounds of prairie-chickens courting. More importantly, on Texas' coastal prairie they are the sounds of Attwater's greater prairie-chicken. For a century now, each spring has heard fewer of these birds than the year before.

Prairie-chickens blend in well with their environment. Their entire plumage is coarsely barred brown on buff. This helps them hide in the prairie vegetation, which is mostly grasses. The male sports a blackish brown tail, the female a brown tail. The male has elongated feathers on the side of the neck. These are paired with

Attwater's greater prairie-chicken is well camouflaged, blending into its environment. The brown-on-buff plumage helps these birds hide in prairie vegetation, which is mostly earth-toned grasses and brush.

air sacs, one on each side. The sacs are bare and colored bright orange, and a small wattle over each eye is the same color. During courtship, the male erects the long neck feathers so they stand above his head like great horns. He also inflates the air sacs.

Grounded courtship

Each spring, males congregate on flat ground with short, sparse vegetation. Each male fights off other males to defend a territory. The males strut about calling and cackling. The sight and sound serves to intimidate other males and attract females. Once the females have mated, they fly off to build nests in taller prairie grasses, sometimes quite distant

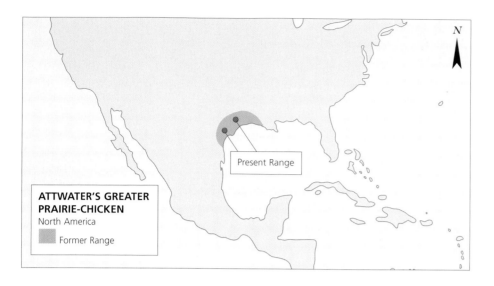

ATTWATER'S GREATER
PRAIRIE-CHICKEN
North America

Former Range

Present Range

N

from the courting grounds. They build the nest, lay and incubate the eggs, and rear their young with no assistance from the males. The communal courting areas are called leks. In popular terms they are known as booming grounds because of the calls of the strutting males.

Attwater's greater prairie-chicken is a subspecies of the greater prairie-chicken. The species once ranged over much of the Great Plains and prairies into the Northeast. The heath hen (*Tympanuchus cupido cupido*) was another subspecies, and this died out in the early 1930s. It inhabited the Atlantic coastal prairies from New Hampshire to Chesapeake Bay. The Attwater's subspecies occupied similar habitat on the Gulf of Mexico from Louisiana to Mexico.

Before white settlement began in Louisiana and Texas in the 1800s, Attwater's greater prairie-chicken probably numbered nearly one million birds. It was so plentiful that it attracted the interest and energies of commercial hunters. The prairie-chickens were pitifully easy to slaughter on their leks every spring. Entire populations were destroyed to put the prairie-chicken on restaurant and private menus. By the early decades of the 1900s, the Attwater's subspecies had declined to less than 20,000 birds. The entire subspecies was estimated at just 8,700 birds in 1940. The 1988 estimate included only 926 birds. By 1997, the wild population numbered just 58 birds at three locations and is now dependent on releases of captive-bred chicks for its survival. Obviously, the decline persisted for decades even after unrestrained hunting had ended.

The urban plight
Ornithologists blame the 97 percent loss of coastal prairie habitat for the decline of the Attwater's greater prairie-chicken. Light livestock grazing is not detrimental to the bird's habitat needs, but heavy grazing is disastrous. Occasional fires can even improve or maintain essential prairie-chicken habitat. But the birds cannot tolerate urbanization.

Some important work to preserve habitat has been accomplished in the last 20 years. The American branch of the World Wildlife Fund purchased some important habitat for the Attwater's greater prairie-chicken in the 1960s. Soon after this, private citizens donated land to the Arkansas National Wildlife Refuge to establish the Attwater's Prairie Chicken National Wildlife Refuge. The success of conservation partnerships with adjacent landowners has been exemplary. More land has been purchased for the prairie-chicken, but other factors may be working against it.

Population concern
Despite habitat acquisitions and careful management, populations continue to dwindle. Problems of defining the minimum size of undisturbed habitat, protecting the leks, restricting human developments, and diminishing predation by feral house cats and dogs need to be addressed. Even natural predators may be problems. Red foxes (*Vulpes vulpes*), coyotes (*Canis latrans*), raccoons (*Procyon lotor*), and striped skunks (*Mephitis mephitis*) thrive around people. They eat pets and garbage, while also taking wild prey. The problem appears to be reduced breeding success, and it may be that the courtship behavior that ensures natural levels of productivity is no longer stimulated because the population is now so low.

Captive breeding
Attention is now being directed toward captive breeding of the Attwater's greater prairie-chicken, as this is now essential to maintain the wild population. Ornithologists are also trying to discover ways to return the wild breeding success rates to their normal levels.

Kevin Cook

PRAIRIE DOGS

Class: Mammalia

Order: Rodentia

Family: Sciuridae

Members of the squirrel family, prairie dogs are prodigious diggers, and each family group (a coterie) occupies a deep, extensive burrow system. These can have from one to five entrances. In a typical burrow, the entrance shaft descends at a 45-degree angle for about ten feet (3 meters), then branches into several horizontal nesting tunnels, each of which ends in a grass-lined chamber. These individual burrows are combined with others to form massive settlements that sprawl for hundreds of acres.

Because they located their settlements in areas of well-drained soil with sufficient moisture for vegetative growth, prairie dogs became a pest to 19th-century U.S. settlers, especially ranchers. These animals were poisoned and shot to control their populations, and these practices diminished prairie dogs in many regions where they were once common.

Mexican Prairie Dog

(Cynomys mexicanus)

ESA: Endangered

IUCN: Endangered

Weight: 26–42 oz. (750–1,200 g)

Head-body length: 10¾–12¾ in. (27.5–32.5 cm)

Diet: Herbivorous

Gestation period: About 30 days

Habitat: Prairielike mountain valleys and basins

Range: Northeastern Mexico

NATIVE TO A small area in northeastern Mexico, the Mexican prairie dog lives farther south than any other species of prairie dog in North America. Found in valleys at elevations ranging from 5,200 to 7,200 feet (1,600 to 2,200 meters), its distribution is also very restricted, occupying only around 320 square miles (800 square kilometers). When first discovered in 1881, the Mexican prairie dog was known only from a single small colony. However, in 1891, a colony covering a large area and containing abundant numbers of individuals was found. As late as 1949, this colony was still described by naturalists as having abundant numbers of prairie dogs. Since then several smaller colonies have also been discovered.

As abundant as the individuals within a given colony might have been, it is believed that this species has always had a tiny distribution. It is presumed that it evolved from a population of black-tailed prairie dogs (*Cynomys ludovicianus*) that became separated from most of its population. It is known that the black-tailed prairie dog once occurred in this southern range during the last ice age before retreating to its present distribution in the great plains of North America.

A grizzled burrower

The Mexican prairie dog shares many traits with the black-tailed prairie dog. They are the two largest species in the genus *Cynomys*, and both have black hairs on the tip of the tail, although the Mexican prairie dog also has many black hairs on its head. The overall coat is dominated by a

The Mexican prairie dog evolved from a population of black-tailed prairie dogs (*Cynomys ludovicianus*) that became separated from the majority of its population.

buff color with some black hairs, but there are also many hairs which have four bands of color: black, white, red, and yellow, giving it a grizzled appearance.

Like other members of its genus (and other burrowing members of the squirrel family), this species has short ears and legs, as well as a short tail.

However, the black-tailed and the Mexican prairie dog also have a number of nearly identical genetic characteristics which distinguish them from the other prairie dog species.

Little is known about the reproduction and growth of this species, and what is known is based on a single litter of six young that were born and raised in captivity. Born hairless and blind, the young are completely furred after three or four weeks, and have their eyes open by four to five weeks. Like the black-tailed prairie dog, this species is social and, by the time the young are weaned at 41 to 50 days, they possess a well-developed set of vocalizations.

No winter naps

Unlike all other species of prairie dog, the Mexican form has a prolonged breeding season. While other species breed and bear their young during a one-month period in the spring, the Mexican prairie dog is reported to be sexually active from January to at least May, possibly into July. Owing to their southerly distribution, this species also differs from other prairie dogs by not hibernating during winter.

The Utah prairie dog, like most others in its genus, does not store food for the winter. It is a true hibernator, relying on its fat reserves.

The Mexican prairie dog digs extensive burrow systems that descend to three feet (one meter) or more underground, then radiate horizontally. While in many cases these burrows are located in settlements containing 50 or fewer individuals, some, in areas with extensive deposits of well drained soil, occur in enough numbers to support colonies of hundreds of individuals. The burrows are occupied by family groups consisting of one male, several reproductive females, and their offspring. Burrows are also shared with other vertebrates such as spotted ground squirrels (*Spermophilus spilosoma*) and burrowing owls (*Athene cunicularia*), as well as a number of invertebrate species.

Unfortunately, these same burrows, which are a benefit to others in the greater prairie community, may prove to be the Mexican prairie dog's downfall now that farming has come to dominate the area. All prairie dogs are viewed as agricultural pests, not only because they eat some crops, but because their burrows result in broken legs for many livestock. Prairie dogs have, therefore, been subjected to thorough eradication attempts in the form of both poisoning and shooting.

It will be difficult to initiate protective measures for this prairie dog in areas where the human population is growing very rapidly and the economy is strongly linked up with agriculture. A combined effort must be made to educate local people about this endangered species and to set aside land where the Mexican prairie dog will be safe and protected.

Utah Prairie Dog

(*Cynomys parvidens*)

ESA: Threatened

IUCN: Lower risk

Weight: 24½–49 oz. (700–1,400 g)
Head-body length: 10¾–13 in. (28–33 cm)
Diet: Herbivorous
Gestation period: 28–32 days
Longevity: Up to 8 years
Habitat: Short-grass prairie
Range: South-central Utah

WHEN EUROPEAN-Americans first explored and settled the American west, they encountered many natural wonders. Along with the spectacular vistas and endless herds of bison, many written accounts mentioned the extensive towns built by medium-sized rodents known as prairie dogs. The towns of the black-tailed prairie dog (*Cynomys ludovicianus*), native to the great plains, were typically around 250 acres (100 hectares) in size, but could be even more massive. One in west Texas occupied 25,600 square miles (64,000 square kilometers) and was estimated to contain hundreds of millions of individuals. Towns of white-tailed prairie dogs (genus *Cynomys*, to which the Utah prairie dog belongs) were smaller, and they were found mostly on the plateaus and high prairies of the Great Basin area, west of the Continental Divide.

The Utah prairie dog is a ground-dwelling member of the squirrel family. Due to its burrowing habits, its tail, ears, and legs are short. It is a grayish buff color, with the underside being slightly paler than the back. Prairie dogs live together in family groups called coteries. These groups typically consist of an adult male, and several adult females, as well as their offspring from the past two years.

Individual Utah prairie dogs have sizable home ranges, each covering from 3 to 20⅓ acres (1.2 to 8.2 hectares). Home ranges of males are, on average, twice as large as those of females. From the time the young are born in April until the time they are weaned in mid-June, adult prairie dogs tend to stay within 66 yards (60 meters) of their burrow, which is usually near the center of their home range. After the young are weaned, adults are much more likely to be seen near the periphery of their home range, as much as 109 to 328 yards (100 to 300 meters) from the burrow.

Keeping a watchful eye

While each family group occupies an area from which it excludes all other prairie dogs, the close association of these territories (which form towns) is important in defending against predators. This species is adapted to living in areas of short, lush vegetation. This allows some individuals in each group to watch for predators, while the rest of their relatives have their heads down eating. If a predator is spotted, an alarm is sounded and all within earshot scurry for the safety of the burrow. This watchful behavior may play an important role in both the natural expansion and the managed

transplanting of colonies. There may be a lower limit to a population size that can exist at a site and still be able to effectively scan for predators. Some evidence from colony transplants carried out in the late 1970s suggests that predation, especially by badgers, affects population numbers in new colonies, but has little effect on established colonies. The depth and complexity of burrows, as well as the number of watchful eyes, may play a role in this difference. Further study will be required to determine the factors important to predation in new colonies.

Human risk

While the Utah prairie dog's natural enemies do not appear to have a noticeable effect on large, established colonies, the same cannot be said of their newest predator, humans. The numbers of prairie dogs are estimated to have been around 95,000 in the 1920s, but declined to around 8,800 by 1970. Most of this decline is attributed to direct shooting and poisoning of the

species, especially during the massive poisoning campaigns of 1933, 1950, and 1960.

As bad as the situation was in 1970, it became more grim one year later when only 5,700 members were left. When the drop in numbers continued to a low of 3,300 in 1973, the Utah prairie dog was officially listed as endangered. After listing, its numbers started to improve and, as of the late 1980s, were estimated at 30,000.

While the Utah prairie dog's population is still well below its 1920s level, the large increase of the late 1970s and early 1980s has resulted in the reclassification of the species as lower risk rather than endangered. The population of the Utah prairie dog seems to have stabilized. However, the species is still in jeopardy because so many of its members inhabit areas of private land. There needs to be a continuing effort to identify and prepare transplant sites on protected public lands in order to accommodate new prairie dog towns.

Terry Tompkins

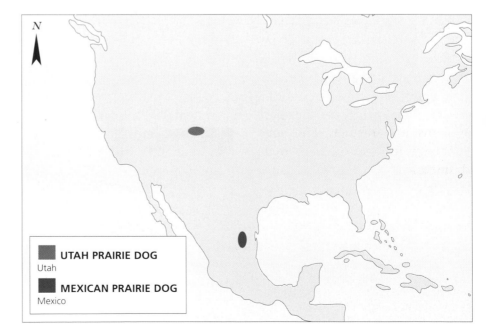

N

UTAH PRAIRIE DOG
Utah

MEXICAN PRAIRIE DOG
Mexico

Price's Potato Bean

(Apios priceana)

ESA: Threatened

IUCN: Vulnerable

Order: Magnoliopsida
Family: Leguminosae
Flower: Greenish white or pink
Habitat: Mixed oak forests, clearings on river bottoms and ravines, on well-drained loam soil
Range: Alabama, Kentucky, Mississippi, and Tennessee

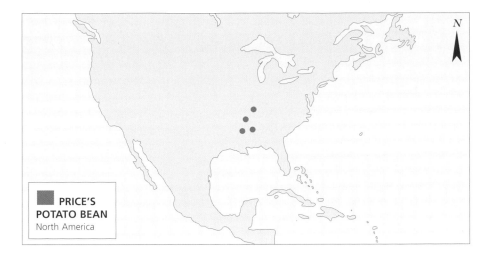

PRICE'S POTATO BEAN

PRICE'S POTATO BEAN
North America

This species was listed as threatened by U.S.F.W.S. in January 1990, and a recovery plan has been developed for it. More research is needed to find out how the flowers are pollinated, what can be done to ensure that plenty of seeds are produced, and that the seedlings thrive.

Sara Oldfield

PRICE'S POTATO BEAN (*Apios priceana*), also called Price's ground nut, is now known only from 25 populations in Alabama, Kentucky, Mississippi and Tennessee. It is a twining, perennial, herbaceous vine growing from a thick, roundish tuber. Price's potato bean is thought to be extinct in the state of Illinois. Most of the sites where the plants grow have less than 25 individuals, so these tiny populations can easily be wiped out unless they are carefully looked after. Populations that used to grow in Illinois are already extinct. The perennial vine grows in mixed-oak forests and clearings on river bottoms and ravines. The soils where it is found are usually well-drained loams. The main threats to Price's potato bean are destruction of habitat caused by cattle grazing and trampling and by tree felling.

Loss of habitat, trampling, and tree felling have contributed to the decline of Price's potato bean. A recovery plan has been developed for the plant.

PRONGHORN

Class: Mammalia

Order: Artiodactyla

Family: Antilocapridae

The American pronghorn is the only survivor of a once large group of ungulates numbering up to 12 genera, originating in the Eocene and finally ending in the Pleistocene, except for today's surviving pronghorn. It is classified in its own family with no close living relations. The American pronghorn is found today only in North America and is represented by five subspecies. Its habitat is usually located in dry grassland plateau. Temperature is not a defining factor for this ungulate; the animal is found in the colder temperatures of Canada and in the warmer climate of Mexico. It is diurnal in its habits and is primarily a grazing animal, although if given the opportunity it will browse. It is still found in some numbers in part of its range, but two subspecies are in jeopardy due to encroachment by man. This unusual animal, which is the sole surviving representative of what was once a very large family, is well adapted to what is often an extremely challenging environment.

There is a surviving population of about 500,000 today, divided up into the following five subspecies:

Common Pronghorn
(*Asntilocapra americana americana*)

Mexican Pronghorn
(*Antilocapra americana mexicana*)
IUCN: Lower risk

Western Pronghorn
(*Antilocapra americana oregona*)

Peninsular Pronghorn
(*Antilocapra americana peninsularis*)
IUCN: Critically endangered

Sonoran Pronghorn
(*Antilocapra americcana sonoriensis*)
IUCN: Endangered

The pronghorn is the only member of its subfamily. It is not closely related to deer or antelope, even though it is often erroneously referred to as an antelope. Its closest bovine relatives died a long time ago and are known only from fossils. The pronghorn, therefore, is a unique animal in this century.

Both males and females have a special form of horn that consists of a permanent, bony core emerging from the skull and an outside horny layer that is shed once a year. This is a similar process to that which occurs in the antlers of deer. The pronghorn's hair feels like fine straw to the touch. On microscopic examination, the hairs are found to be hollow, giving the animal considerable insulation. This hair coat is shed once a year. The pronghorn's upperparts are reddish brown to tan in color, and the underparts are white. The neck has a black mane, except for two bands of white underneath. The horns are longer than the ears.

Former range

Pronghorns were once found from eastern Washington state and southern Manitoba in Canada all the way to Baja California. They preferred to live in a semi-arid habitat. Although the present day pronghorn is a lone survivor of what was once a very large family, it has survived because it has been very successful in meeting the demands of its environment. It was so successful that the original population at the time Columbus reached the New World numbered 40,000,000. Because of destruction of their environment and intrusion by man, as well as a great slaughter, their numbers reached an all time low of about 15,000 in 1910. They now number about 500,000. The pronghorns became another in a long list of species that fell victim to unrestricted hunting and competition with livestock for open range land.

Fast movement

Pronghorns live primarily on grasses and herbs. They rely on their ability to run to escape from danger. They are the fastest four-footed animal in the Western hemisphere, capable of speeds of at least 57 miles (92 kilometers) per hour, although some observers claim that they can run at even higher speeds. This makes them potentially even faster than the African cheetah. They also combine speed with endurance, being able to run 25–30 miles (40–48 kilometers) an hour for long distances. To add to their abilities, pronghorns are also good swimmers.

Sexual maturity occurs at 15–17 months. While does often

mate at this age, bucks generally do not mate until they are older and have established dominance, usually at 3 years of age.

Pronghorn group size and structure varies with the changing seasons. Loose groups of mixed sexes and ages form at the end of the breeding season during late fall and winter. During spring and summer the herd breaks up into smaller groups segregated by sex. More dominant males scent-mark and defend territories, and collect harems of females during the breeding season, or rut, in the wild. This occurs over a 2 to 3 week period during September or October.

Daily and seasonal movements depend on the resources available. In the winter, herds may need to cover an area of 2 to 6 miles (3.2–9.7 kilometers) to find enough food resources.

Twin offspring

The young are usually born in the late spring (May and June), and first-time mothers usually have single babies. Thereafter, however, twins are the rule. Females ovulate four to seven eggs at mating time. Usually four fertilized eggs implant in the uterus, though not all embryos will survive, as some are killed when they are punctured by projections that grow from the embryos destined to survive. This means that females typically give birth to two offspring at a time.

The female leaves her babies at dawn and forages most of the day, returning in the evening and feeding them during the night. The babies are hard to detect: their hair coat works as a camouflage, and they are almost odorless, which offers them protection for the first two weeks of their lives, after which they accompany their mother when she forages through the day.

Pronghorns mark their territory with well-developed scent glands. They are quite sociable and can communicate by movement. When excited, the white patch on their rump stands out like a flag. They also communicate by vocalization. Calves bleat when they are separated from their mother; mothers, in return, call their calves. Males and females blow through their nostrils when they are angry. Males can also roar at each other during tests of dominance.

High death rate

Despite their many adaptations to danger, there is still a high mortality rate among pronghorns due in part to their harsh

Despite their natural wariness, pronghorns are also curious and unafraid to approach a strange object if there is no obvious threat.

environment. That, combined with hunting, reduced their numbers to just 20,000 in the early part of the twentieth century.

Two aspects of pronghorn behavior work against them. First, they are not capable of jumping, and even a short fence is an insurmountable barrier (they will try to crawl under it). Second, due to their curiosity, it is easy to lure them; one of the old techniques for killing them was to wave a cloth from behind a bush to attract their attention.

Fortunately, with protection and management, the overall pronghorn population is more than 500,000 today and is relatively stable. However, of the two subspecies listed, the Sonoran pronghorn (*Antilocapra americana sonoriensis*) is classified as endangered and the Peninsular pronghorn or Baja Californian pronghorn (*Antiolocapra americana sonoriensis*) is listed as critically endangered. Both are smaller and paler than their northern cousins. In both cases they are endangered because of loss of habitat and predation by people. The Peninsular subspecies, found in Baja California, is down to about 100 individuals; the Sonoran pronghorn, found in south-central Arizona and central and northeastern Sonora (Mexico), is down to about 500. The population of Mexican pronghorn (*Antilocapra americana mexicana*) is larger and this subspecies is classified as lower risk. Although these subspecies are given protection by the Mexican government, enforcement is lacking and their numbers continue to decline. The remainder of the subspecies numbers appear to be stable.

The pronghorn has been held in captivity, but management is difficult. Despite this, groups have been set up in zoos.

Sonoran Pronghorn
(Antilocapra americana sonoriensis)

| **ESA:** Endangered |
| **IUCN:** Endangered |

Weight: 80–150 lb. (30–70 kg)
Diet: Grasses, leaves, shrubs
Habitat: High, semi-arid grasslands
Range: South-central Canada to northern Mexico and Baja California. Nebraska, Oklahoma, Kansas, Texas to California, Oregon, and Washington

SONORAN PRONGHORN are lightly built and streamlined for speed, which is their primary method of survival when pursued by predators. Their upper parts are a warm, rufous tan with a pronounced neck mane. The underparts are white, together with two white bands on the neck and a large, white rump patch. The hairs on this patch can be raised, so the animal uses it like a signaling device.

Special adaptations
The Sonoran pronghorn has a number of special characteristics and adaptations. Speed is its salvation, and it is the fastest four-footed animal in North America. According to some reliable observers, it rivals the cheetah in being the fastest four-footed animal in the world.

The added difference with the Sonoran pronghorn is its stamina. The cheetah's speed is explosive, but short-lived. Pronghorns can maintain, for several miles, a speed of 47 miles (75 kilometers) per hour, and one

A young pronghorn baby is hard to detect because it is almost odorless. This helps to protect it from predators.

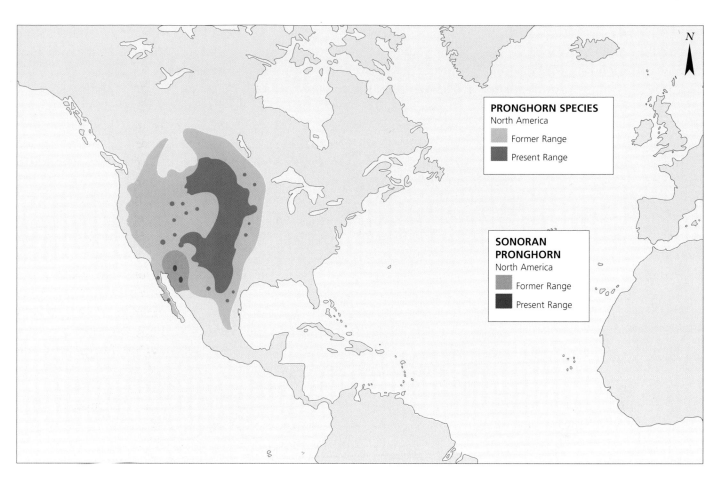

female was clocked in a sprint at over 70 miles (112 kilometers) per hour. Oddly enough, for all their athletic ability they appear to be incapable of jumping. Moving over a low fence seems to be impossible, though they are adept at digging under it.

Sonoran pronghorn have a few other unusual characteristics. They have scent glands near their rump, under their ears, on their lower back, and on the backs of their toes. This is very important to the males during the breeding season. They shed their hair coat, or molt, in the spring at which time the old hair falls out and the new hair grows in. The hair is unusually constructed, in that each hair grows as a hollow tube that provides very efficient insulation during the winter. The thickness of the coat is determined by the stimulus of cold

weather. Their horns have a unique structure. There is a bony process on each side of their skull called the cornul process, similar to that found on cattle. To this is attached a specialized horn, the outer coating of which is shed each year, a similar process to that occurring in deer. The horn can grow to over 12 inches (30 centimeters) in length and has an end spike and a mid-spike or prong, hence the origin of the name pronghorn. Females have very short horns with no prong. The horns themselves are composed of fused hair.

Sonoran pronghorn live in small groups of from 5 to 50, although males are often seen solitarily. The rutting season is September to October and the young are born in May and June. Occasionally singles are born, but usually it is twins, and

occasionally triplets. Pronghorn seem to have a unique system of reproduction. The female apparently produces four eggs at a time. These are all fertilized by the male; they implant in the uterus and begin development. Some of the embryos far exceed the others by developing more rapidly. They literally crowd out their siblings to the point that the less advanced fetuses are reabsorbed and only the vigorously developing fetuses reach maturity and birth. When the young are born, they weigh 4–10 pounds (1.8–4.5 kilograms), and for the first several days they are almost completely odorless. This acts as a protective device from predators. They are gray in color and remain wherever their mother hides them when she leaves to forage. The young do not stay together, but are placed

50–70 yards (46–64 meters) apart. The mother attends them from dusk to dawn. During the day, she is isolated from them, and their feeding is done at night.

Growth and change

Sonoran pronghorn develop rapidly. A fawn two weeks old can run 35 miles (56 km) per hour. By their third month they are almost their mother's size. Females are sexually mature by 16 months.

The Sonoran pronghorn inhabits this grassland area near Elkhart, Kansas. This species can survive in desert conditions where the temperature is high, and there is little vegetation.

The original population of pronghorn at the time when Columbus reached the New World was about 40,000,000. Because of intrusion by humans their numbers reached a low of 15,000 by 1910. The total population of all pronghorn is now around 500,000.

Distribution

The Sonoran pronghorn is mainly located in the Sonoran desert of Arizona, where the temperatures are high and available vegetation scarce, and the mountain valley grasslands of Mexico. The population of Sonoran proghorn is estimated to be 164 to 216 in Arizona and 250 in Mexico, and it is classified as endangered by IUCN.

Population threats

In Arizona the population has been reduced by habitat loss due to overgrazing by livestock, drought, and the damming and diversion of rivers. In Mexico, where it is also threatened by habitat loss, poaching still poses a threat to the Sonoran pronghorn.

Hunting was also once a problem for Sonoran pronghorn in the United States, but the subspecies has been protected for several decades.

Warren D. Thomas

Puaiohi

(Myadestes palmeri)

IUCN: Critically endangered

Class: Aves
Order: Passeriformes
Family: Muscicapidae
Subfamily: Turdinae
Length: 6–6½ in. (15.2–16.5 cm)
Clutch size: 1–2 eggs
Diet: Small fruits, insects
Habitat: Dense undergrowth of forested ravines
Range: Alakai Swamp on Kauai in the Hawaiian Islands

DEEP IN THE Hawaiian forest, where sunlight seldom reaches the ground and daily rains keep the soil wet, the short cry of a seemingly invisible bird can be heard. This is the sound of the puaiohi.

Differences

Closely resembling the larger kamao (*Myadestes myadestinus*), the puaiohi has a thinner, longer beak and pale, flesh-colored legs. It also displays distinctive behavior. Whereas the kamao frequently sings from treetops above the forest canopy, the puaiohi seldom leaves the security of the forest undergrowth.

The puaiohi was never abundant, even from the time it was first discovered by ornithologists in 1893. People of western North America are well acquainted with the Townsend's solitaire (*Myadestes townsendi*),

Almost uniformly brownish gray, the puaiohi has a few flecks of white over the eye, and darker streaks at the sides of the throat.

which spends its summers eating insects and its winters eating small fruit—particularly the juicy cones of junipers (*Juniperus* sp.). In posture and physique, the puaiohi very closely resembles the much more abundant Townsend's solitaire.

Island change

The Polynesians arrived in Hawaii between C.E. 500 and C.E. 800 and permanently settled on the islands. During the next thousand years and before the Europeans arrived, they altered island plant communities and managed to drive perhaps three or more dozen bird species into extinction. They cleared forests to grow vegetable crops and pili grass, which they used to thatch their buildings. They also introduced exotic mammals such as Polynesian rats (*Rattus exulans*), which eat the puaiohi's eggs and compete with native insectivorous birds for food resources. Pigs (*sus scrofa*) were imported by both Polynesian, and later, European settlers, but it was the European breeds of pigs that colonized and severely damaged native forests. Europeans also introduced sheep (*Ovis aries*), goats (*Capra hircus*), and cattle

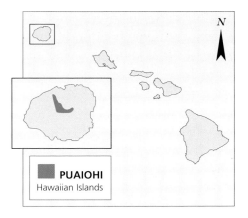

(*Bos taurus*), which contributed to the havoc wreaked on native island habitats.

The Alakai Swamp is the last area in Hawaii in which the unique plants and animals that evolved naturally on the island still thrive. In the early 1970s, ornithologists estimated the puaiohi population at 177 birds. The population is currently estimated at about 200, possibly up to 300, birds. It was the puaiohi's fondness for sheltered ravines that saved it from the devastation wrought on Kauai's forests by hurricanes in 1982 and 1992.

Save the species

An intensive recovery program is underway to save this species from extinction. A captive population is now breeding successfully, and releases back into the wild were planned to start in March 1999. Baits laced with rat poison are stationed in areas where puaiohi are known to breed, and this protects both eggs and nestlings from predators.

The steep slopes and harsh climate found in the Alakai Swamp make fieldwork difficult, but saving the puaiohi from extinction makes the effort more than worthwhile.

Kevin Cook

Northern Pudu
(Pudu mephistophiles)

IUCN: Vulnerable

Range: Equador and Peru

Southern Pudu
(Pudu pudu)

ESA: Endangered

IUCN: Vulnerable

Class: Mammalia
Order: Artiodactyla
Family: Cervidae
Subfamily: Odocoilinae
Weight: 12–20 lb. (5.5–9 kg)
Shoulder height: 12–14 in.
(30.5–35.5 cm)
Diet: Grass, leaves, fruit
Gestation period:
Approximately 180–210 days
Longevity: 10–15 years
Habitat: Dense forest, swamp,
and grasslands
Range: Argentina, Chile

THE PUDU IS THE smallest deer in the world. This dwarf deer is found in two populations separated by around 2,000 miles (3,200 kilometers). The southern population is mainly found in Chile and Argentina, and the northern form ranges from Ecuador to Peru. The pudu has a thick, piglike body and short, stubby legs. The head is much smaller than that of a pig, and although the height is similar, a pig is heavier than a pudu.

The northern pudu is buff, with a dark brown back and underparts that change from buff to rufous. The face and feet are nearly black, while the ears are gray. The southern pudu is a more reddish brown color than its northern relation.

The pudu is very secretive and seldom seen in the wild. Its main diet is vegetation such as leaves, vines, and ferns. When searching for leaves and shoots, the pudu pushes over small plants and stands on top of them to reach the upper foliage. In its native habitat it is rarely seen drinking water because it obtains moisture from the lush vegetation.

The pudu creates a network of trails that are almost like tunnels through the dense foliage. A pudu will have regular resting places along these trails, which are usually found in conjunction with dung piles.

The male pudu has short, spiky antlers that measure only a few inches. These are shed annually around the middle of July, then grow back by mid-November. Breeding occurs in April, May, and June, and the female usually produces just one baby. A male pudu's territory covers up to 60 acres (24 hectares).

The southern species has declined due to habitat destruction and internal parasites.

The pudu prefers rain forests, bamboo thickets, and other heavy vegetation in the valleys and lowlands of the Andes Mountains.

However, the overall population is still substantial and is considered stable. The northern pudu's status is less well determined, but it is known that centuries of hunting and agricultural clearing have reduced its range. These are the same problems faced by deer worldwide, and they must be addressed to save this animal from extinction. There are no northern pudu in captivity, but 150 southern pudu can be found in North America and Europe.

Warren D. Thomas

	NORTHERN PUDU
	Ecuador to Peru
	SOUTHERN PUDU
	Argentina, Chile

Pungu
(Pungu maclareni)

IUCN: Critically endangered

Class: Actinopterygii
Order: Perciformes
Family: Cichlidae
Length: 4¾ in. (12 cm)
Reproduction: Egg layer
Habitat: Inshore areas among debris
Range: Lake Barombi-Mbo, Cameroon

IN CAMEROON THERE is a crater lake called Barombi-Mbo, where a number of species of cichlid are threatened with extinction. One of these is the pungu.

This fish lives in this small, relatively infertile freshwater lake, which is just 1½ miles (2.4 kilometers) in diameter. The local fishers from the village of Barombi guard their right to fish this lake and that includes fishing for the pungu, a fish found nowhere else on earth.

With such a limited range, any species is vulnerable to natural catastrophes or human short-sightedness. Prolonged over-fishing is a key problem for the pungu and its fellow cichlids.

Colorful appearance
The pungu is a brightly colored fish, with yellow as its dominant background color; the back is slightly darker yellow than the more creamy yellow belly. The body has short horizontal lines and small patches of contrasting black scattered within the yellow. The head is almost entirely black, with only a hint of dark yellow over both eyes. The chin, throat, and breast are black to match the head.

Black and blue
The gill covers are mainly black, but a bold blotch of sky blue dominates the upper third. Blue is also found in a faint band in the dorsal fin on the back and as a large spot at the base of the tail fin. This blue spot is flanked by black, and the end of the tail fin varies between a dark and a medium shade of yellow. The body has large scales, but the head and gill covers are, for the most part, scaleless.

All cichlids are rounder and flatter in appearance than other streamlined or torpedolike fish. They normally scrape algae, a small part of the pungu's diet, from underwater surfaces, or crush hard foods with their teeth.

The pungu has thick, fleshy lips that only partially cover impressive jaw teeth. In addition to teeth on the jaws, these fish also have hundreds of teeth on a platelike bone situated at the base of the throat.

The pungu uses its large teeth to bite off pieces of sponge, the preferred food of the pungu, as well as to pry other foods from rocks and wood. It also eats insect larvae, general organic material known as detritus, some algae, and tree fruits that have dropped into the lake from the shore.

The pungu, if it behaves like other cichlids, is probably a mouth brooder. The parents actually take fertilized eggs into their mouths until they hatch, and will even take the little hatchlings into their mouths in order to protect them from predators.

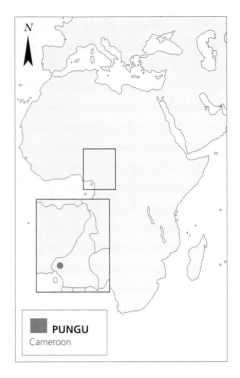

PUNGU
Cameroon

The pungu produces relatively few young, only about 15 per female per breeding cycle. With so few babies to perpetuate the species, it becomes extremely important to take care of them.

Controlled fishing
The Barombi villagers intend to maintain exclusive fishing rights on their lake, and this may be beneficial to the pungu and other cichlids because villagers apparently have the knack of keeping a workable balance between their required catch and the natural supply of fish.

Other steps to protect the pungu would help. Locals should be careful not to introduce harmful non-native fish into the lake, such as the large and aggressive Nile perch (*Lates niloticus*). This mistake has previously been made elsewhere, with devastating results.

William E. Manci
See also Leka Keppe, Myaka-myaka, Otjikota Tilapia, and Unga.

Puntius
(Puntius spp.)

IUCN: Data deficient

Class: Actinopterygii
Order: Cypriniformes
Family: Cyprinidae
Length: 2½–6 in.
(6–15 cm)
Reproduction: Egg layers
Habitat: Small and medium streams
Range: Philippines, Sri Lanka

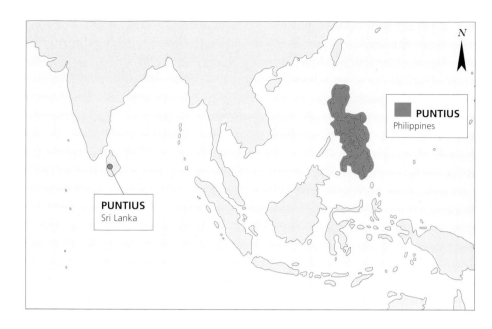

THE PUNTIUS group of fish belongs to the large family Cyprinidae. Many cyprinids are commonly called barbs because of the barbels (whiskers) at the corners of their mouths. Most of the barbs are small, and rarely exceed a length of 5–6 inches (13–15 centimeters). However, the giant mahseer (*Barbus tor*) can have a length greater than 5 feet (1.5 meters) and weigh over 100 pounds (45.5 kilograms).

The puntius has an internal organ known as the Weberian apparatus. The organ is really a set of bones that connects the gas bladder of the fish to the inner ear. The gas bladder helps regulate the fish's buoyancy, but the organ also acts as an amplifier of sound, just like a drum.

The puntius is found in schools and generally prefers clear water. The female scatters her eggs over vegetation, and a special sticky outer layer of the eggs allows them to attach to aquatic plants. The male fertilizes the eggs by spreading sperm (milt) over the eggs.

Because of their small size, bright colors, and prolific repro-duction in captivity, barbs have become favorites of aquarium enthusiasts. Males are often brilliantly colored during spawning, which adds to their desirability as aquarium fish.

The puntius has no teeth in the mouth at all, but in the back of its throat it has comblike teeth called pharyngeal teeth that perform the same function.

The puntius is important ecologically because it is often found in great numbers, serving as an important food for other fish, reptiles, birds, and mammals. Unfortunately, many barb species are now threatened due to habitat loss, introduction of non-native fish, and capture for the aquarium trade.

The Philippines are home to a number of fish within the Puntius group. These tropical river fish are under pressure from human activities and are plagued by many of the problems that threaten or endanger other members of this genus.

Eleven Philippine fish are currently considered to be critically endangered. Five others are listed as vulnerable.

The puntius prefer pristine conditions consisting of clean water and a stream bottom that is free of silt. Given the Philippines' need to provide jobs for its people and develop an export economy, land needs to be cleared for agricultural and industrial purposes. The resulting deforestation has proved devastating to the puntius that inhabit its island streams. Lumbering and slash-and-burn agricultural practices destabilize soil that is quickly washed into nearby streams during the frequent heavy rains. Sediments in the water and on the stream bottom not only cover and kill the preferred food of the puntius, but also render historic spawning grounds unusable. Eggs clinging to vegetation are smothered.

Species loss

General ignorance about the sensitivity and vulnerability of the puntius to non-native fish has also contributed to the loss of individuals within these species. Non-native fish are often aggressive and compete both directly and indirectly with the native populations; puntius are food for many non-native invaders, which drive them into poorer river habitats.

Aquarium capture

Finally, the demand for colorful puntius as aquarium fish has meant that some fish are captured and removed from their natural range, further reducing the wild population. This problem does have an advantage: many aquarium keepers understand the predicament of the puntius and other fish and are aware that aquariums help safeguard all kinds of threatened and endangered fish populations. Often, aquariums become a species' final haven.

In recent decades much of the native range of the Sri Lankan puntius has been drastically altered due to deforestation, and this fish is one of many native species of Sri Lanka to suffer from environmental change. However, at present there is insuffient data available to calculate the effect this will have on the puntius' status. In regions that have been spared from deforestation, fishing for puntius in order to support the aquarium trade has further reduced its numbers and increased the probability of extinction occurring. Colonization by people, resulting in biological and chemical pollution of streams, has also had a negative impact.

The puntius is only found in the Kalu River in the Knuckles Hills in Sri Lanka, which is polluted by silt washed down from the gem mines that are further upstream. The Sri Lankan puntius is unable to live in murky water and could become extinct. It is thought that there are now too few fish there to be exported for the aquarium trade.

William E. Manci

PUPFISH

Class: Actinopterygii

Order: Cyprinodontiformes

Family: Cyprinodontidae

Pupfish are similar to species commonly called perritos or cachorritos in Mexico, and are located in various areas of the western United States. The name *perrito* or *cachorrito* for the Mexican form refers to a little whelp or pup—hence, the name *pupfish*.

Pupfish are part of the rather large and widespread group of fish known as killifish (*Cyprinodontidae* and other families). Representatives of this group are found in temperate and tropical climates throughout most of the world. Killifish are found in North America, South America, Africa, southern Asia, southern Europe and the East Indies, but are not native to Australia.

In comparison to most freshwater fish, killifish are able to inhabit some very extreme aquatic environments. They are found in both salt water and freshwater, as well as in waters with a mineral content that is very high.

Pupfish are often quite solitary, or they live with only a few other species of fish. Many are found in closed desert basins and they often rely on springs or spring-fed environments. Most pupfish evolved in isolated habitats that have remained relatively constant over thousands of years. This has allowed certain changes to occur and, over time, these isolated fish have become a unique species.

The diversity of pupfish is reason enough to study and preserve their populations. Some of their adaptations are so impressive (for example, their ability to live in water that is as much as ten times more saline than seawater) that researchers are interested in the application of these mechanisms to human medical science.

For the most part, pupfish are small and very colorful. Most species show a difference in color, markings, or body form between males and females.

Their small size has allowed them to occupy restricted habitats in significant numbers. The mouth of most pupfish is at the top of their somewhat flattened head, and a very large percentage of their feeding occurs at or near the surface of the water.

Changes to the pupfish's favored isolated habitats, generally caused by human activities, have more often than not had a dramatic impact upon these small fish. In addition, pupfish are very vulnerable when larger, more aggressive species are stocked into waters that were previously occupied by fish no larger than themselves. This often happens in areas that are frequented by sports fishers. Also, as water levels in pupfish habitats have decreased, predatory birds have played a significant role in the fish's decline.

Amargosa pupfish, Concho's pupfish, and Desert pupfish were previously listed by IUCN, but were not evaluated by the time that the 1996 Red list was compiled. Until further information is available, they are included here with endangered taxa, because there is a possibility that these species are still at risk.

Amargosa Pupfish

(Cyprinodon nevadensis)

Length: 1½ in. (4 cm)
Reproduction: Egg layer
Habitat: Warm spring outflows
Range: Amargosa River Basin of California and Nevada

AFTER THE LAST Ice Age, when glaciers receded and melted, the Great Basin of the western United States held many large lakes, including Lake Pahrump and others along the southern border between California and Nevada. Warm and dry weather conditions existed, much as they do today. Ancestors of the Amargosa pupfish adapted to the early post-glacial environment and flourished within these lakes. As water from the lakes evaporated and they became smaller, pockets and river beds formed. These receding lakes isolated fish populations and, over time, subspecies evolved based on the unique conditions in each of these pockets of survival.

Today, six subspecies of the Amargosa pupfish are recognized. One of these, the Tecopa pupfish (*Cyprinodon nevadensis calidae*), recently became extinct. At the species level, the Amargosa pupfish is considered a threatened species, but at the subspecies level, its classifications vary. The Amargosa pupfish (*C. nevadensis amargosae*) and the Saratoga Springs pupfish (*C. nevadensis nevadensis*) are listed as subspecies of special concern; the Ash Meadows pupfish (*C. nevadensis mionectes*) is listed as threatened; and the warm springs pupfish (*C. nevadensis pectoralis*) and the Shoshone pupfish (*Cyprinodon nevadensis shoshone*) are listed as endangered.

Regardless of the subspecies, all Amargosa pupfish are plagued by the same kinds of problems. Until recently, all the springs occupied by this species were threatened by the pumping of groundwater for agriculture, which lowered local water tables and reduced the output of the springs. Competition from the more aggressive mosquitofish (*Gambusia affinis*) and predation

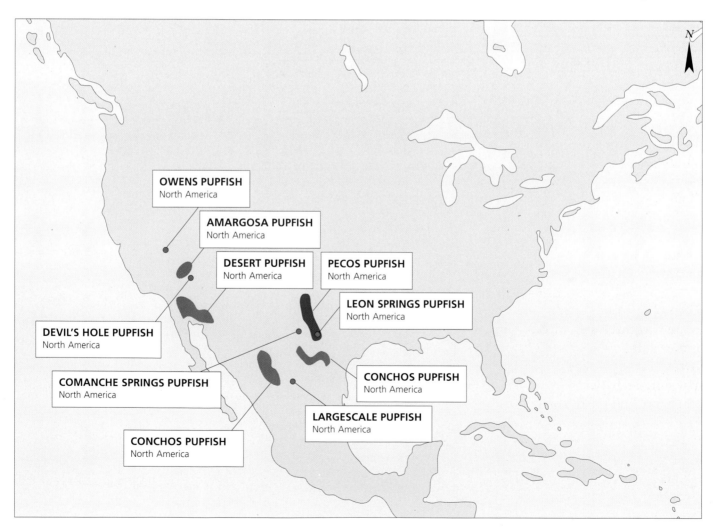

OWENS PUPFISH
North America

AMARGOSA PUPFISH
North America

DESERT PUPFISH
North America

PECOS PUPFISH
North America

LEON SPRINGS PUPFISH
North America

DEVIL'S HOLE PUPFISH
North America

COMANCHE SPRINGS PUPFISH
North America

CONCHOS PUPFISH
North America

LARGESCALE PUPFISH
North America

CONCHOS PUPFISH
North America

by water birds such as the belted kingfisher also posed problems.

Given the isolation that the various subspecies have lived under over the millennia, it is no wonder that significant variety exists in the body coloration of this species. In general, the Amargosa pupfish is blue in color, with several dark purplish vertical bars on the sides; males are more brilliantly blue than the females, particularly during spawning. In some specimens (and in most females), only the gill covers are noticeably blue, and the dominant background color is silver. In others the background is a more yellow color. Most males have body fins edged in blue and orange or just blue, and the tail fin is edged with solid black. The female's fins are predominantly clear, with some blue and black coloration on the dorsal fin at the back.

All Amargosa pupfish have a stout, robust, but quite short body, and a typical pupfish form that includes rounded fins, a dorsal fin set back on the body, and pelvic fins on the belly that are small in relation to the other fins.

Breeding begins in April, and those subspecies that occupy springs may have as many as ten groups of offspring before water temperatures fall in October. River-dwelling subspecies are limited to three sets of offspring in the reproductive season before lower temperatures dampen spawning activity.

Today, establishment of the Ash Meadows National Wildlife Refuge and control over the water rights have provided a degree of protection for the Ash Meadows pupfish and the warm springs pupfish; enforce-ment of the water rights issue is an ongoing battle. Other subspecies must rely on the efforts of the U.S. Fish and Wildlife Service and assistance from groups such as The Nature Conservancy in order to secure their futures.

Comanche Springs Pupfish
(Cyprinodon elegans)

ESA: Endangered

IUCN: Endangered

Length: 2 in. (5 cm)
Reproduction: Egg layer
Habitat: Earthen and concrete irrigation ditches
Range: Springs and canal system near Balmorhea, Texas

THE COMANCHE Springs pupfish never did inhabit a large natural range in western Texas. Today, the range is significantly smaller and has been modified by human activity. Comanche Springs near Fort Stockton, Texas, the name-sake of this species, dried up in the 1950s as a result of the use of groundwater for agricultural irrigation and domestic use. Water is a precious commodity in this dry region, and the needs of fish took second place to the needs of people. The failure of this spring system eliminated a large percentage of the pupfish population.

Today, the only other population center is located near Balmorhea, Texas, about 114 miles (183 kilometers) west of Fort Stockton.

This fish is a silvery brown desert dweller, with both sexes lacking the vertical bars on the sides that are characteristic of other pupfish; instead, the male displays a blotchy and speckled pattern. It also carries a pronounced dark band at the edge of the tail fin. Both males and females have a stout body, rounded fins, a dorsal fin that is set back on the body, and an

The Amargosa pupfish primarily consumes algae and supplements it with small aquatic invertebrates such as mosquito larvae.

The Comanche Springs pupfish begins spawning in spring and may produce several groups of offspring during a breeding season. This fish consumes algae and other plant material and aquatic insects.

upturned mouth that it uses for easier capture of surface-dwelling insects such as mosquitoes.

While the Balmorhea population continues to survive, its habitat has changed dramatically. An irrigation network was developed by farmers to utilize water from Giffin and San Solomon Springs. These springs and the earthen and concrete ditches that form the irrigation network are the only barrier between life and death for the last surviving population of this pupfish.

The irrigation system creates a major problem for this pupfish: the variability in water flow can potentially cause the loss of hundreds of fish during periods when water flow is low.

An additional threat comes in the form of introduced fish species such as the sheepshead minnow (*Cyprinodon variegatus*). Cross-breeding between these two species and direct competition for limited food could bring an end to the Comanche Springs pupfish, even if a plan ensures adequate supplies of water. The Texas Parks and Wildlife Department has created a secure refuge and provides a relatively stable water supply.

Protected population

To provide an additional measure of safety, another population is being maintained at the Dexter National Fish Hatchery in New Mexico. Despite these steps, the Comanche Springs pupfish faces an uncertain future.

Conchos (Devil's River) Pupfish
(Cyprinodon eximius)

Length: 1½ in. (4 cm)
Reproduction: Egg layer
Habitat: Backwaters and margins of small to large streams
Range: West Texas and Rio Conchos Basin, Chihuahua, Mexico

THE CONCHOS OR Devil's River pupfish is not a spring dweller like others within its genus; instead it prefers to occupy streams both large and small, avoiding springs and their outfalls and other headwaters. This fish can be found in the upper reaches of the Rio Conchos Basin in Mexico's Chihuahuan Desert, within the Rio Grande on the U.S.-Mexico border, and in the Devil's River in western Texas. Tolerance of river life gives this fish an advantage over other pupfish. Far from being isolated in small and vulnerable spring systems, the Conchos pupfish has expanded its range across hundreds of miles.

Overall, the Conchos pupfish is silvery in color, with dark vertical bars on the sides that are characteristic of many pupfish. Males gain some body coloration during the breeding season, in particular, when they develop orange-yellow color on the dorsal fin on their backs. The dorsal fin of the female and all juveniles has a dark spot at its base called an ocellus. Also, the males have a prominent black band at the tip of the tail fin.

The Conchos pupfish has a chunky and robust body, small pelvic fins on the belly, and dorsal and anal fins that are set well back on the body. It spawns in the spring and may produce several groups of offspring in one breeding season. Its favorite foods include algae and aquatic invertebrates.

Challenges

Even with its advantage of tolerating river life, this species is challenged by the same forces that jeopardize the well-being of other threatened and endangered desert fish. Diversion of water for human use, such as the construction of dams that help to control river water, has reduced and dramatically altered historical water flow patterns. This can help to prevent migration. As a result, some populations have been lost forever, and their overall range is shrinking. This trend, however, is still far from driving the Conchos pupfish to extinction if steps can be taken to provide the secure habitats they need.

Desert Pupfish
(Cyprinodon macularius)

ESA: Endangered

Length: 2¾ in. (7 cm)
Reproduction: Egg layer
Habitat: Desert streams, springs, and shoreline pools
Range: California, Arizona, and northwestern Mexico

THE DESERT PUPFISH is an amazing creature. It can withstand water temperatures as high as 110 degrees Fahrenheit (43.3 Centigrade), dissolved oxygen levels close to zero, and salinities as high as twice that of normal sea water. Most other fish would perish under these water conditions. This supremely adapted species, however, is well suited to

The desert pupfish is capable of surviving in extraordinary conditions—temperatures of up to 110 degrees Fahrenheit (43.3 Centigrade), dissolved oxygen levels of close to zero, and salinities twice that of normal seawater. Yet even these characteristics could not stop it from joining the list of endangered pupfish.

life in the deserts of the southwestern United States and northwestern Mexico. Today, the natural range of the desert pupfish includes southern California near and south of the Salton Sea; Baja California Norte; Sonora, Mexico; and Arizona near the Mexican border within the Organ Pipe Cactus National Monument. A distinct subspecies of the desert pupfish, the Quitobaquito pupfish (*Cyprinodon macularius eremus*), was named after the spring it occupies within the National Monument.

The range of this fish used to be larger. Despite its hardiness and ability to tolerate poor water quality, the desert pupfish is no match for invading, more aggressive fish species such as the redbelly tilapia (*Tilapia zilli*), shortfin molly (*Poecilia mexicana*), mosquitofish (*Gambusia affinis*), and largemouth bass (*Micropterus salmoides*). These fish compete for space and food, and can consume large numbers of desert pupfish if safe hiding places are not available.

Human activity also helped force the desert pupfish onto the

list of endangered fish. Dam construction on the Salt River and Gila River of Arizona caused many pools on the lower reaches of these rivers to dry up. These pools were favorite breeding areas, as well as safe havens from larger predators.

This fish is not without allies. In an effort to ensure the survival of the desert pupfish, populations have been established in Arizona and California at the Arizona-Sonora Desert Museum, Boyce Thompson Arboretum, Arizona State University, Salton Sea State Park, the Living Desert Reserve, and Anza-Borrego State Park. Dexter National Fish Hatchery in New Mexico, a sanctuary for other endangered fish, also maintains a breeding population. Officials in Arizona are also attempting to establish viable non-captive populations at several locations on land controlled by the U.S. Bureau of Land Management.

A fish of many hues
The desert pupfish is quite attractive and colorful. Like other pupfish, it displays physical

differences between the sexes. Males tend to be larger and show a different pattern of coloration. During the breeding season colors intensify. The body is iridescent medium blue, and the tail and tail fin are yellow orange; all other fins are dark. Females and juveniles of both sexes are silver and display a row of dark blotches on the side that may meet to suggest a horizontal bar. The fins lack pigmentation, except for a dark spot called an ocellus at the base of the dorsal fin on the back. The body of both sexes is stout and chunky, and the mouth slightly upturned.

During spring and summer, the desert pupfish can produce up to three batches of offspring. After eggs are laid on shallow vegetation, the male fertilizes and protects them for three days until they hatch. Young fish and adults consume algae and other small aquatic plants and insects.

Pumping of groundwater has been the principal threat to the Devil's Hole pupfish. Because it lives in a tiny portion of a single spring-fed pool in western Nevada, any changes to its habitat are very damaging.

Devil's Hole Pupfish
(Cyprinodon diabolis)

ESA: Endangered

IUCN: Vulnerable

Length: ¾ in. (2 cm)
Reproduction: Egg layer
Habitat: Cavelike, spring-fed pool
Range: Devil's Hole, Ash Meadows, Nevada

LESS THAN one inch (two centimeters) in length, the Devil's Hole pupfish is one of the smallest in its genus. That is probably fortunate, because this fish is only found around a 10– by–18-foot (3– by 5.5–meter) limestone ledge within Devil's Hole, a spring-fed pool in the Ash Meadows region of western Nevada. All feeding and reproduction occurs on this ledge. This water-filled cave, which is at an altitude of 2,300 feet (700 meters) above sea level, is more than 300 feet (91.5 meters) deep, but the Devil's Hole pupfish only occupies the area immediately over the submerged ledge and the adjacent main pool.

Past problems
Before 1952, when the area around Devil's Hole was included as part of the Death Valley National Monument, this fish's situation was very precarious, and no legal protection was in existence.

Pumping of groundwater was the main threat to this species. During the 1950s the ledge was covered by only three feet (one meter) of water. After Devil's Hole achieved status as a national monument, officials began monitoring the water level within the spring. Unfortunately, during the late 1960s the U.S. Bureau of Land Management traded away a considerable tract of land in the Ash Meadows region to a private company that began sinking wells and pumping water for irrigation. This activity lowered the water level in Devil's Hole and ultimately exposed about 60 percent of the life-sustaining ledge. A court battle ensued that ended in the U.S. Supreme Court in 1976. The Court determined that the Devil's Hole pupfish was worth saving and ordered limits on the amount of water that could actually be pumped from the Devil's Hole Basin.

Males of this species differ somewhat in appearance relative to females. The slightly larger male is bright blue and has dark vertical bars on the tail. The female is yellow-brown in color and lacks the vertical bars of dark pigment, but has a spot called an ocellus instead on the dorsal fin

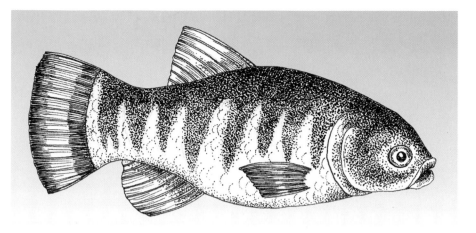

on the back. This fish's fins are rounded and, curiously, both sexes lack a set of pelvic fins on the belly; although pelvic fins are small, they are present on other pupfish.

The Devil's Hole pupfish breeds throughout the year but activity peaks in spring. It uses the algal mats that cover the rock ledge as a food source; small aquatic invertebrates that occupy the algal mats are also consumed.

As a result of the Supreme Court ruling, the U.S. Fish and Wildlife Service was given an opportunity to buy back land that was traded into private hands, but they refused the offer. Today, this large tract of land remains under private ownership and, while water level fluctuations are less of a concern, other factors still threaten the survival of this species. Partial protection has been achieved by transferring and maintaining some of the 300 to 900 individuals to artificial refuges, most notably, a refuge at the base of Hoover Dam.

Largescale Pupfish
(Cyprinodon macrolepis)

IUCN: Endangered

Length: 1½ in. (4 cm)
Reproduction: Egg layer
Habitat: Spring and spring outflow near vegetation
Range: Jimenez, Chihuahua, Mexico

THE LARGESCALE pupfish lives in the Chihuahuan Desert of northern Mexico near the town of

The largescale pupfish breeds throughout the warmer months of the year. It eats algae and small aquatic invertebrates.

Jimenez. The single artesian spring it occupies, known as El Ojo de La Hacienda Dolores, is believed to be the largest in the Chihuahuan Desert. It is supplied by groundwater.

The key to the continued survival of the largescale pupfish is a constant, reliable flow of groundwater from this artesian spring. Unfortunately, the supply for this spring is undermined by the pumping of groundwater from nearby wells for agricultural and domestic use.

Named for their unusually large scales (*macrolepis* means large scales), this pupfish is typical in color for this genus. Overall, the male is blue with orange on the dorsal fin during the breeding season, and the outer margin of the rounded tail fin is black. The female is silver-colored, and both males and females display a row of blotches or short vertical bars on the sides (the blotches are much less pronounced in the male).

In addition to groundwater pumping, diversion of water from the mouth of the El Ojo de

La Hacienda Dolores spring threatens to strand pupfish that live in the outflow. If human demand for the spring's water continues to increase, the spring may fail. Relocation of some fish to other more secure locations may offer a short-term solution to the threat of extinction.

Leon Springs Pupfish
(Cyprinodon bovinus)

ESA: Endangered

IUCN: Critically endangered

Length: 1½ in. (4 cm)
Reproduction: Egg layer
Habitat: Shallow streams in open areas
Range: Diamond Y Spring and Leon Creek, Texas

LOCATED IN THE Pecos River Basin of west Texas, the Diamond Y Spring and its outflow stream called Leon Creek are the only homes for the endangered Leon Springs pupfish. This fish used to occupy nearby Leon Springs sometime before 1938,

The critically endangered Leon Springs pupfish eats vegetation, decaying organic matter, and small aquatic invertebrates.

but these springs dried up as a result of over-pumping of local ground water. This fish is hardy and can tolerate a wide range of environmental challenges, but has not yet adapted to a complete lack of water. Water is a precious commodity, and despite this fish's status as an endangered species, the pumping of groundwater still poses a threat to its long-term well-being.

Compounding the problem is the threat of pollution from a nearby oil refinery. In the past, oil spills at the refinery have made their way to the Diamond Y Spring and Leon Creek and caused the death of significant numbers of Leon Springs pupfish. Some efforts have been made to minimize the potential of future pollution, but one catastrophic event could wipe out the entire species.

A third threat to this fish comes from the sheepshead minnow (*Cyprinodon variegatus*). In 1974 this species of minnow was introduced into Leon Creek; some people speculate that this commonly used bait fish was dumped into the creek by an unwitting fisherman. Shortly after its introduction, the sheepshead minnow and Leon Springs pupfish began interbreeding. Almost certainly, this incident would have spelled the end of the Leon Springs pupfish as we know it today. But after the sheepshead minnows and the hybrids were discovered, officials began a meticulous netting program to rid the creek of the invading fish and their offspring. By the end of 1978, all invaders had been removed. As this episode demonstrated, the continued genetic integrity of the Leon Springs pupfish is by no means secure.

The coloration of this pupfish is somewhat similar to other fish in its genus. The male is almost uniformly blue across the body, with faint darker blotches on the sides and back. The end of the tail fin carries a dark band. In both sexes, pelvic fins on the belly are absent. The less colorful female is dusky gray but has more pronounced dark blotches on the sides, back, and belly than the male. The fins are clear except for the base of the tail fin, which displays a narrow vertical dark band.

This pupfish is capable of breeding at any time during the year, but spawning peaks in the month of July during the summer's warmest weather. After eggs are laid and fertilized, they are guarded by the male for several days until they hatch.

Owens Pupfish
(Cyprinodon radiosus)

ESA: Endangered

IUCN: Endangered

Length: 2½ in. (6 cm)
Reproduction: Egg layer
Habitat: Clean spring pools and sloughs over sand
Range: Fish Slough, Owens Valley, California

BEFORE THE construction of dams to control flooding and diversion channels to carry water to agricultural fields, the Owens River in arid eastern California supported a wide array of aquatic and terrestrial wildlife. In particular, marshes along the river sustained large numbers of the now endangered Owens pupfish. The construction of flood-control dams caused the marshes to dry up completely, and the Owens pupfish was forced to retreat to spring outflows in Fish Slough, a waterway associated with the Owens River. The effect of dam construction and water diversion on this fish was so severe that, for many years before 1956, the Owens pupfish was thought to be extinct.

Today, after efforts were made to secure a safe home for this species, the pumping of groundwater threatens to dry up the springs in Fish Slough that maintain the remaining population. Fish Slough is part of the Owens Valley Native Fish Sanctuary and was established to protect speckled dace (*Rhinichthys osculus*), Owens sucker (*Catostomus fumeiventris*), the endangered Owens tui chub (*Gila bicolor snyderi*), and pupfish such as the Owens pupfish.

The Owens pupfish is under severe pressure from human alteration of habitat—not just in the form of routine human activities, but also from disgruntled or ignorant people who have vandalized structures and equipment designed to maintain the fish's habitat. Incredibly, officials found out that predatory largemouth bass (*Micropterus salmoides*) had been intentionally stocked into the spring areas holding the Owens pupfish. Many of the voracious fish-eaters

were removed, but some still persist today. As a measure of protection, some Owens pupfish may be relocated to Adobe Valley, where there is habitat that is suited to this species.

This fish is small, but it is large for a pupfish. The Owens pupfish is light blue overall, with olive on the back and gray on the lower sides and belly. The tail and sides of the male carry bold purplish gold vertical bars with more faint purplish bars toward the head. The dorsal fin on the back and the anal fin are blue with an orange border; other fins are clear or dark striped. The female lacks the blue cast and carries brown blotches on the sides as well as purplish bars. Both sexes have a stout and chunky body, an upturned mouth, and rounded fins. The male is larger than the female.

Pairs begin mating in April, after the blue color of the male intensifies, and continues in the spring and summer. Females can lay 200 eggs in a breeding season. The male defends its territory, as well as fertilized eggs. Juvenile and adult Owens pupfish eat algae, plankton, insects, and other aquatic invertebrates.

Pecos Pupfish
(Cyprinodon pecosensis)

IUCN: Critically endangered

Length: 2 in. (5 cm)
Reproduction: Egg layer
Habitat: Saline springs, sinkholes, and desert streams
Range: Pecos River Basin, New Mexico and Texas

NAMED AFTER the river basin it inhabits, the Pecos pupfish is found in and near the Pecos River in southern New Mexico and west Texas. The Pecos River is a major river of the southwest and, consequently, is considered a valuable resource within the region. The need of people to control this resource led to the construction of dams and other structures in order to control flooding and to divert water for irrigation purposes.

Dams along the Pecos River hinder natural migration of the Pecos pupfish, isolating populations that may otherwise interact. The dams significantly alter seasonal water flow and water quality. This species also inhabits sinkholes along the river valley and, while dams and water diversions do not directly affect these populations, diversion of water from the river tends to lower the local water tables and water levels within the sinkholes.

With the exception of breeding males, the Pecos pupfish

The Pecos pupfish is an opportunistic feeder, and seeks a wide variety of food, including decaying organic matter and a range of aquatic invertebrates.

displays a brown-green colored background under a series of dark spots and blotches on the back and sides; the base of the tail fin carries a dark crescent. A dark spot called an ocellus, a characteristic of many juvenile and female pupfish, is present in the Pecos pupfish. The belly is usually white or cream, with scattered dark dots. The male is only slightly larger, but is quite different and more spectacular in coloration during breeding. A gray-blue iridescent color dominates the body and most of the head; the belly, cheeks, and gill covers are cream. The dorsal fin on the back and the anal fin are black, and the tail fin carries a dark crescent at its base and a black band at its outer edge. The

pectoral fins are yellow. Like other pupfish, the Pecos pupfish has a stout body, rounded fins, and an upturned mouth for easy capture of surface insects.

Breeding occurs during spring and summer and peaks in May and June. Males defend their breeding territories and may provide fertilized eggs with parental care until they hatch.

In addition to its shrinking habitat, another major problem for the Pecos pupfish is the introduction of the sheepshead minnow (*Cyprinodon variegatus*). This fish readily interbreeds with the Pecos pupfish and other pupfish species. Only a few years ago, the Pecos pupfish was found throughout the Pecos River in Texas. Today, because of inter-

breeding and the hybrid offspring that result, no purebred Pecos pupfish can be found within the main channel of the Texas Pecos River.

Hybrids have been found in Red Bluff Reservoir at the Texas–New Mexico border. Fisheries biologists had hoped that Red Bluff Dam would act as a barrier and hinder upstream migration of the hybrids. It is possible that the hybrids were either purposely or accidentally stocked. In any case, upstream purebred populations are now at risk of hybridization. That means that the future of the Pecos pupfish is unclear.

William E. Manci

See also Cachorritos, Killifish, and Perritos.

Indian Python
(Python molurus)

ESA: Endangered

IUCN: Lower risk

Class: Reptilia
Order: Serpentes
Family: Boidae
Subfamily: Pythoninae
Length: Up to 21 ft. (6.5 m)
Diet: Mammals and birds
Range: Pakistan, India, Nepal, Bangladesh; *Python molurus bivittatus* ssp. in Myanmar, China, Southeast Asia, Hainan, Borneo, Sulawesi, Java, and Sumbawa; *Python molurus pimbura* ssp. in Sri Lanka

N

INDIAN PYTHON
Asia

PYTHONS HAVE the honor of claiming three of the world's four largest snakes among their subfamily: *Python reticulatus*, *Python sebae*, and *Python molurus*, or the Indian python. In fact, some researchers believe that the reticulated python, *Python* reticulatus, is actually the world's biggest snake. Pythons differ from their relatives, the boas, in that they lay eggs. Boas are ovoviviparous, meaning that the eggs

develop within the maternal body and hatch within or immediately after extrusion. These snakes probably hunt by day or night, and feed mainly on mammals and birds.

Subspecies

The Indian python exists in three geographic subspecies: P. *molurus molurus*, P. *molurus pimbura*, and P. *molurus bivittatus*. The latter is the most common, as well as the largest, growing up to a maximum length of around 21 feet (6.5 meters).

Reproduction

The Indian python is a docile creature in captivity, and has been successfully captive-bred many times. Sexual maturity is reached between three and five years of age. Clutch sizes of 25 to 60 eggs have been reported, and incubation takes about 100 days.

There are several thousand Indian pythons in captivity, both in zoos and kept by private individuals. Such large numbers mean the survival of these animals is fairly secure.

Clutches of up to 50 eggs have been reported in the wild. The female guards the eggs, coiling around them and leaving only occasionally to drink. The temperature of the eggs can be elevated to a level much higher than their surroundings. Heat is generated from the muscle contractions produced by twitching movements that are often made by the female during the brooding period.

In India, the python's skin has long been a popular export item. Increasing human population has led to habitat disturbance. In China, snakes are prized as food. It can also be assumed that the python, like most snakes, has faced persecution from people who have learned to fear and dislike these reptiles.

The Wildlife Act of 1972 has protected *P. molurus molurus*, and *P. molurus bivittatus*. They are both listed by the Convention on International Trade in Endangered Species of Wild Fauna and Flora, a treaty that is observed by many nations.

Some Indian scrubland habitat of the snake is considered to be wasteland by native peoples, and in these areas the Indian python is relatively safe. This area must be recognized as an important ecological region and given sanctuary status. The economic value of this rodent-eating python should be widely publicized so that people within this reptile's range will come to recognize it as useful and symbiotic. The Indian python is classified by IUCN as lower risk.

Snake enthusiasts, as well as zoo programs, should consider the importance of keeping large groups of single snake species to form breeding groups, rather than collecting a wide assortment of species that cannot sustain themselves.

Elizabeth Sirimarco

Merriam's Montezuma Quail

(Cyrtonyx montezumae merriami)

ESA: Endangered

Class: Aves
Order: Galliformes
Family: Phasianidae
Subfamily: Odontophorinae
Length: 8–9 in. (20.3–22.9 cm)
Weight: Males, 7 oz. (195 g); females, 6⅓ oz. (175.7 g)
Clutch size: 6–14 eggs
Diet: Bulbs and tubers (particularly of *Cyperus* sp. and *Oxalis* sp.), small fruits and seeds, invertebrates
Habitat: Pine-oak woodlands with undergrowth of herbaceous (non-woody) plants
Range: Mount Orizaba in Veracruz, Mexico

A COYOTE CREEPS through the tall grass, its nose directing it toward an animal its eyes have not yet seen. Slowly it advances, moving one paw at a time, its muscles quivering, its legs bent for a quick spring. It pauses. The strong scent tells it that Montezuma birds are very close. But it cannot pounce on what it cannot see. The coyote waits. A blade of grass moves in perfectly still air. The hidden group of birds cannot smell the coyote, because birds cannot smell as well as mammals. Relaxing its guard, one quail takes a step. When the grass moves again the coyote pounces, and the quails scatter.

Grouping call

After scattering, the group of quails sit motionless and quiet for a few minutes. Then, one by one, quavering whistles (quail calls) rise out of the grass, helping the birds reunite. On hearing their neighbors whistle, the birds walk toward each other and reform their group.

Coyotes (*Canis latrans*) and Montezuma quails have coexisted for tens of thousands of years. In fact, the Montezuma quail has survived despite having many predators: coyotes, foxes, skunks, weasels, certain snakes, and birds of prey, as well as cats. It has also survived parasites, occasional fires, and other natural phenomena, but the entire species has noticeably declined through the 20th century. By the 1980s, one subspecies—the Merriam's Montezuma quail—was imperiled by an enemy it could not recognize. Nothing in the quail's history had prepared it for domestic cattle.

Plumage

A very short tail, a short neck, and a plump, round body make the Montezuma quail look a little like a small feathered ball. The face is white, extending down and across the throat in a narrow band. A thin, black band starts at the side of the neck and borders the white throat stripe. The black chin and cheek are separated by a thin white line along the jaw. An even thinner white line crosses the cheek. A thin black ring encircles the dark eye, and a thin black line starting at the base of the upper beak streaks up the forehead and onto the crown.

A caramel colored crest arches back from the crown and puffs slightly out from the back of the head and the nape. The back is patterned, as each feather shaft is pale brownish tan and the feather vanes are cinnamon and black. The wings are strongly patterned in grayish tan with black spots. The breast and belly are uniformly cinnamon, but a broad swath of white spots on a gray background decorates the bird's side from neck to belly. The female lacks the zebralike face. She also has no spotted sides, and her underparts are more spotted and streaked than those of her mate.

Distribution

The Montezuma quail occurs in portions of southeastern Arizona, southwestern New Mexico, extreme southwest Texas, and in widely separated areas of western and eastern Mexico.

Its habitat demands are so rigid that it is not really abundant anywhere, and places where it was once common now have no Montezuma quails left at all. The Merriam's subspecies lives only in the woodlands of Veracruz, Mexico, between 3,500 and 10,000 feet (1,067 to 3,049 meters) above sea level.

Birds in the bush

A terrestrial bird, Merriam's Montezuma quail inhabits the dense herbaceous undergrowth of woodlands where pines and oaks grow. Herbaceous plants, such as grass, are not woody (as are trees and shrubs) but are soft and often live only for a single growing season. Among the thick growth, the quail searches for wood-sorrel (*Oxalis* sp.),

nutsedge (*Cyperus* sp.), and various lilies. With elongated claws on its toes, the quail easily digs up these plants to eat their bulbs and tubers.

Enemy protection

As an extra benefit, the tall herbaceous plants hide the quail from its enemies. Unfortunately, those areas where plants grow lushly enough to attract Merriam's Montezuma quail also attract ranching. The herbaceous plant life fattens up cattle (*Bos taurus*) cheaply, but grazing has hidden costs.

When livestock animals are overgrazed, the consequences are almost always disastrous. Overgrazing not only reduces the number of plants available to animals, it also alters the character of plant communities as habitat. Excessive grazing by cattle also eliminates the way that plants protect the soil from water.

The resulting erosion usually permanently damages the soil

and impairs its ability to regrow native plants. Wherever excessive grazing causes the loss of soil, habitat for birds such as the Merriam's Montezuma quail is lost forever. If they are not grazed too heavily, however, plant communities can eventually recover.

Montezuma quail habitat has been heavily grazed throughout the bird's range. Even though modern-day ranchers have learned how to prevent serious overgrazing, allowing herbaceous plants time to regenerate, their activities still cause too dramatic a change in the habitat to benefit the Montezuma quail.

Only solution

Merriam's Montezuma quail needs tall herbaceous plants in which to hide and build its peculiar domed nest. The only answer to the problem is to prohibit grazing entirely within the living range of Merriam's Montezuma quail.

Kevin Cook

QUAIL
North America

Gray-headed Quail-dove

(Geotrygon caniceps)

IUCN: Lower risk

Class: Aves
Order: Columbiformes
Family: Columbidae
Length: 11 in. (27.9 cm)
Clutch size: 1–2 eggs
Habitat: Lowland and montane forests
Range: Cuba, Dominican Republic, and possibly Haiti, Caribbean

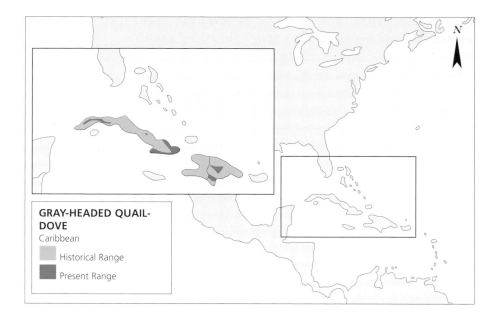

GRAY-HEADED QUAIL-DOVE
Caribbean

Historical Range
Present Range

GRAY-HEADED quail-doves greeted Christopher Columbus when he reached the islands of Hispaniola (Dominican Republic and Haiti) and Cuba in 1492, but the European explorer and his crew took more interest in the Arawak and Carib people who occupied the islands. Perhaps 100,000 people lived scattered about the islands of the Greater Antilles when Columbus arrived, and the quail-doves outnumbered them. First, the Caribs and the Arawaks disappeared. Then, forests and woodlands vanished. Now, the gray-headed quail-dove may follow.

A pale gray forehead and a slightly darker gray crown, face, and throat lend the bird its name. The medium gray continues across the breast but fades to a dingy white belly patch and pinkish color undertail. A deep, shiny purple colors the back and rump, and a dull purple covers the side between the wing and belly. Both wing and tail are a dark gray color, although the wing shows a little orange-brown in flight. Beyond where it lives and what it looks like, ornithologists know very little about the quail-dove.

Population decrease

The gray-headed quail-dove is slowly vanishing from Cuba and Hispaniola because people left it very little habitat. Since the arrival of Columbus, the human population on Cuba has topped 10 million, with another 12 million on Hispaniola. Once the native Arawak and Carib peoples

Quail-doves normally feed on the ground, and the gray-headed species is probably no exception. Its usual diet includes small fruits, seeds, and small invertebrates.

disappeared from these small islands, imported slave laborers cleared native trees in order to plant sugarcane and coffee.

Cuba measures only 44,218 square miles (114,967 square kilometers) and the island of Hispaniola measures 29,418 square miles (76,487 square kilometers) in area. Now the island forests have diminished to just strips and patches left in ravines and gullies, where the land does not support agriculture well. The gray-headed quail-dove barely survives in those remnant patches of forest and woodland.

Where it does still occur on Cuba, it is heavily hunted for food, using drop traps baited with orange seed.

The quail-dove typically prefers good forest undergrowth. The gray-headed quail-dove on Cuba prefers the lowland forests, but on Hispaniola it prefers the wetter montane forests. The destruction of these forests on both islands has greatly endangered this dove.

Preservation problems

No estimates of population are known, and very little deliberate action has been taken to help the gray-headed quail-dove. In the Dominican Republic, hunting of the species was prohibited in 1978, and a reassessment of the protected areas system has proposed six new montane forest reserves. However, the political and social problems on both islands make wildlife preservation work very difficult. The most important preservation steps to take now are to stop the clearing of any more primary forest and woodland on the two islands, to conduct natural history research on the species, and to initiate ongoing surveys to determine population size and actual distribution on the islands. There is no other way to help this species.

Kevin Cook

QUETZALS

Class: Aves
Order: Trogoniformes
Family: Trogonidae

Members of the Trogonidae family are all brightly colored. They have long wedge-shaped tails and short beaks that are strong and slightly hooked.

The male quetzal has been poached for its magnificent green and red feathers, and for display in private museums. The bright green tail coverts can reach a length of up to 40 inches (100 centimeters). This full length is only reached when the male quetzal is three years of age.

The female quetzal is a duller green and brown, and she does not have long tail coverts.

The quetzal was revered by the Mayas and the Aztecs, and the bird has become the emblem of Guatemala. The country's currency also takes its name from this bird. Tourism and habitat destruction have been the main problems for this bird.

Eared Quetzal

(Euptilotis neoxenus)

IUCN: Endangered

Length: 13–14 in. (33–35.5 cm)
Clutch size: 2–3
Diet: Berries, fruit, and insects
Habitat: Pine or pine-oak forest between 6,000–10,000 ft. (1,800–3,000 m)
Range: Northwest Mexico

Past the town of San Juan de Michilía, Mexico and 7,000 feet (2,000 meters), up a winding road, lies the territory of the eared quetzal. The landscape of this region is extremely rugged, with deep canyons and valleys clad in pine and oak forest lying between steep-sided ridges.

The eared quetzal sings in a hollow and eerie quavering series of notes: first single notes, then double notes, then triple. The sound is soft at first, then louder. The song comprises as many as 24 or more whistles in a series, and the result has a particularly eerie quality.

Colorful appearance

The eared quetzal is a colorful bird. The male's upper breast is bottle green and its belly is scarlet, in contrast with a white undertail. The bird has a dark head and a small gray bill. Its

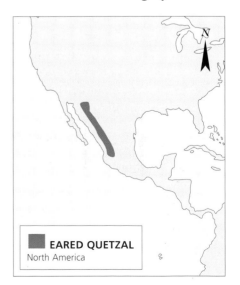

EARED QUETZAL
North America

Although they have bright plumage, eared quetzals spend a lot of time perched motionless on the branches of trees, so they are easily overlooked.

upperparts are green, apart from black flight feathers and a dark blue tail. In the New World, most male quetzals have dark green upper-parts, with red or yellow bellies. Fine plumes protrude from behind the eyes. These are inconspicuous, and although they do not resemble ears, they are responsible for the bird's name. The female bird has similar colored plumage on the upperparts and belly, but the green on the upper breast is gray brown. The female call to the male is an ascending squeal which ends in a clucking sound.

Hidden bird

Although they have very bright plumage, all the world's quetzals spend a lot of time perched motionless on the branches of trees, and so are easily overlooked. The rarity of the eared quetzal means that catching sight of one is unlikely, although it is more mobile than many members of the species.

Its family is spread around the world's tropical regions in Central and South America, Africa, the Indian subcontinent, and Southeast Asia. The eared quetzal is a limited-range species, breeding only in northwest Mexico and in the provinces of Michoacán, Jalisco, Zacatecas, Nayarit, Durango, Sinaloa, Sonora, and Chihuahua. It is a rare visitor to southern Arizona, in the United States. Its range is larger than that of many endangered species, and thinly spread.

Suitable environment

Its favored habitat is pine or pine-oak forest at a height of 6,000–10,000 feet (1,800–3,000 meters), and it appears to show a preference for canyon environments. Although they are usually observed singly or in pairs, small parties of the birds are sometimes seen together and about 16 were observed in lush riparian forest at 7,000 feet (2,000 meters) at Monte Oscuro, Durango, in January 1995; this situation is exceptional, however.

Eared quetzals eat small fruit. They also consume insects, either picking them off leaves or making short aerial flights to catch them. Their breeding season runs from June to October, and the female lays two or three eggs in a tree cavity.

One of the problems facing this species is the destruction of such large trees for nesting. As in so many of the world's forested regions where valleys are relatively easy to access, much good habitat has been destroyed by logging. In addition, fires have damaged forest, dead trees have been uprooted by hurricanes. Until more is known of this quetzal's ecological requirements and seasonal movements, it is difficult to develop a plan to preserve it.

Protective measures

There are a large number of places where the bird is known to reside, there is much more suitable forest that has not been searched but that may hold a reasonable number of individuals, and there is a 135 square mile (35,000-hectare) biosphere reserve at La Michilía, Durango, where quetzals have been observed. Protected areas and tighter controls on commercial forestry would seem to be the best way forward to help this endangered bird.

Tim Harris

Resplendent Quetzal

(Pharomachrus mocinno)

ESA: Endangered

IUCN: Lower risk

Class: Aves
Order: Trogoniformes
Family: Trogonidae
Length: 14–15 in. (35.6–38.1 cm); male has tail 20–30 in. (50.8–76.2 cm) long
Weight: 7½ oz. (210 g)
Clutch size: 1–2 eggs
Incubation: 18 days
Diet: Fruits, insects, spiders, frogs, and lizards
Habitat: Montane forests
Range: Southern Mexico into Panama

IN THE RAIN-SOAKED forests of Central America, few birds are more beautiful than the resplendent quetzal (pronounced ket-SAL).

Its upperparts are bright grass green and shiny. In fact, they are frequently described as glittering. An erect, brushlike crest originates at the base of the beak and extends across the forehead and crown, down the back of the head onto the nape. The face, chin, throat, and upper breast are the same deep, grass green color. The green ends in a smooth line across the mid-breast. The lower breast is maroon and fades to brilliant, shining red on the sides and belly. The underside of the tail feathers is white. The usually short small feathers of the wing are elongated, and they sweep forward over the sides.

The most startling part of a male quetzal are the great plumes that look like tail feathers. They arise from the lower rump and are feathers that ornithologists term *tail coverts* because they cover the base of the tail feathers. The four central tail coverts may grow 2½ feet long (nearly 1 meter). The tail coverts also possess a glittering quality. The female has a gray breast and a paler red belly and sides. Her tail is more barred than that of the male, and she lacks the plumes, although the rump feathers may be slightly elongated.

All this fine plumage earned the resplendent quetzal honors long before Europeans settled into Central America. The ancient peoples of Central America revered the quetzal and placed high value on the male's great plumes. The bird figured prominently in religious ceremonies. The resplendent quetzal was formally described in 1832 and it quickly became a popular

Quetzals live where cloudbursts soak the land every day. Rain measures 150 inches (381 centimeters) in most years. Trees grow 150 feet (45.7 meters) tall and are abundantly festooned with orchids, bromeliads, ferns, and vines.

bird for the many private museums of the day. Thousands of resplendent quetzals were killed and stuffed, not so much for their scientific value as for the prestige of owning a set of specimens.

Birds are still illegally trapped and sold to those people who want caged birds and are willing to pay high prices for rare species. However, this practice appears to have been reduced throughout much of this quetzal's range, but may persist in parts of southern Mexico. The reasons for the quetzal's continuing decline are the loss and fragmentation of montane forest.

Typically good soils and slightly cooler temperatures make the cloud forests where the quetzal lives attractive for agriculture, and the tall trees are irresistible for cutting into lumber. Consequently, the cloud forests that were once fairly continuous from southern Mexico into northern South America are now reduced to smaller, unconnected fragments. Estimates published in the mid-1980s claimed 100,000 to 150,000 acres (40,000 to 60,000 hectares) of cloud forest were being cut each year in Central America, which does not help the resplendent quetzal's chances for survival.

Nutritional changes

The resplendent quetzal starts life eating insects, spiders, small frogs, lizards, and other animal foods that the parent birds can catch. The quick growth of a nestling bird means that they need a large amount of protein, and animal food provides this far better than fruit. As a young bird matures, it gradually eats fewer animals and more fruit, and an adult will eat strictly fruit. Various plants in the laurel family (Lauraceae) are its preferred food, but researchers have found that the quetzal actually consumes fruit from nearly four dozen plant species. Not all plants are in fruit at the same time, so in any given season the quetzal may be eating only a dozen or so different kinds.

Location

In tropical climates most plants flower and bear fruit year-round. This arrangement means the quetzal's food supply is constant but scattered. The quetzal adjusts by moving up and down the mountains where it lives in order to find adequate food. This seasonal movement is known as

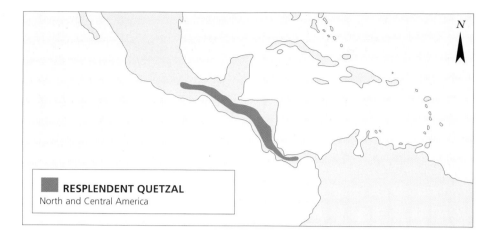

RESPLENDENT QUETZAL
North and Central America

altitudinal migration. Usually, the resplendent quetzal ranges between 5,000 and 10,000 feet (1,500 to 3,000 meters). It is entirely arboreal, flies somewhat weakly, and does not occur in dense numbers. When the cloud forests are restricted to patches here and there, the quetzal becomes isolated and has little or no chance to move about between patches. Roads built to carry logs out of a cutting area also give access to trappers, who can now trap even more quetzals.

Nature protection

All Central American countries have established national parks or nature reserves, either specifically for the resplendent quetzal or for the cloud forests in general. The first was Guatemala's Volcano Atitlan in 1972. Reserves are not always enough, however. Many of the parks are too small to accommodate the quetzal's seasonal migrations. Governments do not always support their parks with funding to sustain protection. Some national parks have become havens for soldiers fighting civil wars, especially in southern Mexico. Soldiers shoot the quetzal and other wildlife both for food and for target practice.

Those who would protect this quetzal have no opportunity to reason with such desperate people. Nor can they reason with those who stand to make financial profit from cutting the cloud forests for lumber. Small farmers also cut down parts of the cloud forests. They cut undergrowth, then set fires to burn the land clear. These fires often burn for weeks at a time and consume far more forest than the people can use for crops. In high rainfall areas erosion follows, and the potential to farm or recover the forests lessens.

In addition to habitat destruction, tourism is also a threat: local people sell quetzal plumes and stuffed quetzals as souvenirs.

Protective measures

Preserving the resplendent quetzal requires only that its habitat is protected and that people stop taking it into captivity. Protecting the habitat depends on resolving complex human problems of overpopulation, inefficient farming, profiteering of natural resources, political turmoil, as well as increasing economic stability. Securing the future for this bird is surely a demanding task under these circumstances.

Kevin Cook

RABBITS

Class: Mammalia

Order: Lagomorpha

Family: Leporidae

Rabbits, which belong to the family Leporidae, have been introduced throughout the world. There are some 47 species, from the Americas to Australia to Java, and they generally thrive wherever they live.

Rabbits can be found in many types of habitat, such as forests, grasslands, or barren mountains. Their hearing and smell are their best-developed senses, and help to protect them from predators. Some rabbits are good runners, while others are more cautious and remain close to their burrows or other shelter.

The flesh and fur of rabbits have always made them popular targets for hunters. Because rabbits often feed on and harm crops, they are routinely trapped and killed by farmers.

Biologists still argue about whether lagomorphs such as pikas, rabbits, and hares should be considered a suborder related to rodents. Many are convinced that these two groups belong together, while others are equally convinced that there are no significant similarities between them to justify such a grouping.

There is some resemblance between rabbits and rodents, but the most obvious physical differences are the rabbits' long ears and short, furry tails.

Rabbit eat just about any variety of vegetation. They are also known for passing feces that they then eat again to get the maximum food value out of anything they ingest. Eventually, they pass drier inedible pellets.

Certain species found in the family *Leporidae* have existed in North America for longer than 50 million years. Their sure-footed ways and prolific breeding abilities have no doubt helped these species to survive the test of time. However, a number of rabbit species have not been so fortunate, and many are facing an uncertain future.

In 1999, a new species of rabbit was found in Laos. It looked similar to the Sumatran rabbit, but DNA analysis by scientists at the University of East Anglia confirmed that the animals were genetically distinct and therefore belonged to a new species.

Amami Rabbit

(Pentalagus furnessi)

ESA: Endangered

IUCN: Endangered

Head-body length: 16½–18½ in. (42–47 cm)

Weight: 4–6 lb. (2–3 kg)

Diet: Grass and acorns

Gestation period: 180–210 days

Habitat: Forests

Range: Amami and Tokumoshima Islands in the Ryukyu Archipelago southwest of Japan

THE AMAMI RABBIT, which is also known as the Ryukyu rabbit, is unique among lagomorphs because of its very dark, thick fur, which is not typical of this order of animals. It is known locally as the black rabbit of Amami. Additional differences include its small eyes and ears, a long snout, and short limbs with relatively long nails for digging.

This rabbit has been recognized by the government of Japan as an endangered species, and has also been designated as a special natural monument by that government. Unfortunately, even though this animal enjoys this special designation and governmental protection, its existence is not widely known in Japan. While it is protected from hunting by governmental decree, little attention is paid to the management of its habitat.

An ancient line

Scientists recognize this rabbit as a sort of living fossil; its physical traits are similar to fossil species found as far back as the Miocene era (26 million years ago), making the Amami rabbit one of the most primitive lagomorphs in the world. This rabbit is found only on Amami Oshima and Tokunoshima, two Japanese islands of the Ryukyu Archipelago. Originally thought to exist only in the primary forests that once covered both islands, signs of this rabbit have been seen in younger secondary forests in the less densely wooded regions of

AMAMI RABBIT
Asia

these islands. Presumably, this rabbit's dark fur is a natural camouflage that helps it hide in dark forest shadows. The Amami rabbit is nocturnal, emerging from its burrow to forage for food at night, using passages through the underbrush as natural cover.

Mating occurs in November and December, and the young rabbits (kits) first appear above ground six to seven months later in April or May.

Seasonal diet

The Amami rabbit feeds on a variety of plants in the forest, including grass, leaves of the Japanese sweet potato, bamboo sprouts, acorns, and the bark of forest trees. It appears to feed mostly on the leaves of the Japanese pampas grass during summer, and on the acorns of the pasania tree in winter. The importance of these seasonal choices is not yet known.

Recent sightings indicate the Amami rabbit is found in cutover areas and forest edges covered by Japanese pampas grass. This rabbit is not found in cultivated, residential, or urban areas frequented by people. The first population estimate was made in 1977, placing the total at about 6,000 rabbits. However, this number was disputed because it originated from a small group of individual studies. A revised estimate was made in 1987, placing the total population on Amami Island at 3,700 rabbits. The population on Tokonoshima Island has never been estimated.

The human threat

The main threat to these animals today is human activity. Selective logging of the old forests has reduced the size of old growth forest to less than 5 percent of its original range, but a considerable area has returned to secondary growth. The Amami's primary natural predators have been feral cats and dogs.

Considering the rarity and obvious value placed upon the Amami rabbit by the Japanese government, it is very odd that no extensive food, habitat, and behavior studies have been conducted by scientists. Perhaps this work will be completed before any further damage to this rabbit's habitat pushes it closer toward extinction.

Sumatran Rabbit

(Nesolagus netscheri)

IUCN: Critically endangered

Length: 14½–16 in. (37–40 cm)
Diet: Various fruit and vegetables
Habitat: Mountain forests
Range: Barisan Mountains, Sumatra

THE SUMATRAN rabbit is presumed to be the rarest of all lagomorphs. It is about the same size as a European rabbit, but has unusually short ears. Its tail is barely visible, having only 12 bones, as opposed to the European species with 17 to 19 bones.

The fur on the Sumatran rabbit is very soft and short. The rabbit may be distinguished by wide black or dark brown stripes on its yellowish gray body. These become rusty brown toward the rear. The fur on the underbelly, chin, and hind legs is whitish. The ears are black and so short that, when they are folded forward, they reach only to the eye.

Distribution

The Sumatran rabbit lives in remote, inaccessible areas of montane forest in the Barisan Mountains of west and southwest Sumatra. Experts believe that it populates the entire range. Mostly nocturnal, the Sumatran

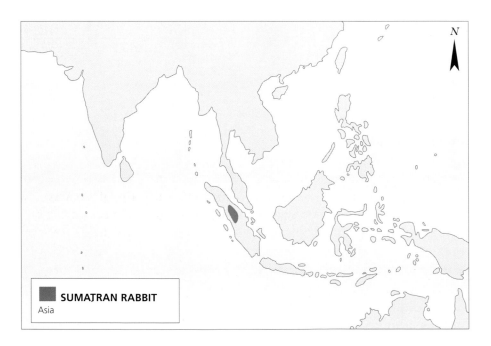

SUMATRAN RABBIT
Asia

rabbit hides during the day in dark places at the base of trees, in burrows, or in holes in the ground protected by the forest undergrowth. Even captive specimens showed this behavior, feeding only at night and remaining nearly motionless during the day. The natural food of this rabbit is probably grasses, seeds, and bark of the forest trees and underbrush. Specific classes of food are unknown. Animals in captivity appear to thrive on rice, fruit such as bananas, and cultivated vegetables.

There is nothing recorded about the reproductive life of this rabbit in the wild or in captivity. When originally discovered in 1880, the rabbit was already so rare that the locals did not have a name for it. No accurate population studies have been made since its original discovery.

Museum preservation

About 12 museum specimens exist, collected between 1880 and 1916. No Sumatran rabbits exist in captivity. Sightings continue to provide hope that this mysterious little rabbit will continue to thrive in its high mountain domain, where its habitat remains undisturbed.

In 1998, the Sumatran rabbit was captured on film in Kerinci Seblat National Park, Sumatra. The photograph, thought to be the first of this rabbit in the wild, was taken with a phototrap camera by researchers from Fauna and Flora International, a U.K.-based conservation organization.

The immediate threat to this rabbit is the destruction of its habitat, mainly caused by the clearing of the forests for coffee plantations.

Volcano Rabbit
(Romerolagus diazi)

| **ESA:** Endangered |
| **IUCN:** Endangered |

Weight: 17½ oz. (500 g)
Diet: Grasses, herbs, forest seeds, and bark
Habitat: Mountain pine forests
Range: Central Mexico

THE VOLCANO rabbit is considered to be one of the most primitive living rabbits. It is tiny, weighing barely 1 pound (0.45 kilogram) as an adult, with the female being slightly larger than the male. The only smaller rabbit among lagomorphs is the pygmy rabbit (*Brachylagus idahoensis*).

The volcano rabbit's hind legs and feet are short, the ears are small and rounded, and the tail is rather inconspicuous. The fur is short and dense, with the upperparts and flank dark brown to black in color. The volcano rabbit is found only in central Mexico and only on the pine-forested

Cottontails, such as this brush rabbit, are one of the most widely scattered game species in the United States, with many millions killed each year. One subspecies of brush rabbit (*Sylvilagus bachmani riparius*), however, is found only in California's San Joaquin Valley and is in danger of extinction.

slopes of four volcanos. These are Popocatepetl and Iztaccihuatl in the Sierra Nevada mountain range and El Pelado and Tlaloc in the Sierra Chichinautzin mountains. This amounts to a total range of roughly 108 square miles (280 square kilometers).

The rocky slopes this rabbit prefers contain a dense undergrowth of bunch grass, which grows at an altitude of between 9,187 and 14,600 feet (2,800 and 4,450 meters).

Most of the area of this rabbit's range has winter drought and summer rains, with an annual rainfall of nearly 60 inches (about 150 centimeters).

There is little evidence that this rabbit is a burrower, yet some observers report that the rabbit uses burrows that have been abandoned by ground squirrels, pocket gophers,

ally has plumage differing from an adult bird of the same species

in captivity: a species that exists in zoos, captive breeding programs, or in private collections, perhaps because the species can no longer be found in the wild

incubation: the period when an egg is kept warm until the embryo develops and hatches

indigenous species: any species native to its habitat

inflorescence: a group of flowers that grow from one point

insular species: a species isolated on an island or islands

interbreed: when two separate species mate and produce offspring; see hybrid

invertebrate(s): any organism without a backbone (spinal column)

juvenal: a bird with an intermediate set of feathers after its downy plumage molts and before growing hard, adult feathers

juvenile(s): a young bird or other animal not yet mature

lore(s): the irregularly shaped facial area of a bird between the eye and the base of the beak

mesic: describes a plant that requires a moderate amount of moisture for survival

migrate, migratory: to

move from one range to another, particularly with the change of seasons; many species are migratory

milt: the reproductive glands of male fishes; also, the breeding behavior of male fishes

mollusca: the Latin scientific name for mussels, clams, and snails

montane forest: a forest found in mountainous regions

nocturnal: active at night; some animals are nocturnal, while others are active by day (see diurnal)

nomadic species: a species with no permanent range or territory; nomadic species wander for food and water

old growth forest: forest that has not experienced extensive deforestation

omnivore: any species that eats both plants and animals

ornithologist(s): a scientist who studies birds

pelage: the hairy covering of a mammal

pelagic: related to the oceans or open sea; pelagic birds rarely roost on land

perennial: persisting for several years

plumage: the feathers that cover a bird

predation: the act of one species hunting another

predator: a species that preys upon other species

primary forest: a forest of native trees that results from natural processes, often called virgin forest

primate(s): a biological ranking of species in the same order, including gorillas, chimpanzees, monkeys, and human beings (*Homo sapiens*)

range: the geographic area where a species roams

recovery plan(s): any document that outlines a public or private program for assisting an endangered or threatened species

relict: an isolated habitat or population that was once widespread

reptilia: the Latin scientific name for reptiles

riffle(s): a shallow rapid stretch of water caused by a rocky outcropping or by an obstruction in a stream

riparian: relating to plants and animals close to and influenced by rivers

roe: fish eggs

rufous: in bird species, plumage that is orange-brown and pink

secondary forest: a forest that has grown back after cutting, forest fire, or another kind of deforestation; secondary forests may or may not contain exotic tree species, but they almost always differ in character from primary forests

sedentary species: one that does not migrate

siltation: the process of sediment clouding and obstructing a body of water

terrestrial: living in or adapted for living principally on the ground; some birds are terrestrial and seldom, if ever, ascend into trees (see arboreal)

territory: the area occupied more or less exclusively by an organism or group, usually defended by aggressive displays and physical combat

threatened species: any species that is at risk of becoming endangered

tribe: a more specific classification within the biological rankings of family or subfamily

tubercle: a prominent bump on a fish's body connected to a spine

umbel: umbrella-shaped cluster of flowers

veldt: a grassland region with some scattered bushes and virtually no trees; other terms are *steppe*, *pampas*, and *prairie*

ventral: on or near the belly; the ventral fin is located on the underside of a fish and corresponds with the hind limbs of other vertebrates

vertebrates: any organism that has a backbone (spinal column)

weir: a dam or other

obstruction in a stream or river that diverts water from its natural path

woodland: a plant community in which trees grow abundantly but far enough apart that their crowns do not intermingle, so no overhead canopy is formed

xerophyte: a plant adapted for life with a limited water supply

INDEX